Many Gods and Many Voices

Many Gods and Many Voices

The Role of the Prophet in English and American Modernism

Louis L. Martz

University of Missouri Press
Columbia and London

Library of Congress Cataloging-in-Publication Data

Martz, Louis Lohr.
    Many gods and many voices : the role of the prophet in English and
American modernism / Louis L. Martz.
        p.   cm.
    Includes bibliographical references (p.   ) and index.
    ISBN 0-8262-1148-8 (alk. paper)
    1. American poetry—20th century—History and criticism.
    2. Modernism (Literature)—United States.   3. Lawrence, D. H. (David
Herbert), 1885–1930—Characters—Prophets.   4. Modernism
(Literature)—Great Britain.   5. Prophecies in literature.
    6. Religion and literature.   7. Prophets in literature.   8. Gods in
literature.   I. Title.
    PS310.M57M37   1997
    811'.5209112—dc21   97-40320
                                                                            CIP

∞™ This paper meets the requirements of the American National Standard
for Permanence of Paper for Printed Library Materials, Z39.48, 1984.

Designer: Stephanie Foley
Typesetter: BOOKCOMP
Printer and binder: Thomson-Shore, Inc.
Typefaces: Bellevue and Galliard

For permissions, see Acknowledgments, p. 225.

For Bobbi, Olivia, and Andrew

Contents

Illustrations

Preface

LOOKING OVER the contents of this volume, I feel rather like Pound in his Canto 46: "Seventeen / Years on this case . . . nineteen / Years on this case." For over this many years, and more, I have been pondering the "case" for the genre of prophetic poetry. The present volume expresses views that have been presented in classrooms, public lectures, essays, introductions, and reviews— drawn together, I hope, in a sequence of ten essays, followed by a group of four essays related in various ways to the long sequence. Most of the writing here is either new or published over the past decade, but some older materials have also been included, as indicated in the notes and on the permissions page. Under such circumstances, the book cannot be expected to present a seamless robe, but there is, I believe, a persistent thematic emphasis, and certain writers tend to recur, especially Pound and Lawrence. I have had in mind something like the "musical" organization that Pound follows in the *Cantos.*

I wish to express my gratitude to the John Simon Guggenheim Foundation for a fellowship that enabled me to explore the Lawrence country and to study the manuscripts in the Lawrence Collection at the University of Nottingham, and also to study the manuscripts of *Quetzalcoatl* and *The Plumed Serpent* in the Harry Ransom Humanities Research Center of the University of Texas at Austin.

Many Gods and Many Voices

The sea has many voices,
Many gods and many voices.

—Eliot, "The Dry Salvages"

Part I

Prophetic Voice in Modern American Poetry

1.

The Voices of Prophecy

*P*ROPHETIC VOICE: what is a prophet? First of all, along with William Blake, we should reject the modern view that the prophet's primary function is to foretell the future. "Prophets, in the modern sense of the word, have never existed," Blake declares. "Jonah was no prophet in the modern sense, for his prophecy of Nineveh failed. . . . A prophet is a Seer, not an Arbitrary Dictator. It is man's fault if God is not able to do him good, for he gives to the just and to the unjust, but the unjust reject his gift."[1] Thus the biblical prophets spend a great deal of time—indeed, most of the time—denouncing the misdeeds of the unjust at the present moment, evils that derive from the people's worship of false gods. Prophecies of the future appear, but these are often prophecies of the disasters that will fall upon the people, or will continue to fall upon them, if they do not mend their unjust ways. The Hebrew prophet is a reformer: his mind is upon the present.[2] But then he also offers the consolation of future good, the

---

1. *Poetry and Prose of William Blake,* ed. Geoffrey Keynes (London: Nonesuch Press, 1951), 961. I am grateful to Professor Rodney Barrie for calling my attention to this passage.
2. Biblical scholars of the prophets have over the past fifty years frequently stressed the prophet's relation to the social and religious situation in his day, that is, to history. See, for example, the opening chapter of Abraham J. Heschel's classic *The Prophets* (New York: Harper and Row, 1962), and Alan Cooper, "Imagining Prophecy," in *Poetry and Prophecy,* ed. James L. Kugel (Ithaca and London: Cornell University Press, 1990), 26–44; Cooper's extensive notes (188–98) provide what amounts to a bibliography of biblical scholarship on the prophets over the past fifty years. Especially important for literary students are two short books by Walter Brueggemann, *The Prophetic Imagination* (Philadelphia: Fortress, 1978) and *Hopeful Imagination: Prophetic Voices in Exile* (Philadelphia: Fortress, 1986). Many insights into prophecy are also found in *Poetic Prophecy in Western Literature,* ed. Jan Wojcik and

possibility of redemption, if the people give up their unjust ways and return to worship of the truth.

Thus the voice of the prophet tends to oscillate between denunciation and consolation, between despair and hope, between images of desolation and images of redemption, between the actual and the ideal. He does not tell a story, as the epic bard does; he relates visions of good and evil, and he does so in what we call prose and what we call poetry, though in the Bible it is hard to distinguish these modes: poetry and prose flow together within the immense range of the prophetic voice, which can intermingle the most vicious language with the most exalted lyrics. The following passage from Isaiah will illustrate this characteristic movement:

> How is the faithful city become an harlot!
> It was full of judgment; righteousness lodged in it;
> But now murderers.
> Thy silver is become dross,
> Thy wine mixed with water:
> Thy princes are rebellious, and companions of thieves:
> Everyone loveth gifts, and followeth after rewards:
> They judge not the fatherless,
> Neither doth the cause of the widow come unto them.
> Therefore saith the Lord, the Lord of hosts, the Mighty One of
>   Israel,
> Ah, I will ease me of mine adversaries,
> And avenge me of mine enemies:

But here the prophecy takes a surprising turn: the threatened destruction is purgative, not deadly.

> And I will turn my hand upon thee,
> And purely purge away thy dross,
> And take away all thy tin [base alloy]
> And I will restore thy judges as at the first,
> And thy counsellors as at the beginning:
> Afterward thou shalt be called,
> The city of righteousness, the faithful city.
> Zion shall be redeemed with judgment,
> And her converts with righteousness.

Then the prophecy turns back to the threat:

Raymond-Jean Frontain; except for Whitman, the essays in their collection do not deal with the writers treated in the present book.

With a few exceptions, works listed in the bibliography are in the footnotes identified only by title.

> And the destruction of the transgressors and of the sinners
>   shall be together,
> And they that forsake the Lord shall be consumed.[3]

By persistent repetition of these dual themes the prophet seeks to achieve a change of heart, a moral and spiritual change in the minds of his people.

At the same time, as this passage shows, the true prophet never speaks for himself. In the basic Greek meaning of the word, a prophet is "one who speaks for another"—for God, for the gods, or for other human beings. Thus the voice of the Lord came to Ezekiel in ancient Babylon, saying:

> Son of man, stand upon thy feet, and I will speak unto thee. And the spirit entered into me when he spake unto me, and set me upon my feet that I heard him that spake unto me. And he said unto me, Son of man, I send thee to the children of Israel, to a rebellious nation that hath rebelled against me: they and their fathers have transgressed against me, even unto this very day. For they are impudent children and stiffhearted. I do send thee unto them; and thou shalt say unto them, Thus saith the Lord GOD. And they, whether they will hear, or whether they will forbear, (for they are a rebellious house), yet shall know that there hath been a prophet among them. (Ezek. 2:1–5)

As with Ezekiel, during the Babylonian captivity, prophetic writing is born out of disaster or the threat of disaster, out of the human need to believe in more than destruction. And in our century the genre of prophetic writing has again come alive. It was first created out of the ashes of World War I, by D. H. Lawrence, H.D., Ezra Pound, and T. S. Eliot: all born within a three-year period, 1885–1888. They read each other's writings and were linked by friendship: it is no accident that their voices joined in a prophetic chorus. They shared the basic view expressed by Lawrence in one of his letters of 1915, when the war that could not happen had happened, with no end in sight for three more years:

> When I drive across this country, with the autumn falling and rustling to pieces, I am so sad, for my country, for this great wave of civilisation, 2000 years, which is now collapsing, that it is hard to live. So much beauty and pathos of old things passing away and no new things coming: this house of the Ottolines—It is England—my God, it breaks my soul—this England, these shafted windows, the elm-trees, the blue distance—the past, the great past, crumbling down, breaking down, not under the force of the coming buds but under the weight of many exhausted, lovely yellow leaves, that drift over the lawn and over the pond, like the soldiers, passing away, into winter

3. Isa. 1:21–28, quoted in the versified arrangement of the Authorized (King James) Version in *The Reader's Bible* (Oxford: Oxford University Press, 1951). Other biblical quotations are taken from the standard Oxford editions of the King James Version.

and the darkness of winter—no, I can't bear it. For the winter stretches ahead, where all vision is lost and all memory dies out.

But a week earlier he had taken a more optimistic view:

> Let the leaves perish, but let the tree stand, living and bare. For the tree, the living organism of the soul of Europe is good, only the external forms and growths are bad. Let all the leaves fall, and many branches. But the quick of the tree must not perish. There are unrevealed buds which can come forward into another epoch of civilisation, if only we can shed this dead form and be strong in the spirit of love and creation.[4]

Here again is the characteristic oscillation of prophecy.

In this state of mind, during World War I, Lawrence turned toward America, with thoughts of emigrating to Florida or South America, and with extensive reading of American authors of the nineteenth century—Fenimore Cooper, Hawthorne, Melville, Dana, Whitman—and gradually the series of essays took shape that were ultimately published under the title *Studies in Classic American Literature* (1923), essays that would be the first to reveal to England the greatness of these American authors. For Lawrence, Whitman in particular became a major prophetic voice: "Whitman, the one man breaking a way ahead. Whitman, the one pioneer. And only Whitman. No English pioneers, no French. No European pioneer-poets."

> Whitman was the first heroic seer to seize the soul by the scruff of her neck and plant her down among the potsherds.
> "There!" he said to the soul. "Stay there!"
> "Stay there, stay in the flesh."

Whitman, he declares, gives "the American heroic message." "The soul is not to pile up defences round herself. . . . She is to go down the open road, as the road opens, into the unknown, keeping company with those whose soul draws them near to her."[5]

But in what sense could Walt Whitman be called a prophet? For whom does he speak? What disasters does he recognize? What consolations does he offer? The answers to all these questions are implicit in his *Leaves of Grass* of 1855, the opening of which came to be called "Song of Myself"—but what a self!

> Walt Whitman, an American, one of the roughs, a kosmos,
> Disorderly fleshy and sensual. . . . eating drinking and
>   breeding,

4. To Lady Cynthia Asquith, November 9, November 2, 1915, in *The Letters of D. H. Lawrence,* vol. 2, ed. George J. Zytaruk and James T. Boulton (Cambridge: Cambridge University Press, 1981), 431–32, 425.

5. Lawrence, *Studies in Classic American Literature* (New York: Seltzer, 1923), 253–57.

> No sentimentalist. . . . no stander above men and women or
>   apart from them . . . . no more modest than immodest.

And then he describes the core of his prophetic function:

> Through me many long dumb voices,
> Voices of the interminable generations of slaves,
> Voices of prostitutes and of deformed persons,
> Voices of the diseased and despairing, and of thieves and
>   dwarfs,
> Voices of cycles of preparation and accretion,
> And of the threads that connect the stars—and of wombs, and
>   of the fatherstuff,
> And of the rights of them the others are down upon,
> Of the trivial and flat and foolish and despised,
> Of fog in the air and beetles rolling balls of dung.[6]

Whitman's self incorporates the voices of every man and every woman and indeed "speaks" for every thing, even "beetles rolling balls of dung." A prophet is one who speaks for another. This prophet desires to speak for all Americans, diverse as they are; he desires to bind them all together by the power of his voice. Thus in his enormous catalogs, based upon the vistas of the biblical prophets, he includes every aspect of human existence: the baby in its cradle, the lovers, the suicide, the "pure contralto," the carpenter, the pilot, the duck shooter, the spinning girl, the lunatic, the printer, the "quadroon girl" sold at auction, the "groups of newly-come immigrants," the Indian squaw, the peddler, the bride, and the opium eater, along with the president and the "crew of the fish-smack." Listening intently, he hears "the blab of the pave. . . . the tires of carts and sluff of bootsoles and talk of the promenaders," "the clank of the shod horses on the granite floor," "the hurrahs for popular favorites, the fury of rous'd mobs" (146–49). Then come the crucial lines that reveal the core of his poetic technique and his prophetic mission:

> What living and buried speech is always vibrating here. . . .
>   what howls restrained by decorum.
> Arrests of criminals, slights, adulterous offers made,
>   acceptances, rejections with convex lips,
> I mind them or the resonance of them. . . . (157–59)

His aim is to hear and express this "living and buried speech" that he hears all about him:

---

6. *Leaves of Grass: The First (1855) Edition*, ed. Malcolm Cowley, lines 499–501, 509–17. For Whitman as prophet in the biblical tradition see Dennis K. Renner, "Tradition for a Time of Crisis: Whitman's Prophetic Stance," in *Poetic Prophecy*, ed. Wojcik and Frontain, 119–30.

> This is the grass that grows wherever the land is and the
>   water is,
> This is the common air that bathes the globe. (358–59)

These voices are his leaves of grass—the leaves of his book. It is a book that shows his deep belief in the creative power of human consciousness, but if that power is not put into words, we do not know it. He is the one who will give us the words.

> It is you talking just as much as myself. . . . I act as the
>   tongue of you,
> It was tied in your mouth. . . . in mine it begins to be
>   loosened. (1244–45)

What would have prompted such a desire to assume the prophetic voice in the year 1855? It seems that Whitman, journalist and traveler, was well aware of the divisions arising in the land, soon to break forth in the war that he would include in the later editions of his *Leaves of Grass:* "Over the carnage rose prophetic a voice," as he says in "Drum Taps." The voice of the prophet arises out of disaster or the threat of disaster. Thus in the latter part of his "Song of Myself" Whitman brings in every kind of human suffering: the voice of the wife as "They fetch my man's body up dripping and drowned" (816–17), the terror of those on the sinking ship (819–25), the "hounded slave" (829–39), the horrors of war (856–62), "the murder in cold blood of four hundred and twelve young men" (864–89), and much more. But throughout all this agony the prophet offers redemption by his presence. "I am the man. . . . I suffered . . . , I was there" (827). Like the skipper who stays by the "crowded and rudderless wreck," he is "faithful of days and faithful of nights" (820–21). This poetry, like all prophetic poetry, is (to adapt the title of a book on Williams) "a poetry of presence,"[7] the presence of a consciousness that observes and absorbs the physical world and its people, while affirming a sustaining power derived from the awareness of some transcendent presence.

---

7. Bernard Duffey, *A Poetry of Presence: The Writing of William Carlos Williams.*

Fig. 1. Ezra Pound in old age; portrait by Lotte Frumi, 1972. Yale Collection of American Literature, Beinecke Rare Book and Manuscript Library, Yale University.

2.

Pound as Prophet

*I*N THEIR ADMIRATION for Whitman, Ezra Pound and D. H. Lawrence truly meet, although their personal relationship was brief and never close. They annoyed each other. "Detestable person," Pound wrote of Lawrence to Harriet Monroe in 1913, "but needs watching," he added with his usual eye for new talent: "I think he learned the proper treatment of modern subjects before I did." And of course he got Lawrence published in *Poetry,* as well as in the *Egoist.* "Lawrence, as you know, gives me no particular pleasure," Pound wrote to Harriet a few months later. "Nevertheless we are lucky to get him. . . . I *recognize* certain qualities of his work. If I were an editor I should probably accept his work without reading it. As a prose writer I grant him first place among the younger men."[1]

Lawrence was at first dazzled by Pound, though one can discern within this letter of 1909 the seeds of their later dislike:

> He is a well-known American poet—a good one. He is 24, like me,—but his god is beauty, mine, life. He is jolly nice: took me to supper at Pagnani's, and afterwards we went down to his room at Kensington. He lives in an attic, like a traditional poet—but the attic is a comfortable well furnished one. He is an American Master of Arts and a professor of the Provençal group of languages, and he lectures once a week on the minstrels [at] the London polytechnic. He is rather remarkable—a good bit of a genius, and with not the least self consciousness. . . . He knows W. B. Yeats and all the Swells.[2]

1. *The Letters of Ezra Pound, 1907–1941,* ed. D. D. Paige, 17, 22.
2. To Louie Burrows, November 20, 1909, in *The Letters of D. H. Lawrence,* vol. 1, ed. James T. Boulton (Cambridge: Cambridge University Press, 1979), 145.

Yet their relation, direct and indirect, is significant. They shared a friendship with
H.D. during the London years, and in this way Lawrence developed more than
a superficial acquaintance with Imagism.

Lawrence saw Pound as an aesthete: "his god is beauty." Lawrence did not
see, perhaps it was too early to see, that underneath the pre-Raphaelite trappings
of *A Lume Spento* lay the sense of an enormous mission akin to Lawrence's own
growing sense of a prophetic mission: to redeem the dying civilization of the
West. As far back as 1909, when Pound wrote his brief essay "What I Feel about
Walt Whitman," his sense of an immense mission was in evidence. Whitman
is, Pound declares, "The only one of the conventionally recognised 'American
Poets' who is worth reading. . . . The vital part of my message, taken from the
sap and fibre of America, is the same as his."

> Mentally I am a Walt Whitman who has learned to wear a collar and a
> dress shirt (although at times inimical to both). Personally I might be very
> glad to conceal my relationship to my spiritual father and brag about my
> more congenial ancestry—Dante, Shakespeare, Theocritus, Villon, but the
> descent is a bit difficult to establish. And, to be frank, Whitman is to my
> fatherland . . . what Dante is to Italy and I at my best can only be a strife for
> a renaissance in America of all the lost or temporarily mislaid beauty, truth,
> valour, glory of Greece, Italy, England and all the rest of it.[3]

Pound aims to energize the dying strains of late Victorian poetry by bringing
in something of Whitman's freedom of subject and verse form to alleviate the
"Crepuscular Spirit in Modern Poetry," as he says in a poem of 1909:

> I would shake off the lethargy of this our time, and give
> For shadows—shapes of power
> For dreams—men.[4]

His "Salutation" (1913) becomes a declaration of his kinship with Whitman in
movement, imagery, and attitude:

> O generation of the thoroughly smug
>   and thoroughly uncomfortable,
> I have seen fishermen picnicking in the sun,
> I have seen them with untidy families,
> I have seen their smiles full of teeth
>   and heard ungainly laughter.

And in the same year his poem "A Pact" declares the essential relationship:

---

3. Pound, *Selected Prose, 1909–1965,* ed. William Cookson, 115–16.
4. "Revolt," from *Personae* (1909), in *Collected Early Poems of Ezra Pound,* ed. Michael
John King, 96; hereafter cited as *CEP.*

I make a pact with you, Walt Whitman—
I have detested you long enough.
I come to you as a grown child
Who has had a pig-headed father;
I am old enough now to make friends.
It was you that broke the new wood,
Now is a time for carving.
We have one sap and one root—
Let there be commerce between us.[5]

At the same time, to carve the new wood, to give it form and shape, Pound felt that he must fuse into Whitman's "barbaric yawp" the culture of the European past from Homer to Dante and the troubadours, and later on the culture of ancient China. Clearly it is with this sense of mission that he wrote in 1912 his "Epilogue (To my five books containing mediaeval studies, experiments and translations)":

I bring you the spoils, my nation,
I, who went out in exile,
    Am returned to thee with gifts.

I, who have laboured long in the tombs,
    Am come back therefrom with riches.

Behold my spices and robes, my nation,
My gifts of Tyre.

Here are my rimes of the south;
Here are strange fashions of music;
Here is my knowledge.

Behold, I am come with patterns;
Behold, I return with devices,
Cunning the craft, cunning the work, the fashion.[6]

Within the late Victorian archaisms of this strange poem one can hear, I think, the rhythms of Whitman striving for release: the ancient and the modern have come together here in an awkward and uneasy combination as Pound tries to create the guise of a wizard, a seer, a prophet, and a conqueror.

The same vein of hope is found throughout *Patria Mia,* which was published in *New Age* in seventeen installments during 1912 and 1913. Here he tells

5. Both of these poems were published in *Poetry* (April 1913) as part of a series entitled "Contemporania." See Donald Gallup, *Ezra Pound: A Bibliography,* 230, item C76. *Personae,* rev. ed. by Lea Baechler and A. Walton Litz, 86, 90.
    6. *CEP,* 209.

his British audience of his belief that America will undergo an "awakening," a renaissance, that "will have its effect not only in the arts, but in life, in politics, and in economics"—an "American Risorgimento" in which, following Whitman's "American keynote," Pound might play a leading role. And in this hope he wrote:

> One wants to find out what sort of things endure, and what sort of things are transient; what sort of things recur; what propagandas profit a man or his race; to learn upon what the forces, constructive and dispersive, of social order, move; to learn what rules and axioms hold firm, and what sort fade, and what sort are durable but permutable, what sort hold in letter, and what sort by analogy only, what sort by close analogy, and what sort by rough parallel alone.[7]

These are the words of a man pondering a deep mission.

Pound dons the prophet's robes in a poem that he sent to Harriet Monroe in 1913, "From Chebar"—the river beside which the prophet Ezekiel during his Babylonian exile "saw visions of God" and "heard a voice of one that spake," saying, "Son of man, stand upon thy feet, and I will speak unto thee."[8] Pound knew his prophets well; while still a student at Hamilton College he wrote to his mother in February 1905: "untill you can show me men of today who shall excell certain men some time dead, I shall continue to study Dante and the Hebrew prophets."[9] Pound knew well what he was doing when he wrote from Chebar: he adopted the prophetic voice of Ezekiel with the cadences and imagery of Whitman, just as Whitman himself had invented his *Leaves of Grass* out of the cadences and catalogs of the Hebrew prophets. As Whitman said in his preface to the 1855 *Leaves of Grass*, "The expression of the American poet is to be transcendent and new. It is to be indirect and not direct or descriptive or epic. Its quality goes through these to much more. Let the age and wars of other nations be chanted and their eras and characters be illustrated and that finish the verse. Not so the great psalm of the republic. Here the theme is creative and has vista."[10]

So Pound proceeds with his own vista, writing from his exile by the Thames:

> I can see the coast and the forest
> And the corn-yellow plains and the hills,
> The domed sky and the jagged,

7. *Patria Mia and the Treatise on Harmony,* 26–27, 45, 49. For details of publication see Gallup, *Ezra Pound,* 82, item A63.

8. Ezek. 1:1, 28; 2:1.

9. Family Letters, Ezra Pound Archive, Beinecke Library; hereafter cited as Family Letters. (Listed as "Family Correspondence" in typescript catalog.)

10. *Leaves of Grass* (1855), ed. Cowley, 8. Note that the phrase "great psalm" identifies the biblical tradition, in contrast to epic.

> The plainsmen and men of the cities. . . .
> I have seen the dawn mist
> Move in the yellow grain,
> I have seen the daubed purple sunset;
> You may kill me, but I do not accede,
> You may ignore me, you may keep me in exile,
> You may assail me with negations, or you
>   may keep me, a while, well hidden,
> But I am after you and before you,
> And above all, I do not accede.

With a witty self-awareness of his style here he adds, "There is no use your quoting Whitman against me, / His time is not our time, his day and hour were different." But the rhythms we hear are the same. Then he gives the goal, the ideal:

> The order does not end in the arts,
> The order shall come and pass through them.
>
> The state is too idle, the decrepit church is too idle,
> The arts alone can transmit this.
> They alone cling fast to the gods,
> Even the sciences are a little below them.[11]

Thus poetry and the other arts become a civilizing, a redeeming force, preserving the "gods"—that is, the ideals and beliefs and inspirations of the past that will convey an ordering power into the present and the future.

But all this was fermenting in Pound's mind before 1914, before the disaster of the war, which struck Lawrence and Pound and H.D. with horror and despair as they watched what they judged to be the suicide of Europe. Pound, in Canto 16, reveals his revulsion against the slaughter, as, like Whitman, he hears voices: "j'entendis des voix"—in French, because most of the voices and scenes that follow are French, or set in France. He seems to be saying, as Whitman did, "What living and buried speech is always vibrating here"—and declaring, as Whitman did, "Through me many long dumb voices."

So here in Canto 16 he hears Plarr's narration of Gallifet's famous charge in the Franco-Prussian war, followed at once by old Admiral Percy's vivid account of finding Lord Byron

> Dead drunk, with the face of an A y n. . . . .
> He pulled it out long, like that:
>   the face of an a y n. . . . . . . gel.

---

11. *CEP*, 269–72. For Pound's condition of exile and his differences from Whitman in this poem see Stephen Cushman, *Fictions of Form in American Poetry*, 104–6.

Suddenly, out of these voices from older wars, he shifts to a long catalog of his friends who have died or have been caught up in the recent war:

> They put Aldington on Hill 70, in a trench
> >   dug through corpses
> With a lot of kids of sixteen,
> Howling and crying for their mamas,
> And he sent a chit back to his major:
> >   I can hold out for ten minutes
> With my sergeant and a machine-gun.
> >   And they rebuked him for levity.
> And Henri Gaudier went to it,
> >   and they killed him.
> And killed a good deal of sculpture,
> And ole T. E. H. he went to it,
> With a lot of books from the library,
> London Library, and a shell buried'em in a dug-out,
> And the Library expressed its annoyance.

"And Wyndham Lewis went to it," and Windeler, and Ole Captain Baker, each with his vignette;

> And Ernie Hemingway went to it,
> >   too much in a hurry,
> And they buried him for four days.

Then follows in French the long passage describing, in the voice of an eyewitness, the collapse of the soldiers into a world without order, a world of wild beasts, with the official list of the dead, five million. Then abruptly follows the voice from Mitteleuropa, taunting a "bolcheviki" in broken English:

> Looka vat youah Trotzsk is done, e iss
> >   madeh deh zhamefull beace!!

And next a clearly American voice, reporting the scene at the outbreak of the Russian Revolution:

> That's the trick with a crowd,
> >   Get 'em into the street and get 'em moving.

Then comes the voice of "a man there talking," the voice of Lenin, filtered through the voice of an American reporter (Lincoln Steffens), witnessing the outbreak of violence:

And when it broke, there was the crowd there,
And the cossacks, just as always before,
But one thing, the cossacks said:
    "Pojalouista."

And finally, the scene shifts back to wartime England in the midst of Butcher Haig's command, with the voices of soldiers on leave nursing an illusory hope:

So we used to hear it at the opera,
That they wouldn't be under Haig;
    and that the advance was beginning;
That it was going to begin in a week.[12]

Those are the closing words of the book that appeared in 1925 with that most tentative title, *A Draft of XVI. Cantos of Ezra Pound for the Beginning of a Poem of Some Length*. Pound's method of hearing voices was now firmly established; as he wrote to his father toward the end of 1924: "As to Cantos 18–19; there aint no key. Simplest paralell I can give is radio where you tell who is talking by the noise they make. If your copies are properly punctuated they shd. show where each voice begins and ends." But what was he writing as he composed his medley of voices ("my big long endless poem that I am now struggling with," as he said to his father in 1915)? He was not sure. "Have done cantos 5, 6, and 7, each more incomprehensible than the one preceding it; dont know what's to be done about it," he wrote to his father in 1919.[13] Is it an epic? In the "tirade" sent to his mother in 1909, he denies that an "Epic to the West" is possible—except perhaps as Whitman did it: "Whitman expressed America as Dante did mediaeval europe." "An epic in the real sense," he says, "is the speech of a nation thru the mouth of one man." He is defining epic in terms of prophecy: "Just at present I can see America producing a Jonah, or a Lamenting Jherimiah. But the american who has any suspicion that he may write poetry, will walk very much alone, with his eyes on the beauty of the past of the old world, or on the glory of a spiritual kingdom, or on some earthly new Jerusalem." Right now, the only prophetic vision he can summon up is satirical: "So I behold a vision—Rockfellow marches in purple robes thru a cloud of coal smoke, Morgan is clothed in samite, and the spirits of the 3d heaven foster their progress enthroned on trolley cars."[14]

What then was he writing? As he wrote on May 7, 1924, to Bill Bird, his printer and publisher of *Draft of XVI. Cantos,* "It ain't an epic. It's part of a

12. Quotations from the *Cantos* are taken from the thirteenth printing (1995) of the New Directions text.
13. Family Letters, November 29, 1924; December 18, 1915; December 13, 1919.
14. Family Letters, to his mother, 1909.

long poem."[15] So far as I know, this is all he would call his poem up to this point, a "long poem." Pound appears to have been working under the inchoate impulse of a mighty intuition: he had a mission in the world; a long poem would convey that mission, but how, exactly, could it be expressed in a long poem? The role of the biblical prophet showed a way. The prophet's poem is a poem including history—the history of his people's misdeeds and occasional glories. The prophet is a religious reformer: he sees and threatens disaster while he offers a mode of redemption. His way of speech is exhortation, denunciation, excoriation, satire. Thus we have Pound's sly response to his father, who had apparently objected to the satire in Cantos 18 and 19: "Satire, my dear Homer," he wrote in mock amazement, "SATIRE!!! Wotcher mean by satire?!? Those are just the simple facts . . . wot have taken me a number of years to collect. And all of 'em by word of mouth or from the original actors. . . . You understand the NAMES dont matter; what I am trying to give is the STATE of rascality and wangle."[16] Yes, a poem including history—of rascality and wangle. But the prophet denounces these things in order to recall his people to the good ways of the past and to create the good ways of the future: the true, the eternal, the just. He offers also the poetry of consolation. And he offers all this in a work that often modulates toward prose and sometimes indeed includes prose. Robert Alter begins his discussion of prophetic poetry by pointing to "the many passages, long and short, in Jeremiah, Ezekiel, and the late Minor Prophets that were written in prose. Some of these prose prophecies make use of loosely parallel semantic-syntactic structures that distantly recall the background of poetry."[17] One thinks of Pound and Lawrence and Whitman. Is it characteristic of prophetic writing in all ages to show this sort of variation in style?

But what was this endless long poem? Perhaps Pound discovered what it was when he helped to make *The Waste Land* what it became under his deleting and shaping hands: a poem purged of extraneous matter, so that the prophetic voice becomes dominant, from the warning words "Son of Man" at the outset, on to the prophet Tiresias in the center of the poem, and finally to the Sanskrit prophecies at the close. Pound helped to shape the poem so that it became essentially a prophetic utterance addressed to the falling cities of the Western world. Eliot's own natural mode was introspective, diffident, as in Prufrock's "I am no prophet—and here's no great matter." Pound, I believe, saw in Eliot's sprawling and diffident manuscript the new wood, half carved, and set about sharpening the planes of that incipient prophetic carving.

---

15. *Letters,* ed. Paige, 189.
16. Family Letters, March 4, 1926.
17. *The Art of Biblical Poetry* (New York: Basic Books, 1985), 137. Alter's chap. 6, "Prophecy and Poetry," provides an account of prophetic technique that throws light on the "vocative" qualities of the *Cantos:* "The overarching purpose is reproof (and not, I would contend, prediction), and this general aim is realized through three related poetic strategies: (1) direct accusation; (2) satire; (3) the monitory evocation of impending disaster" (141).

Perhaps it was the presence of Tiresias in Eliot's poem that gave Pound the insight into his own true mode of writing and led him in the year after the appearance of *The Waste Land* to shear away most of those first three Cantos of 1917, leaving only, as Canto 1, the voyage to the underworld, the meeting with Tiresias. If so, the suggestion was earned, for perhaps it was the appearance of Tiresias in those early Cantos that led Eliot to place Tiresias in his poem, just as the example of the seven Cantos that Eliot surely read before 1922 provided the mélange of voices that make up the method of Eliot's prophetic poem.

When we take Odysseus as the central figure of the *Cantos*—a mask of Pound—we must not forget that without Tiresias, Odysseus would have lost his way. Tiresias, the name of the prophetic voice, is indeed essential as a controlling figure in the *Cantos*. It is in searching for Tiresias that Odysseus finds the shades of the past flocking all about him: Tiresias, we might say, is the magnet that draws the iron filings into the shape of the rose. And in what is now the second Canto, the priest of Bacchus warns King Pentheus to heed the warning of Tiresias. Was this one reason Pound moved what was originally Canto 8 to become Canto 2: in order to stress the gods, and the prophet of the gods? Then in Canto 39, in the midst of this fertility celebration, he gives in Greek the words of Circe to Odysseus concerning Tiresias, which form the opening of the next fertility Canto, number 47:

> Who even dead, yet hath his mind entire!
> This sound came in the dark
> First must thou go the road
>   to hell
> And to the bower of Ceres' daughter Proserpine,
> Through overhanging dark, to see Tiresias,
> Eyeless that was, a shade, that is in hell
> So full of knowing that the beefy men know less than he,
> Ere thou come to thy road's end.

Then in the prison camp, in Canto 80, we have another echo of this Greek passage, altered in memory to Pound's own Greek—but followed by the words "Still hath his mind entire."

Perhaps, then, Pound knew what he was saying, long before, in *The Spirit of Romance,* when he wrote about the *Lusiad* of Camoens, saying how much it belonged to the spirit of its age: "His work is utterly dependent upon the events and temper of his time." And then he noted: "An epic cannot be written against the grain of its time: the prophet or the satirist may hold himself aloof from his time, or run counter to it, but the writer of epos must voice the general heart."[18]

18. *The Spirit of Romance* (London: Dent, 1910), 227, 228.

That sentence may tell us much about the *Cantos*. For Pound knew well that his age was not an age for epic, and that he himself could not accede to the demands of his age. Perhaps the *Cantos* should be called prophecy and satire. Or perhaps the term *prophetic poem* or *prophetic voice* will do, since violent denunciation of evil forms an essential part of the prophetic voice. Seeking the ideal for his people, the prophet reacts with fierce revulsion from what he sees as the corruption of his people; to save them, he denounces them in fearsome terms—but always with the indestructible ideal in mind: *dove sta memoria* (Canto 76).

I would like to urge, then, that we might consider this "long poem" as a work closely related to the prophetic tradition, along with the epic. The practice of calling the poem an "epic" is firmly established, and the term is justified if we are using it to describe the poem's immense length and range of reference, along with its many allusions to ancient epic. But the term *epic* may also lead us to search for certain qualities in the poem: a heroic protagonist and some sort of plot or sequence—qualities that exist in the *Cantos* only in terms of the poet as speaker and the events in his career: these are the essential qualities of the biblical prophets. At the same time prophecy provides an alternative, or a supplement, to Pound's view, expressed around 1933, that "an epic is a poem including history."[19] The books of the biblical prophets arise from the history of the Hebrew people and from the personal experience of the prophet. I think that consideration of the texture of the Hebrew books of prophecy will help to solve some of the difficulties and show some of the virtues of the *Cantos*.

Prophecy and epic flow together in the *Cantos,* a confluence of genres such as we find in Dante's great poem. Stephen Sicari glimpses this blending of traditions in his treatment of the *Pisan Cantos,* where he sees one aspect of prophecy in Pound's stance as "prophet of the ideal order"—"the prophet who keeps the dream of ideal justice alive for the rest of humanity." Sicari sees these prophetic elements as contained within a larger "narrative line surrounding the figure of the wanderer," in the tradition of epic.[20] All this is true, but I would reverse the emphasis. I would see the fragmentary allusions to ancient epic as contained within a larger fabric of prophecy, in biblical terms. The *Pisan Cantos* bear a striking similarity to the Book of Jeremiah; Jeremiah also suffered imprisonment and opprobrium but never gave up hope that some day his people might heed his violent denunciations. Like Pound, Jeremiah is constantly present amid his poetry and occasional prose, reminding us of his enemies in high places, and even among his neighbors. Like these cantos, the Book of Jeremiah oscillates between denunciation and hope, between the abyss and the ideal, and all these

19. See Pound, *ABC of Reading* (London: Routledge, 1934), 30, and *Letters,* ed. Paige, 247 (to Harriet Monroe, September 14, 1933). Pound was still using the definition in his famous interview in *Paris Review* 28 (1962): 22–51.
20. *Pound's Epic Ambition: Dante and the Modern World,* 115, 116, 16.

variations in mood and tone and literary method, ranging from prose to delicate lyric—all this is held together by the prophetic voice.

I was struck some time ago by the following description of a book that, according to this critic, "makes, at least on first trial, extremely difficult reading."

> Nor is this entirely because it so often alludes to persons, situations, and events of which the reader can hardly be expected to know, or because they presuppose viewpoints, develop concepts, and use terminology unfamiliar to him. . . . What makes these [poems] particularly, and one might say need-lessly, difficult is the very manner of their arrangement—or, to be more accurate, their apparent lack of arrangement. . . . All seems confusion. There is no narrative for him [the reader] to follow, nor can he trace any logical progression running through them and binding their parts together into a coherent whole. No sooner has he grasped a line of thought, and prided himself that he is following it tolerably well, than it breaks off and something quite different is being discussed. The impression he gains is one of extreme disarray; one can scarcely blame him for concluding that he is reading a hopeless hodgepodge thrown together without any discernible principle of arrangement at all.[21]

This may represent the initial response of a good many readers to the *Cantos* of Ezra Pound, but this critic is describing, accurately, I think, the initial impact of reading the prophetic Book of Jeremiah. Such a mode of writing seems to be inherent in the very nature of prophetic utterance. The prophet is one who speaks from inspiration. Sometimes his vision soars into exalted poetry, sometimes it shifts into violent denunciation of the sins of the people, their deviations from truth; at other times the writing is expository, historical, descriptive, plain prose. Everyone who has ever read the Hebrew prophets has remarked upon this disconcerting variation in style and subject, caused partly by the fact that no one can write constantly in the white heat of the divine coal applied to the lips of the prophet Isaiah. "The prophetic books," our biblical critic explains, "are indeed not books" in the ordinary sense of that word. "They are, rather collections of prophetic sayings and other material which have a long and complex history of transmission behind them."[22] Something of the sort might well be said of the modern prophetic poem, which represents a "long and complex history of transmission" through the poet's mind.

As biblical scholars have noted, the books of prophecy include an immense variety of literary forms and modes: "lyrical fragments, prose narratives, in parable or direct speech, curt oracular style or the various literary forms of exhortation, diatribe, sermon, proverb, formal psalms, love songs, satire, funeral

21. *The Anchor Bible: Jeremiah,* ed. John Bright, 2d ed. (New York: Doubleday, 1965), lvi–lvii.
22. Ibid., lvii.

lament, etc."[23] (This could almost be a description of Pound's *Cantos*.) Yet all this abundant variety is not without its peculiar unity. The ancient editors of the prophetic books have set their materials together in such a way that repetition of theme, phrase, and sentence serves to link the materials within the presence of the dominant voice. The Books of Isaiah, Ezekiel, and Jeremiah move toward resounding finales: Isaiah with the splendid redemptive poetry of "Second Isaiah" (chapters 40–55); Ezekiel with the chapters (40–48) realizing his goal, the rebuilding of the Temple, "a blueprint for the religious and political rehabilitation of the Israelite nation in Palestine";[24] and Jeremiah with the longest and most eloquent of all his poems, the series of "Oracles against the Nations" (chapters 46–51).

A similar unity may be found in the immense variety of Pound's *Cantos*. I believe that, up through Canto 51,[25] we can trace the powerful oscillations of the prophetic voice, its movements from denunciation to exaltation, and find the *Cantos* cohesive, convincing, and successful. It is with the virulent opening of Canto 52, published, with blacked-out lines, in 1940, and now at last completely printed,[26] that the troubles begin and the prophetic voice falters. For now, from Canto 52 on through Canto 71, we have voices of quite a different kind: first the voice of the history teacher chronicling the story of ancient China, and second the voice of another history teacher patching together the story of John Adams and his times. This is not the medley of voices that Pound invented, it is not at all the prophetic voice. With the onset here, for the first time in the *Cantos,* of an overt anti-Semitism, the prophetic voice collapses, then wanders desperately through the radio broadcasts into the prison camp at Pisa, and there, in the *Pisan Cantos,* struggles to recover the voice of the prophet in the midst of ruin, and does, at times, truly recover, as in the great lynx hymn of Canto 79 or in the biblical voice that emerges from the vision of the eyes at the close of Canto 81, speaking with a double voice, both to the self and to the public:[27]

> What thou lovest well remains,
> > the rest is dross

23. *The Jerusalem Bible* (Garden City, N.Y.: Doubleday, 1966), 1116. See also Alter, *Art of Biblical Poetry,* 142: "the prophets occasionally adapt to their purposes a nonprophetic poetic genre, such as elegy, parable, supplication, thanksgiving psalm."

24. *The Jerusalem Bible,* 1411.

25. I am struck by the coincidence that Jeremiah's prophecy also ends with his chapter 51: "Thus far are the words of Jeremiah." Chapter 52 is clearly an appendix.

26. In the tenth printing of the New Directions edition, 1986; also in the notes to the Italian edition and the translation of the *Cantos* by Mary de Rachewiltz.

27. The point has been sharply debated: is the passage addressed to the "vanity" of the victors of World War II, or to the self? The first view is borne out by Pound's line at the end of Canto 83: "The States have passed thru a / dam'd supercilious era." But the element of self-address seems to be firmly established in the opening and closing lines ("What thou lovest well remains . . ."; "Here error is all in the not done . . ."). For both sides of the issue see Peter D'Epiro, "Whose Vanity Must Be Pulled Down?"

What thou lov'st well shall not be reft from thee
What thou lov'st well is thy true heritage
. . . .
Pull down thy vanity
                          How mean thy hates
Fostered in falsity,
                          Pull down thy vanity,
Rathe to destroy, niggard in charity,
Pull down thy vanity,
                          I say pull down.

The difference between the prophetic voice and the personal voice is then driven home by the next lines: "But to have done instead of not doing / this is not vanity":

                    To have gathered from the air a live tradition
             or from a fine old eye the unconquered flame
             This is not vanity.
                 Here error is all in the not done,
             all in the diffidence that faltered,

The final comma of the first edition, intended or not, seems right: it marks the "not done." The "diffidence," perhaps, indicates a recognition that he has not kept faith with his poetic mission, did not have sufficient faith in the "arts" to work their ordering power. He turned to politics, and the poetry faltered. I do not find that prophetic voice emerging often after the *Pisan Cantos.* Canto 116, the last complete canto, in its muted introspective voice seems to me to sum up poignantly both the success and the failure of Pound's prophetic mission.

3.

Pound and *The Waste Land*

It was in 1922 [says Eliot] that I placed before [Pound] in Paris the manuscript of a sprawling chaotic poem called *The Waste Land* which left his hands, reduced to about half its size, in the form in which it appears in print. I should like to think that the manuscript, with the suppressed passages, had disappeared irrecoverably; yet, on the other hand, I should wish the blue pencilling on it to be preserved as irrefutable evidence of Pound's critical genius.[1]

*T*HE MANUSCRIPT HAS, of course, been preserved and published.[2] It turned up in the New York Public Library in 1968, as part of John Quinn's papers, for Eliot had sent the manuscript to Quinn in 1922. Quinn had told Eliot that *The Waste Land* "is one of the best things you have done. . . . It is for the elect or the remnant or the select few or the superior guys, or any word that you may choose, for the small numbers of readers that it is certain to have."[3] As it turned out, Eliot had sent him what was to become the best-known English poem of the twentieth century, throughout the world: it has been translated into more than twenty different languages: Chinese, Czech, Danish, Dutch, Finnish, French,

1. *An Examination of Ezra Pound,* ed. Peter Russell, 28.
2. *The Waste Land: A Facsimile and Transcript of the Original Drafts, Including the Annotations of Ezra Pound,* ed. Valerie Eliot.
3. Ibid., introduction, xxiii.

German, Greek, Hebrew, Italian, Norwegian, Iranian, Polish, Russian, Spanish, Swedish, Arabic, Korean, Bengali, Lithuanian, Malayan, Romanian, and perhaps more. From its first publication its concentrated voice of prophecy aroused a strong and ever-spreading response. By comparison, Pound's *Cantos,* even when sixteen of them appeared together in 1925, met with only a limited and rather tepid respect. Pound, with his uncanny literary instinct for excellence, almost predicted this result, in one of the letters that he wrote from Paris to Eliot in London, about the manuscript of *The Waste Land,* which he had been reading, cutting, marking up, while suggesting dozens and dozens of alterations, large and small, mainly aimed at shaping the poem. Thus, on January 24, 1922, he wrote to Eliot, "Complementi, you bitch, I am wracked by the seven jealousies, and cogitating an excuse for always exuding my deformative secretions in my own stuff, and never getting an outline."[4] In other words, he felt that his own works—the seven Cantos that he had thus far published—were formless, filled with "deformative secretions," whereas Eliot's poem had an "outline." But the irony is that the shape, the outline, of the poem as we now have it is largely due to Pound's critical insight. Thus, when Eliot wanted to tack on three more pages after the concluding "Shantih," Pound said no, "The thing now runs from April . . . to shantih without break. That is 19 pages, and let us say the longest poem in the English langwidge. Don't try to bust all records by prolonging it three pages further."[5]

So the *shape* of the poem as we now have it (for Pound suggested only one word, "demobbed," and perhaps helped Eliot decide upon another, "demotic")[6] —the *shape* carved out of Eliot's words is largely the work of Ezra Pound. We do not know whether Pound was directly responsible for cutting out the opening fifty-four lines of the manuscript that present the voice of the rowdy Bostonian Irishman telling of a night on the town, but Pound was certainly responsible for removing seventy lines of the poor imitation of Pope's couplets that originally began "The Fire Sermon" and distracted from the Buddhist meaning of that title; and he was also responsible for removing the eighty-two lines of blank verse that originally began the section "Death by Water"—the voice of a sailor narrating the voyage made by an American fishing boat from Massachusetts to the North Pole. These enormous cuts remove the only American materials in the poem (materials that might have pleased William Carlos Williams), leaving it wholly European. But more important, what Pound did by removing Eliot's "deformative secretions" was to focus on the prophetic voice, and to allow that

4. Pound, *Letters,* ed. Paige, 169; also in *The Letters of T. S. Eliot,* ed. Valerie Eliot, 1:498. In both collections the letter is misdated December 24, 1921, through a misunderstanding of Pound's reference to the *Little Review* calendar: "24 Saturnus An I." For the calendar see Forrest Read, *'76: One World and the Cantos of Ezra Pound* (Chapel Hill: University of North Carolina Press, 1981), 39.
5. Pound, *Letters,* ed. Paige, 169; Eliot, *Letters,* 1:497.
6. *The Waste Land: A Facsimile,* 2, 3.

voice to emerge in all its dramatic power. Thus, after the timid voice of one who is afraid that spring will bring him life, and the fragmentary voices of a Europe in decline, the voice of an Ezekiel emerges, asking:

> What are the roots that clutch, what branches grow
> Out of this stony rubbish? Son of man,
> You cannot say, or guess, for you know only
> A heap of broken images, where the sun beats,
> And the dead tree gives no shelter, the cricket no relief,
> And the dry stone no sound of water.

Or, in the midst of the scene in the pub where Lil is suffering from the effects of her abortion and worried about Al's coming home from the war, an insistent voice five times cries out, "HURRY UP PLEASE ITS TIME." This is more than the voice of a bartender. It is the voice that cries like a prophet: Repent, for the end is near. Then we hear the great central voice emerging out of a sordid sexual scene, the voice of the Greek prophet three times identified as "I Tiresias," merging all the other voices identified by the capital letter "I":

> (And I Tiresias have foresuffered all
> Enacted on this same divan or bed;
> I who have sat by Thebes below the wall
> And walked among the lowest of the dead.)

Eliot knows well what he is saying when in his note he tells us, "Tiresias, although a mere spectator and not indeed a 'character', is yet the most important personage in the poem, uniting all the rest. . . . What Tiresias *sees*, in fact, is the substance of the poem." Tiresias, we might say, is the name of the prophetic voice that dominates this poem and emerges at the close in the most powerful voice of all, the voice of the Thunder, uttering its Sanskrit commands. Without the intervention of Pound's critical genius, we would still have had an interesting poem, but the voices brought together by "I Tiresias" would have been blunted and obscured.

Pound, as far as I can see, made only one big mistake in his comments on *The Waste Land,* and that was when he queried Eliot's original epigraph from Conrad's *Heart of Darkness:*

> Did he live his life again, in every detail of desire, temptation, and surrender during that supreme moment of complete knowledge? He cried in a whisper at some image, at some vision,—he cried out twice, a cry that was no more than a breath—
> "The horror! the horror!"[7]

7. Ibid., 4.

The passage leads well into the opening lines, with their fear of revelation, their fear of full consciousness; and it also relates to the lyric of Phlebas, who "passed the stages of his age and youth / Entering the whirlpool." Nevertheless, in his letter of January 24, 1922, Pound objects: "I doubt if Conrad is weighty enough to stand the citation." Eliot in a troubled tone replied, "Do you mean not use Conrad quot. or simply not put Conrad's name to it? It is much the most appropriate I can find, and somewhat elucidative." About Conrad, Pound replied, "Do as you like": "Who am I to grudge him his laurel crown."[8] But in March, Eliot wrote that he had "substituted for the J. Conrad" the epigraph from Petronius[9]—the obscure and learned passage in Latin and Greek that no doubt was designed to please Pound. But along with its pretentious obscurity, I find it misleading, because it presents a despairing picture of the *end* of prophecy, whereas the poem itself is full of the prophetic voice. The cry of Kurtz—"The horror! the horror!"—may not be an empty cry of despair. Conrad's narrator is not a wholly reliable authority, but after he himself has nearly died, Marlow comes to admire Kurtz's last cry: "He had summed up—he had judged," says Marlow.

> "The horror!" He was a remarkable man. After all, this was the expression of some sort of belief; it had candour, it had conviction, it had a vibrating note of revolt in its whisper, it had the appalling face of a glimpsed truth. . . .
> It was an affirmation, a moral victory paid for by innumerable defeats, by abominable terrors, by abominable satisfactions. But it was a victory.

So the Conrad epigraph hints at a possible redemption amid the apparent despair—and this is, as Eliot says, "somewhat elucidative."

Of course, in this context of prophecy, I also regret that Eliot chose to accept Pound's deletion of one line in the opening section, the parenthesis, toward the end of the speech of Madame Sosostris, "(I John saw these things, and heard them)"[10]—a line that stresses the difference between true prophet and modern soothsayer.

The Waste Land owes to Pound much more than this. For Pound was the inventor of the inner method of the poem, that innovative mingling of varied voices in many languages—Italian, French, German, Latin, and, going Pound one better, Sanskrit. This technique of creating a poetical medley of voices seems greatly indebted to Pound's example in his early cantos,[11] the first three that were published in 1917, along with Canto 4, published in October 1919, just at the

8. Cited in the notes to *The Waste Land: A Facsimile*, 125. See Pound, *Letters*, ed. Paige, 169–71; Eliot, *Letters*, 1:497, 504–5.

9. Eliot, *Letters*, 1:506.

10. *The Waste Land: A Facsimile*, 9.

11. The mingling of "voices" is of course also found in Joyce, as in the "Sirens" episode, but Joyce does not mingle languages in Pound's way.

time when Eliot was pondering the composition of his "long poem."[12] Now we discover from Christine Froula's study that an early draft of Canto 4 contains a long monologue given in the voice of an English soldier reminiscing about his experiences in Poland, Hungary, and Germany before and during World War I, a passage of sixty lines.[13] This was a deformative secretion that Pound did not include in his published poem, but Eliot may well have read this manuscript. If so, the long deformative secretions in *The Waste Land* manuscript may be due to Pound's example, because the early manuscript of Canto 4 would have suggested the possibility of using long monologues within the medley of voices. But a more important precedent may be found in Canto 7.

We learn from the new edition of Eliot's letters that Pound, late in November or early in December 1919, had left with Eliot a manuscript of the recently written Canto 7. This explains the cryptic postcard Eliot sent across London on December 2, 1919, opening with the exclamation, "Ελέναus," continuing, "I am absorbing this matter slowly," and ending with the query, "Who is Tyro?" This can only be an allusion to the lines in the middle of Canto 7: "But *is* she dead as Tyro? In seven years? / Ελέναus, ἕλανδρος, ἑλέπτολις"—the words of Aeschylus describing Helen of Troy that also occur in what is now Canto 2, but which was originally Canto 8, written several years later than Canto 7.[14] This postcard is highly important for the composition of *The Waste Land*, because later in this month of December, Eliot declared in a letter to his mother that one of his New Year's resolutions was "to write a long poem I have had on my mind for a long time."[15]

In Canto 7, Pound for the first time reaches a full synthesis of many "voices"— contrasting the past and the present, and presenting the theme of the search for buried beauty and "drowned Eros" for the first time in its full power.[16] This is a poem in which, through the medley of many voices, one feels the pulsating power of the search for redemption of a dead land where one hears "Words like the locust-shells, moved by no inner being; / A dryness calling for death."

The medley of voices opens with two words of Aeschylus, "Ελανδρος and Ελέπτολις," then moves to a passage greatly expanded in the later Canto 2 (8): "poor old Homer blind, / blind as a bat"—but, like Pound, with an "Ear, ear for the sea-surge; / rattle of old men's voices." Then come the voices of Ovid and Bertrans de Born, and one luminous word from Dante's *Paradiso*: "ciocco"; then three lines of concrete detail concerning a room from Flaubert, moving the scene toward modern France. And then we turn to quite a different room, some

12. See Eliot's letter to his mother of December 18, 1919, in *Letters*, 1:351.
13. *To Write Paradise: Style and Error in Pound's Cantos.* For the monologue see 70–73.
14. Eliot, *Letters*, 1:350. We know from the letter Pound wrote to his father on December 13, 1919, that Pound had "done cantos 5, 6, and 7" by that date.
15. Eliot, *Letters*, 1:350
16. For a discussion of the relation of Canto 7 to *The Waste Land* see Ronald Bush, *The Genesis of Ezra Pound's Cantos*, 225–30.

kind of large, formal meeting hall, where the poet-prophet hears again "The old men's voices, beneath the columns of false marble." And from here we move to the passage generally regarded as a memory of Henry James, with "the great domed head," accompanied by phrases from Dante and Vergil: "And the old voice lifts itself / weaving an endless sentence."

From here the poem turns to visit a place where the speaker has formerly lived, in Paris:

> Knocking at empty rooms, seeking for buried beauty;
> But the sun-tanned, gracious and well-formed fingers
> Lift no latch of bent bronze, no Empire handle
> Twists for the knocker's fall; no voice to answer.

The current scene, after seven years' absence, seems degraded: "Four chairs, the bow-front dresser, / The panier of the desk, cloth top sunk in."

> Beer-bottle on the statue's pediment!
> That, Fritz, is the era, to-day against the past,
> Contemporary.

Pound is addressing an old friend of the Paris days, Fritz vander Pyl, a Belgian poet.

But already Pound has introduced a countertheme, "seeking for buried beauty," and he has just mentioned, in the midst of all this contemporary detritus, the title of an old poem of his, "Ione, dead the long year," published in 1914 in memory of a young and talented dancer (Jeanne Heyse), who had killed herself in 1912. The image of this dancer, a vital buried beauty, occurs twice in the poem:

> Nicea moved before me
> And the cold grey air troubled her not
> For all her naked beauty, bit not the tropic skin,
> And the long slender feet lit on the curb's marge
> And her moving height went before me,
>   We alone having being.

And again the dancer occurs:

> Square even shoulders and the satin skin,
> Gone cheeks of the dancing woman . . .

Then he cries out in the voice of Dante's *Paradiso*, "O voi che siete in piccioletta barca," the first line of Dante's second canto: "O you that are in your little bark, eager to hear, following behind my ship that singing makes her way, turn back to see again your shores. Do not commit yourselves to the open sea, for perchance, if you lost me, you would remain astray."[17] This is Dante's warning that for many readers the rest of his poem will be difficult to follow.

Pound does not make his poem any easier by the lines that here follow:

> Dido choked up with sobs, for her Sicheus
> Lies heavy in my arms, dead weight
>   Drowning, with tears, new Eros . . .

The poet feels "Passion to breed a form in a shimmer of rain-blur,"

> But Eros drowned, drowned, heavy-half dead with tears
> For dead Sicheus.

What does this mean? I think it represents, like the memory of the dancer, an irrepressible passion to recover life amid these dead and dry husks. And this, surely, is the central urge of Eliot's *The Waste Land*. Eliot has done it better, as Pound recognized, but he could never have done it at all, without Pound's example in these early cantos and without Pound's final touches of editorial genius.

At the top of some of the typed pages of the manuscript of *The Waste Land* is a title indicating that Eliot may not at first have thought of calling the poem by its present title; at the beginning of the first two sections appears: "He Do the Police in Different Voices: Part I," "He Do the Police in Different Voices: Part II." This is a sentence from Dickens's *Our Mutual Friend* (chapter 16), where the boy Sloppy is described as a "beautiful reader of a newspaper. He do the Police in different voices."[18]

Voices, voices—both Eliot and Pound and later William Carlos Williams seem to be working in the American prophetic tradition begun by Walt Whitman when he wrote, "Through me many long dumb voices," and exclaimed, "What living and buried speech is always vibrating here." The voices that Pound and Eliot hear are, of course, quite different from those of Whitman, for along with many modern voices we hear the voices of ancient poets and sages. Still, how could we find a better description of *The Waste Land,* the *Cantos,* and *Paterson*? "Living and buried speech is always vibrating here."[19]

17. *Paradiso,* trans. Charles S. Singleton.

18. For an illuminating, but quite different, use of this quotation see Calvin Bedient, *He Do the Police in Different Voices: The Waste Land and Its Protagonist.* The echo of Dickens was perhaps prompted by the way in which *Our Mutual Friend* is so deeply concerned with death by water in the Thames and with the ordure, rubbish, and corruption on land in London.

19. The place of Whitman as father of "the Pound Tradition" has been fully recognized in many studies, but nearly always in the context of epic, not of prophecy. See the books by Roy Harvey Pearce, James E. Miller Jr., Jeffrey Walker, Stephen Tapscott, and Mutlu Konuk Blasing listed in the bibliography. Miller, for example, argues that Whitman has invented a "new kind of epic" in "a form without precedent." He shrewdly analyzes the qualities in which Whitman's poem differs from traditional epic, but these are exactly the qualities of biblical prophecy (*The American Quest for a Supreme Fiction: Whitman's Legacy in the Personal Epic,* 33–36).

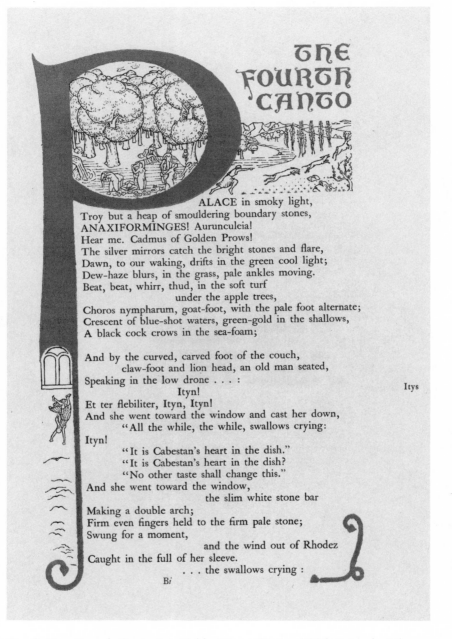

THE
FOURTH
CANTO

PALACE in smoky light,
Troy but a heap of smouldering boundary stones,
ANAXIFORMINGES! Aurunculeia!
Hear me. Cadmus of Golden Prows!
The silver mirrors catch the bright stones and flare,
Dawn, to our waking, drifts in the green cool light;
Dew-haze blurs, in the grass, pale ankles moving.
Beat, beat, whirr, thud, in the soft turf
                under the apple trees,
Choros nympharum, goat-foot, with the pale foot alternate;
Crescent of blue-shot waters, green-gold in the shallows,
A black cock crows in the sea-foam;

And by the curved, carved foot of the couch,
        claw-foot and lion head, an old man seated,
Speaking in the low drone . . . :
                Ityn!   Itys
Et ter flebiliter, Ityn, Ityn!
And she went toward the window and cast her down,
        "All the while, the while, swallows crying:
Ityn!
        "It is Cabestan's heart in the dish."
        "It is Cabestan's heart in the dish?
        "No other taste shall change this."
And she went toward the window,
                        the slim white stone bar
Making a double arch;
Firm even fingers held to the firm pale stone;
Swung for a moment,
                and the wind out of Rhodez
Caught in the full of her sleeve.
                . . . the swallows crying :
        Bi

Fig. 2. Ezra Pound, Canto 4; initial by Henry Strater, 1925. Beinecke Library, Yale University.

4.

Pound and Joyce
Fugal Variations

*I*N THE THREE UR-CANTOS published in 1917 and composed sometime between 1913 and 1916, Pound had already invented his basic technique of juxtaposing voices from varied cultures—Renaissance, Provençal, Greek, and Roman. Then, from December 1917 on, when Joyce sent Pound the first installment of *Ulysses*, up through the publication of *Ulysses* in 1922, the composition of the *Cantos* ran parallel with Pound's excited and admiring perusal of Joyce's work. As Ronald Bush has shown, the impact of Joyce is apparent in the drastically different style that suddenly appears in Canto 4, the style of "compression, intensity" that Pound praised in a note to Margaret Anderson, the style that Christine Froula has also examined, with special attention to the repetitive mode of Canto 4. As her study makes clear, the early fragments assigned to Canto 4 played little part in creating its final form: "the first enabling inspiration for Canto IV came only in 1918"—"early in 1918"—with manuscript evidence "that inspiration came suddenly."[1]

What had happened, I think, is that Pound's reading of the first three chapters of *Ulysses*—the "Telemachia"—which reached him in December and January 1917–1918, showed Pound a way of condensing the long, diffuse passages from ancient cultures that appeared in the ur-cantos, while at the same time

---

1. Bush, *Genesis of Pound's Cantos*, 194–205. For the note to Margaret Anderson see *Pound/Joyce: The Letters of Ezra Pound to James Joyce, with Pound's Essays on Joyce*, ed. Forrest Read, 130. Froula, *To Write Paradise*, 55–56.

alerting him to the "fugal" technique of repetition, leitmotiv, that Joyce would use throughout *Ulysses*. Pound did not read the "Sirens" episode, with its explicit fugal technique, until he received it in Toulouse in June 1919, but the technique was already apparent in these early chapters, especially in the opening chapter, which Pound greatly admired. "Early in 1918," then, Pound was deeply involved with these chapters; in February 1918 he sent them to the *Little Review*, which published them in the three subsequent months.[2]

In the opening chapter he would have noted the intricate series of repetitions and echoes: the memories of Stephen's dream about his mother, the repetition of Stephen's "symbol of Irish art"—"The cracked lookingglass of a servant"— the repeated quotations from Yeats's "Who Goes with Fergus," the repetition of "Agenbite of inwit," the numerous echoes of *Hamlet*, and especially the words of the Catholic ritual, "*Liliata rutilantium* . . . ," which first occur a quarter of the way through the chapter and are then repeated six lines from the end. This last repetition seems closely akin to the way in which Pound frames his Provençal legend in Canto 4, where the doubling of the line "It is Cabestan's heart in the dish" appears about a quarter of the way into the canto, and then the final repetition comes a dozen lines from the end. I am not concerned here with cadenced repetition of single words and phrases closely linked: "with leaves, with leaves," "Beneath it, beneath it," or "Gold, gold," "Blaze, blaze"—for these are not Joycean, but seem to be part of an effort to achieve the lyric movement of Provençal poetry. The Joycean element is found in the distanced echoing of longer passages: "Not a ray, not a sliver, not a spare disc of sunlight," "Not a splotch, not a lost shatter of sunlight," "Not a patch, not a lost shimmer of sunlight." Most significant is the repetition in this middle passage:

> Ply over ply, thin glitter of water;
> Brook film bearing white petals. . . .
> Ply over ply
> The shallow eddying fluid,
> beneath the knees of the gods.

As Froula notes, the meaning of the repeated phrase is illuminated by Pound's manuscript versions, where we read:

> ply over ply—behind them the
> floating images   behind them the
>   recrossing images,
> behind them the lasting gods—

2. For the dates of Pound's reading of *Ulysses* and the publication of early sections see *Pound/Joyce*, 128–30, 156–57; Richard Ellmann, *James Joyce*, rev. ed., 441–42; and A. Walton Litz, *The Art of James Joyce*, 143–45.

As Froula says, here is "the structural principle Pound has found for Canto IV"[3]—and, one might add, for his whole *Draft of XVI. Cantos,* his *Draft of XXX Cantos,* and the unified sequence of his first fifty-one cantos.

The phrase "ply over ply" had occurred in ur-Canto 2, with reference to the layers of ancient life found on Salisbury plain: "Ply over ply of life still wraps the earth there." Here in Canto 4 the phrase describes the ever-present technique of the *Cantos,* passages from human experience in many ages, floating and recrossing, while within them or behind them we catch intimations of those "eternal states of mind," the "gods" revealed by the monuments of human culture.[4] This is the mode of organization that Pound evidently had in mind when he made his famous statement to Yeats in 1928: "Now at last he explains that it [the *Cantos*] will, when the hundredth canto is finished, display a structure like that of a Bach Fugue."[5]

Pound was well aware of the fugal pattern in the "Sirens" episode of *Ulysses,* so elaborately explained to George Borach by Joyce in June 1919: "I finished the Sirens chapter during the last few days. A big job. I wrote this chapter with the technical resources of music. It is a fugue with all musical notations: piano, forte, rallentando, and so on. A quintet occurs in it, too, as in *Die Meistersinger.*" In August 1919 he wrote to Miss Weaver that the chapter contained "all the eight regular parts of a *fuga per canonem.*"[6] In June, Joyce had sent the "Sirens" chapter to Pound in France, and he received what he regarded as an unfavorable reply, although Pound disapproved mainly of the flatulent ending.[7] It may be

---

3. Froula, *To Write Paradise,* 45, 125. Bruce Comens, in *Apocalypse and After: Modern Strategy and Postmodern Tactics in Pound, Williams, and Zukofsky,* has given a detailed and illuminating analysis of Canto 4 as a poem showing what he calls "apocalyptic structure," with "revelatory moments of vision set against the Armageddon of the Great War" (see 43–54, esp. 53). This is the structure that I have been describing as "oscillation." Biblical scholars tend to make a distinction between the "apocalyptic" and the "prophetic," but for the Old Testament the apocalyptic elements, foreseeing a millennium, form only part of the general prophetic message.

4. See Pound's catechism "Religio" (1918), in Pound, *Selected Prose, 1909–1965,* ed. Cookson, 47–48.

5. William Butler Yeats, *A Vision* (New York: Macmillan, 1938), 4. The words *musical* or *fugal* should be regarded as metaphors describing what Kenneth Burke calls "repetitive form" (see his "Lexicon Rhetoricae," in *Counter-Statement,* 2d ed. [Los Altos, Calif.: Hermes, 1953], 125). The repetitive technique in the *Cantos* has of course been widely recognized. See Hugh Kenner's treatment of "subject-rhyme" in *The Pound Era,* 423–36; Kay Davis, *Fugue and Fresco: Structures in Pound's Cantos,* which provides a detailed account of the many modes of repetition; R. Murray Schafer's introduction to *Ezra Pound and Music: The Complete Criticism,* which stresses that "strictly speaking, the fugue is not a form at all, but rather a procedure" (22); and Stephen J. Adams, "Are the *Cantos* a Fugue?" which sums up all the issues and emphasizes that "by calling the *Cantos* fugal, Pound implied that they were an on-going process, an unfolding development" (70).

6. Ellmann, *Joyce,* 459, 462.

7. See Pound's letter in *Pound/Joyce,* 157–58; in his item 4, he speaks of the section as a "fugue."

significant that the next canto that Pound composed (after December 1919), the original Canto 8, shows powerful signs of musical construction in the deliberately repetitive form with which the beginning and the end of the poem frame the Dionysian episode from Ovid within a pattern of verbal echoes. By moving this canto to become the second in his poem Pound drew attention to musical form, both in the structure of this particular canto and in the fragments that replace the lament for the loss of epic sweep with which this canto originally opened, beginning with a line that links with the Vergilian reference in Canto 7:

> Dido choked up with tears for dead Sichaeus;
> And the weeping Muse, weeping, widowed, and willing,
> The weeping Muse
>   Mourns Homer,
> Mourns the days of long song,
> Mourns for the breath of the singers,
> Winds stretching out, seas pulling to eastward,
> Heaving breath of the oarsmen,
>   triremes under Cyprus,
> The long course of the seas,
> The words woven in wind-wrack,
>   salt spray over voices.
> Tyro to shoreward lies lithe with Neptunus
> And the glass-clear wave arches over them . . . [8]

In 1925 all this was removed and replaced by three lines that look forward to themes to be developed in succeeding cantos:

> Hang it all, Robert Browning,
> there can be but the one "Sordello";
> So-shu churned in the sea . . .

In 1930 Pound expanded this adaptation of the opening line of the first ur-canto by adding the lines:

> But Sordello, and my Sordello?
> Lo Sordels si fo di Mantovana.

Browning's "Sordello" can no longer be a model. Pound's Sordello, as poet, will arise from the original Provençal *vida:* "Lo Sordels si fo di Mantovana"—the line being then echoed at strategic intervals, in Cantos 6, 16, and 36, linking all the allusions to Sordello and his lover, Cunizza da Romano.

The next line, "So-shu churned in the sea," anticipates the same words that occur in the conclusion of this canto and, more significantly, anticipates the

---

8. Quoted from *Dial* 72 (May 1922): 505–9.

Chinese and Japanese materials that occur in Cantos 4 and 13. Equally important is the wave imagery associated with So-shu, as described by Pound in one of his essays: "Yoyu and Shojo [So-shu] stirred up decayed (enervated) waves. Open current flows about in bubbles, does not move in wavelengths."[9] The waves created by the poet (So-shu or Pound) now continue through the sea imagery that follows:

> Seal sports in the spray-whited circles of cliff-wash,
> Sleek head, daughter of Lir,
>   eyes of Picasso
> Under black fur-hood, lithe daughter of Ocean;
> And the wave runs in the beach-groove:
> "Eleanor, ἑλέναυσ and ἑλέπτολισ!"
>   And poor old Homer blind, blind, as a bat,
> Ear, ear for the sea-surge, murmur of old men's voices:

The last three lines are then echoed at the outset of Canto 7, followed later in that canto by the Greek words from Aeschylus, "The sea runs in the beach-groove" and the cry "Eleanor!" The Aeschylean words are finally repeated in Canto 46. Then the following warning of the "doom" that "goes with" Helen, adapted from the *Iliad*, foreshadows the grim opening of Canto 4: "Palace in smoky light, / Troy but a heap of smouldering boundary stones." One should add that the imagery of the seal seems to anticipate the allusion to Proteus in the conclusion of Canto 8, since Proteus was a herdsman of seals. Meanwhile, the phrase "eyes of Picasso," whether evoking the creative power of the artist in person or the bold, slanting eyes of his *Demoiselles d'Avignon,* may be taken to imply a relation to Cubist art.

In all this we may find a precedent in Joyce, especially in the opening of his "Sirens" episode, where Joyce lists, for a page and a half, phrases that will form the notes, chords, themes, motifs of his siren's song. These scraps do not, I think, form a prelude or an overture, as some have described this opening, for these fragments do not make up a music, they make up a cacophony. The fragments suggest the discordant noises of the tuning up of the instruments that Joyce describes near the end of the episode: "Night Michael Gunn gave us the box. Tuning up. Shah of Persia liked that best. Remind him of home sweet home. Wiped his nose in curtain too. Custom his country perhaps. That's music too. Not as bad as it sounds. Tootling."[10] The word "Begin" marks the stroke of the conductor's baton, the beginning of the music, and then, "Bronze by gold," Joyce's music picks up each item of the tuning. The phrases weave,

9. *Selected Prose,* ed. Cookson, 346. Cited by Carroll F. Terrell, *A Companion to the Cantos of Ezra Pound,* 1:5.
10. *Ulysses* (New York: Random House, 1934), 280.

repeat, interweave until at the close a group of final repetitions brings the music
to a close, along with the comic staccato of Bloom's flatulation.

We can see, perhaps, why Pound discarded his original lament for the loss
of Homeric power; by substituting fragments that foreshadow basic themes, he
seems to recognize another model: the Joycean technique of "fugue." In any
case, the musical technique of repetition weaves Canto 8 (2) together in Joycean
fashion. After the passage adapted from the *Iliad,* the creative waves continue
with the reference to Tyro, whom Odysseus met in Hades, explicitly in ur-Canto
3; but here the fate of Tyro must be recalled by those who remember the tale of
her rape by Poseidon:

> And by the beach-run, Tyro,
>   Twisted arms of the sea-god,
> Lithe sinews of water, gripping her, cross-hold,
> And the blue-gray glass of the wave tents them,
> Glare azure of water, cold-welter, close cover.

The words "cold-welter" read "cord-welter" in 1922, a phrase that matches the
repetition in the conclusion of the canto: "white welter of wave-cords." The
whole passage correlates with these lines of the conclusion:

> Lithe turning of water,
>   sinews of Poseidon,
> Black azure and hyaline,
>   glass wave over Tyro . . .

Tyro, of course, recurs, along with the Greek words, in Canto 7.

Then this opening passage modulates into a seascape, preparing for the
emergence of the "wine-red glow," evoking the wine of Dionysus and the
"Naviform rock" that leads into Ovid's story of the transformed ship and sailors:
two poets thus collaborating to produce an epiphany of the god and a warning
from the prophet Tiresias. Then, at the close, with perfect musical harmony, the
waves of imagery recapitulate and recall:

> And So-shu churned in the sea, So-shu also,
>   using the long moon for a churn-stick . . .

And so the myth recedes into the seascape, with many subtle echoes of the
opening: "quiet water, / quiet in the buff sands" echoes "Quiet sun-tawny
sand-stretch"; "Sea-fowl stretching wing-joints" echoes "The gulls broad out
their wings" and the snipe that "bend out their wing-joints"; "glass-glint of
wave" and "Grey peak of the wave" echo "blue-grey glass of the wave"; while
"wine-red algae" and "wave, colour of grape's pulp" echo the "wine-red glow"
of the Dionysiac presence.

After Pound wrote Canto 7 late in 1919, a long pause occurred until Canto 8 (2) appeared in the *Dial* in May 1922. Pound had been occupied with many other projects, including the publication of *Ulysses*. After April 16, 1921, he had read nearly all of *Ulysses*, for on that date Joyce gave to him, in Paris, the "Circe" episode, to which Pound responded with an explosion of enthusiasm. "Magnificent, a new Inferno in full sail," he wrote to his father.[11] Here, perhaps, we have the explanation for Pound's resuming the composition of cantos after the long hiatus. It seems likely that his full recognition of Joyce's repetitive technique, which comes to its culmination in "Circe," inspired Pound to write Canto 8 in a manner overtly "musical" in its use of echoes. With the transference of Canto 8 to its present position as Canto 2, the stage was set upon which the rest of the *Cantos*, up through 51, could perform their fugal variations.

Thus the pastoral, edenic close of the present Canto 2 anticipates the many "paradisal" glimpses to follow, as immediately in Canto 3 we come upon a pastoral scene that precedes the falling of the dew in Genesis:

> Gods float in the azure air,
> Bright gods and Tuscan, back before dew was shed.
> Light: and the first light, before ever dew was fallen.

The word "azure" links with the seascape of Canto 2, since the word occurs once at the beginning and once at the end of that canto. Then again, after the troubles of the Cid, the murder of Ignez da Castro, and the imagery of "drear waste, the pigment flakes from the stone," the pastoral moment reappears at the outset of Canto 4:

> Dawn, to our waking, drifts in the green cool light;
> Dew-haze blurs, in the grass, pale ankles moving.
> Beat, beat, whirr, thud, in the soft turf
>   under the apple trees,
> Choros nympharum, goat-foot, with the pale foot alternate . . .

And the phrase "Choros nympharum" points toward the same phrase in the paradisal Canto 17. The imagery of "green cool light" prepares the way for the "Pale soft light" of Canto 5: "Iamblicus' light." Thus, as Pound says in one of his essays, "The thinking, word-arranging, clarifying faculty must move and leap with the energizing, sentient, musical faculties."[12] Or, as he puts it in Canto 27:

> And the waves like a forest
> Where the wind is weightless in the leaves

---

11. See *Pound/Joyce*, 189. Family Letters, April 20, 1921; cited in *Pound/Joyce*, 189, and by Ellmann, *Joyce*, 508.

12. Pound, *Literary Essays*, ed. T. S. Eliot, 52.

> But moving,
>   so that sound runs upon sound.

This pattern reaches its climax as Pound quite consciously moves toward the conclusion of the first half of his projected one hundred cantos. After the denunciation of *usura* in the famous Canto 45, Canto 46 explicitly speaks of "conclusion" after "seventeen" or "nineteen" years "on this case"—that is to say, the case that he is making to prove the corrosive effects of "usury" upon the very sources of life and art. Canto 47 then picks up the theme of the descent of Odysseus to the underworld to meet Tiresias, while resuming the theme of sexuality and fertility developed in Circean terms in Canto 39. Canto 48 returns to the daily world of financial greed; then Canto 49 presents the paradisal Chinese poem of the "Seven Lakes," with the final line that links with the end of Canto 47: "that hath the power over wild beasts." And of course the tranquil beauty of the Chinese scene links backward to the love of "order" that Kung had set forth in Canto 13. Canto 50 returns to the daily world of debt, taxes, and trade, with reminiscent allusions to John Adams, Leopold of Florence, Napoleon, and the destruction of the old Italian city-states: "Venice, Genova, Lucca." Then Canto 51 brings all together with the longest, most detailed, and most significant reprise of all, the reprise of the Usury Canto, 45. Canto 51 begins with a memory of the divine light that, according to Guinicelli's poem,[13] shines above and within the human mind:

> Shines
> in the mind of heaven God
> who made it
> more than the sun
> in our eye.
> Fifth element; mud; said Napoleon

The echo of the words of Napoleon in Canto 34, stuck in the mud of the Russian disaster, brings the exalted rhetoric of Canto 45 down to our daily, contemporary earth. We have heard the pounding rhetoric, the biblical diction, of the Renaissance preacher, denouncing *usura*, in accordance with the doctrine of the medieval church:

> with usura, sin against nature,
> is thy bread ever more of stale rags
> is thy bread dry as paper,
> with no mountain wheat, no strong flour,
> with usura the line grows thick
> with usura is no clear demarcation

13. See the note in Terrell, *Companion,* 1:197.

and no man can find site for his dwelling.
Stonecutter is kept from his stone
weaver is kept from his loom
WITH USURA
wool comes not to market
sheep bringeth no gain with usura
Usura is a murrain, usura
blunteth the needle in the maid's hand
and stoppeth the spinner's cunning. Pietro Lombardo
came not by usura
Duccio came not by usura

All this is now reduced to a flat, prosaic mode, without energy:

> With usury has no man a good house
> made of stone, no paradise on his church wall
> With usury the stone cutter is kept from his stone
> the weaver is kept from his loom by usura
> Wool does not come into market
> the peasant does not eat his own grain
> the girl's needle goes blunt in her hand
> The looms are hushed one after another
> ten thousand after ten thousand
> Duccio was not by usura

The works of art that the preacher of Canto 45 could see as recent achievements, or as works still being created, though now endangered by greed, are in Canto 51 reduced to a distant memory in a modern industrial scene, far removed from the handicrafts of the Renaissance. The change from *usura* to the modern "usury" (a practice now countenanced everywhere), along with the contemporary language, sets the tone for the passionless, enervated speech of a declining age. The following passage that delineates the fine art of making flies for fishing is ambiguous. Yes, it is an art, and the product is beautiful, made from natural things, but what is this beauty when compared with the art of a Duccio or a Botticelli?

> That hath the light of the doer, as it were
> a form cleaving to it.
> Deo similis quodem modo
> hic intellectus adeptus

("Like God in a certain way, this creative intellect.") Yet the lines in this context carry an ironic overtone, a sense of decline that leads on into the circles of hell on the back of Dante's monster Geryon. This theme of usury, a ground tone of the *Cantos,* has become a notorious point of controversy because, in Canto 52 and some of the later cantos, the wartime radio broadcasts, and some of Pound's prose essays, the theme has become associated with anti-Semitism. But such an association does not apply to the first fifty-one cantos, where the financial attack is leveled at financiers of great ethnic variety, while the meaning of "usury" is broadened to include all the variations of "fraud" represented in the descending circles of Dante's hell and in the monster Geryon:

> "Behold the beast with the pointed tail, that passes mountains and breaks walls and weapons! Behold him that infects all the world!" . . . And that foul image of fraud came onward, and landed his head and his bust, but he did not draw his tail onto the bank. His face was the face of a just man, so benign was its outward aspect, and all his trunk was that of a serpent; he had two paws, hairy to the arm pits; his back and breast and both his sides were painted with knots and circlets.[14]

"Hic Geryon est. Hic hyperusura" (Canto 46); "state by creating riches shd. thereby get into debt? / This is infamy; this is Geryon" (Canto 49). This is the beast on which we descend into the depths of infamy, at the close of Canto 51, as the beast sings his fraudulent song:

> I am the help of the aged;
> I pay men to talk peace;
> Mistress of many tongues; merchant of chalcedony
> I am Geryon twin with usura . . .

It all hangs together, but the effect depends upon patient absorption of these fifty-one cantos as the reader's memory holds in suspension the manifold intricate repetitions of his notes, chords, and motifs. As Joyce said, hurt by the adverse reception of the "Sirens" episode, and explaining his own slowness in composition: "The elements needed will fuse only after a prolonged existence together."[15]

The first "half," then, of Pound's projected hundred cantos is complete: a unified and potent book of prophecy. But what does it all *mean,* this verbal fugue in fifty-one cantos? It is no idyllic vision of the past, set against the sordid present. The vicious murders and betrayals of the past, the moneygrubbing of ancient commerce, the sordid and treacherous political dealings of ancient days— all these are vividly recorded; but the redemptive element is also there: in the Tempio of Sigismundo Malatesta, in the paintings of the early Renaissance, in the songs of the Troubadours, in the poetry of Homer and Dante, and in the poetry of Cavalcanti as represented in the great canzone that Pound translates at the outset of Canto 36. In view of all these allusions to art, was Lawrence then right

14. *Inferno,* 17.1–15, trans. Singleton, 173.
15. Ellmann, *Joyce,* 461.

when he said, "His god is beauty"? Only if we consider that the concept of beauty in the *Cantos* includes the ordering principles of Neoplatonic philosophy, with its divine, creative light, along with the ethical principles of Confucian "order," the political ideals of America's founding fathers, and the creative power of the mind that can apprehend the presence of some eternal power working within the landscapes and seascapes of the earth. As Pound had said, long ago, when he wrote "From Chebar":

> The order does not end in the arts,
> The order shall come and pass through them.

Pound's concept of "beauty" involves what can only be called a deeply religious principle: the belief that all the arts of humankind derive from an omnipresent creative power to which Pound gives the name "gods." These gods are "discontinuous" to human beings, but they are indeed continuous throughout the universe. It is this principle, working within the turmoil and corruption of the daily world, that creates the epiphany of beauty: "In the gloom, the gold gathers the light against it." That repeated epigram sums up the total impact of these fifty-one cantos.

5.

Pound and "Dante *Profeta*"

*A*MONG THE MANY voices vibrating throughout the *Cantos* is the voice of a poet deeply revered by Pound, a poet who also wrote of visions and voices: Dante. We may recall Pound's words in that letter to his mother written while he was still a college student: "untill you can show me men of today who shall excell certain men some time dead, I shall continue to study Dante and the Hebrew prophets."[1] Dante and the Hebrew prophets: this topic has been extensively studied by Italian scholars of *The Divine Comedy* over the past fifty years, with the result that the phrase *Dante profeta* has become increasingly familiar.[2] In this scholarship the relation of individual episodes in Dante's poem to the writings of the biblical prophets has been amply and cogently demonstrated, but one area of this relationship has not been fully explored: the relation of the total movement of *The Divine Comedy* to the oscillating strategies of Isaiah, Ezekiel, and Jeremiah. The preceding pages have

1. Family Letters, Feb. 1905. This chapter is adapted from a lecture delivered at the Symposium "Dante e Pound," held at the Biblioteca Classense in Ravenna, September 8–10, 1995; the complete lecture will be published in a collection of Dante studies issued by the Biblioteca Classense.

2. See Bruno Nardi, *Dante e la Cultura Medievale* (Bari: Gius. Laterza & Figli, 1942), chap. 9. Nicolò Mineo, *Profetismo e Apocalittica in Dante* (Università di Catania, Pubblicazioni della Facoltà di Lettere e Filosofia, 1968). Gian Roberto Sarolli, *Prolegomena alla "Divina Commedia"* (Firenze: Olschki, 1971), chap. 4, "Profezia e Visione: Profilo d'un Genere Letterario." Giuseppe Mazzotta, *Dante, Poet of the Desert* (Princeton: Princeton University Press, 1979), chap. 7, "The Language of Faith." I am indebted to Professor Mazzotta for guiding me toward the above-mentioned studies in Italian. See also the title essay in the volume by Raffaello Morghen, *Dante Profeta: Tra la Storia e l'Eterno* (Milan: Jaca Book, 1983).

spoken several times about the way in which the writers of biblical prophecy alternate moments of denunciation and moments that promise redemption. This movement may be seen in miniature in one of Pound's very last cantos, 113:

> The hells move in cycles,
>> No man can see his own end.
> The Gods have not returned.

But another voice at once declares: "They have never left us." And the earlier voice insists, "They have not returned." But the next line asserts their return: "Clouds processional and the air moves with their living." Evil persists, hell persists, but the imagery of wind and lights promises redemption:

> Pride, jealousy and possessiveness
>> 3 pains of hell
> and a clear wind over garofani
>> over Portofino 3 lights in triangulation

—a sort of Trinity.

Such is the peculiar movement of prophecy: an oscillation, an alternating current of power. No words are too harsh for the biblical prophet to use in denouncing these "abominations" (Ezekiel's word); no words of promise are too idyllic for the prophet to use in his exhortations toward redemption. As he repeats these themes over and over again in his canticles, we become aware that repetition constitutes the chief means by which the prophetic voice can achieve a unity in the book of his total message—a unity contained within the presence of the poet-prophet, who identifies himself in person, conveys something of his personality, and reminds us of the mission that he received from the voice of Jehovah. Thus, after his first five chapters, Isaiah introduces himself exactly in the middle of the opening section, known as the Book of Emmanuel, a distinctly separate composition consisting of eleven chapters, plus a brief pendant known as chapter 12. At first the prophet is reluctant to undertake the task, as he explains in a passage of prose where he sees "the Lord sitting upon a throne" and above him the seraphim:

> Then said I, Woe is me! for I am undone; because I am a man of unclean lips, and I dwell in the midst of a people of unclean lips: for mine eyes have seen the King, the Lord of hosts. Then flew one of the seraphims unto me, having a live coal in his hand, which he had taken with the tongs from off the altar: And he laid it upon my mouth, and said, Lo, this hath touched thy lips; and thine iniquity is taken away, and thy sin purged. Also I heard the voice of the Lord, saying, Whom shall I send, and who will go for us? Then said I, Here am I; send me. (Isa. 6:5–8)

Jeremiah tells us of his calling at the outset and continues to tell about himself and his sufferings throughout the book, recounting, for example, how he was cast into a deep dungeon from which he had to be drawn up by cords with rags under his armpits (Jer. 38). Ezekiel, of course, is the most dramatic of all, as he introduces himself "among the captives by the river of Chebar" where "the heavens were opened, and I saw visions of God"—the famous vision of the glorious chariot, from which he hears the voice that gives him his mission. And again, in the third chapter, as he is sitting among the captives "by the river of Chebar," he receives a reminder:

> And the hand of the Lord was there upon me; and he said unto me, Arise, go forth into the plain, and I will there talk with thee. Then I arose, and went forth into the plain: and, behold, the glory of the Lord stood there, as the glory which I saw by the river of Chebar: and I fell on my face. (Ezek. 3:22–23)

This insistent reference to the river of Chebar is important for Pound because, in 1913, just as he was beginning to write the *Cantos,* Pound wrote from his self-imposed exile by the river Thames the poem entitled "From Chebar," which we have cited earlier—the poem that proclaims his prophetic mission to change the mind of America. What is his mission? To create a new "order" of being (*novus ordo seclorum,* as on the back of the dollar bill)—an order that will mark the redemption of America from its provincial and materialistic condition. And what is the means?

> The order does not end in the arts,
> The order shall come and pass through them.
> The state is too idle, the decrepit church is too idle,
> The arts alone can transmit this.
> They alone cling fast to the gods . . .

The arts—of poetry, painting, sculpture, architecture, music, philosophy—these are the instruments of redemption that will bring back the "gods," the recognition of the eternal values that lie within the monuments of human culture: Homer, Ovid, Dante, Confucius, or the Tempio of Sigismundo Malatesta.[3] And so the *Cantos* come to display the typical oscillating movement of prophecy. Thus in Canto 5 we have the opening vision of light with the echo of Dante's vision of the souls in Paradise arising like sparks from the struck log (*Par.* 18.100):

> Iamblicus' light,
>   the souls ascending,

3. See Lawrence S. Rainey, *Ezra Pound and the Monument of Culture: Text, History, and the Malatesta Cantos.*

Sparks like a partridge covey,
Like the "ciocco", brand struck in the game.
"Et omniformis": Air, fire, the pale soft light.[4]

But then the latter part of the canto is given over to the sordid murder of Giovanni Borgia, accompanied by the words "*Caina attende* / The lake of ice there below me," taking us down to the pit of Dante's *Inferno* (5.107). Or consider the way in which Canto 13, the Confucian Canto, is preceded in Canto 12 by the account of Baldy Bacon's financial manipulations, with the first occurrence of the word *usurers* and the comical tale of the "honest sailor"—and is then followed by the two outrageous "Hell Cantos."

Can we discern the alternating movement of prophecy in Dante's great poem? Pound seems to have sensed something of the sort when he wrote in *The Spirit of Romance:* "The *Divina Commedia* must not be considered as an epic; to compare it with epic poems is usually unprofitable. It is in a sense lyric, the tremendous lyric of the subjective Dante."[5] But what are the works of the biblical prophets, if they are not the tremendous lyrics of the poet's subjective consciousness? Pound seems to be discerning here the basic difference between epic and prophecy. In classical epic the presence of the teller of the tale is recessive: he does not introduce himself as a person or a personality. It is true that in certain later epics, such as the *Lusiad* of Camoens or Milton's *Paradise Lost,* the voice of prophecy merges with the voice of the epic narrator, within the frame of the dominant epic movement. And in Dante too we have a merging of the genres, but here the epic motif of the journey is developed through dominant oscillations of the prophetic voice.

This effect reaches a climax in the *Paradiso,* which proceeds by what might best be called an undulating motion, a series of waves, starting with the "splendor" of light and then, as each voice emerges from that light, turning downward to see and berate the degeneration of earthly affairs. The undulation reaches its most sustained descent exactly in the middle of the *Paradiso,* in Cantos 16 and 17, with Cacciaguida's account of the degeneration of Florence, concluding with the bitter prophecy of what has already happened—Dante's exile. This is the longest, but not the fiercest, of these denunciations: the fiercest comes at the beginning of Canto 27, when Peter denounces the papacy. After this we are surprised to hear Beatrice, the very spirit of grace and compassion, taking up the theme and lamenting the degeneration of human beings after their innocent childhood (27.121–48). From light in heaven to dark on earth, over and over the undulations flow, while denunciation becomes ever more vehement as Dante moves ever upward toward higher realms of being.

---

4. James J. Wilhelm finds in this passage "a Neoplatonic ideogram that lifts us out of the ephemeral blur into a brief and lucid glimpse of something eternal" (*Dante and Pound: The Epic of Judgement,* 104).
5. *The Spirit of Romance,* 161.

This prophetic strategy is especially evident in the *Purgatorio,* with the procession of the seven deadly sins, where each painful account of the punishment measured out for sin is followed by the appearance of an angel and the singing of one of the Beatitudes. Many other redemptive elements appear in the *Purgatorio,* notably in the affectionate meetings with Dante's musical and poetical friends and predecessors: Casella, Sordello, Guido Guinicelli, Arnaut.

But are there also redemptive elements in Dante's hell? They do appear, I think, in many ways. Most obviously a mode of redemption appears in Canto 4, in "the fire, which conquered a hemisphere of the darkness" (4.68–69), where Dante meets first the great spirits of the pagan poets. He goes "onwards to the light" and comes to the "noble castle" with its "meadow of fresh verdure" where, "upon the green enamel, were shewn to me the great spirits" of the pagan past (4.103–20).[6] From this bright scene, where classical figures are redeemed by the quality of Dante's affection, we then move quickly into "a part where there is nought that shines" (4.151). Then in Canto 20 we have another long redemptive passage, as Vergil gives his affectionate account of the origins of Mantua, with its beautiful river and landscape (20.61–81). This reminder of nature's vitality may help to tie together many of the similes by which Dante alleviates the pains of hell. Pound himself points out this effect in *The Spirit of Romance,* where he says, "Dante's love of beauty draws it after him into hell itself, so here, with skill, he relieves the gloom of the canto by retrospection."[7] Then he quotes this passage, making his own translation:

> That is Aruns, who hath his belly behind him, he who, in the mountains of Luni, where hoes the Carrarese who dwells below, had his grotto amidst the white marbles and dwelt therein, and thence with unobstructed sight looked forth upon the stars and on the sea. (*Inf.* 20.46–51)

One could add examples with greater redemptive power: the long simile of the river that flows by Ravenna (16.94–104), or in Canto 24, the long opening simile of the frost and the peasant who fears that snow has come to cover his field, but then is relieved to find that the frost has melted. We have images of beneficent dolphins and lively frogs, of fireflies, starlings, and cranes. These similes provide more than relief: they serve as constant reminders that the "dolce mondo," the "dolce lome," still exists on earth, with nature's vitality surviving. At the same time there are certain similes that remind us of human art and craftsmanship, as with this simile quoted by Pound:[8]

6. I am quoting here the translation of the three little volumes in the Temple Classics that Pound used for his longer translations in *The Spirit of Romance;* his own copies, heavily annotated, are in the Humanities Center of the University of Texas at Austin: *Inferno,* trans. John Carlyle, rev. H. Oelsner; *Purgatorio,* trans. Thomas Okey; *Paradiso,* trans. Philip Wicksteed.

7. *Spirit of Romance,* 125.

8. Ibid., 126. Pound is making his own translation, somewhat inaccurately; he omits "l'inverno" and seems to misconstrue the lines "chi ristoppa / le coste a quel che più viaggi fece" (*Inf.* 21.11–12).

> As in the Venetians' arsenal boils the sticky pitch, for the caulking of damaged keels unnavigable, in which, to save rebuilding, they plug the ribs so that they hold for many a voyage; while some hammer at the prow, some at the stern; some make oars, others twine ropes, and mend the jib or mainsail, so, not by fire but by divine means, there is boiled down there a thick tar which glues the bank in every place. (*Inf.* 21.7–18)

We hear too of how the Flemings and the Paduans build their dikes, we see the tailor squinting at his needle, and, in an intimate glimpse, we see the font at "my beauteous San Giovanni," where Dante broke one of the stones.[9] Again, such images of human industry and art constitute more than relief; they remind us that men and women above are still in some cases demonstrating the creative powers bestowed upon them at the Creation. No wonder that the damned long for "the sweet air that is gladdened by the sun" (*Inf.* 7.122).

Other redemptive moments occur. One, in Canto 15, is the interview with Brunetto Latini that places early in the conversation Brunetto's optimistic words about his friend: "And he to me: 'If thou follow thy star, thou canst not fail of glorious haven, if I discerned rightly in the fair life; and if I had not died so early, seeing heaven so kind to thee, I would have cheered thee in the work' " (*Inf.* 15.55–60). Then follow the six tercets denouncing the Florentines, "avaricious, envious and proud"; after this comes Dante's affectionate expression of gratitude for what he has learned from Brunetto. And at the close of the canto we have an image that suggests that Brunetto's achievements will live on and provide for him some sort of victory over evil: "Then he turned back, and seemed like one of those who run for the green cloth at Verona through the open field; and of them seemed he who gains, not he who loses" (*Inf.* 15.121–24).

Finally, I cannot fail to mention the episode of Paolo and Francesca (5.73–142), where Dante's deep sympathy for the lovers' plight is foreshadowed by the beneficent simile that opens the episode: "As doves called by desire, with raised and steady wings come through to their loved nest, borne by their will, so those spirits issued from the band where Dido is, coming through the malignant air; such was the force of my affectuous cry *[affettuoso grido]*." Francesca is allowed to have her hymn to the irresistible power of *Amor, Amor, Amor:* "Love, which to no loved one permits excuse for loving, took me so strongly with delight in him, that, as thou seest, even now it leaves me not." We have no sense that she regrets this love; that is why she is in hell, not in purgatory. Dante as pilgrim faints with pity for the rigor of their sentence.[10] These two sinners, like Brunetto,

9. *Inf.* 15.4–9, 21; 19.16–21.
10. Mazzotta, *Dante, Poet of the Desert,* 169, argues that the episode "features Dante's own drama as he resists the temptation of succumbing to the pathos of Francesca's story. . . . He faints in the intense awareness, furthermore, that he, as an author, might trap the readers into the illusory self-enclosure of the romance, just as the stilnovistic poetry, which Francesca quotes in her speech, trapped her. Dante's own text . . . acknowledges itself as part of the unavoidable ambiguities of the language of desire."

seem to be redeemed by the poet's affection, even though Dante as author and theologian condemns them to hell.

Thus Pound could have found in his beloved Dante some precedent for his oscillating work of prophecy. But in his first thirteen cantos the presence of Dante is fragmentary, subdued by the prominence of Homer, Ovid, the troubadours, and the historic figures of Italy, the Medici, and above all, Sigismundo Malatesta. In Canto 5, after the "ciocco" and the "*Caina attende,*" Pound brings into his gloomy conclusion the line from Dante's sestina, "Al poco giorno ed al gran cerchio d'ombra," to bring a little light into these tales of murder. It is the line that Pound so poignantly recalls with one of his most effective repetitions, in the last complete canto, 116, with its powerful memory of his debt to Dante, which concludes with the lines that for me make the best possible ending for the *Cantos:* "A little light, like a rushlight / to lead back to splendour"—the *splendor* of Dante's *Paradiso.*

The echoes of Dante resume in Canto 7 with a reprise of the "ciocco" and three more quotations from Dante.[11] But after this the echoes of Dante lapse, until they "bust thru" in the notorious Cantos 14 and 15, where Pound's version of hell is introduced with Dante's line, "Io venni in luogo d'ogni luce muto" (*Inf.* 5.28). What shall we make of these violent cantos, which mimic the postures of some of Dante's sinners, stuck in the excrement, mud, and slime of the *Inferno*? Their obscene and stercoraceous elements are no more virulent than many parts of the *Inferno,* but these are scattered throughout Dante's hell, intermingled with scenes of a different kind and intensity. Pound has packed into two short cantos some of the most scabrous and scatological images in Dante and has matched them with modern images of his own creation. But these two cantos do not create the grim horror and disgust that Dante, for the most part, achieves. Pound's hell is done in the tone of black comedy or farce that Dante adopts in his treatment of the barrators in Canto 22, where the "Navarrese" outwits his tormentors by diverting their attention and then diving off into the muck. This is an episode that Dante introduces by crying out: "O reader, thou shalt hear new sport! *[nuovo ludo]*" (22.118). We may appreciate the wit of Pound's sport here—but it is hard to take it seriously.

In the middle of Canto 15, Pound's poem takes a stronger turn, as Pound, echoing Dante's "E io," brings in his guide:

> And I said, 'How is it done?'
>   and my guide:
> This sort breeds by scission
> This is the fourmillionth tumour.
> In this *bolge* bores are gathered,
> Infinite pus flakes, scabs of a lasting pox.

11. "Con gli occhi onesti e tardi," echoing *Pur.* 6.63 and *Inf.* 4.112. "O voi che siete in piccioletto barca," *Par.* 2.1. "E biondo," *Inf.* 12.110.

Fig. 3. William Blake, illustration to Dante's *Divine Comedy*, 1824–1827. Hell Canto I: "Dante Running from the Three Beasts." Pen, ink, and watercolor over pencil. 37.0 x 52.8 cm. Felton Bequest, 1920. National Gallery of Victoria, Melbourne, Australia.

"Andiamo!" cries the guide, "and he said: close the pores of your feet!"

> and again Plotinus:
>> To the door,
> Keep your eyes on the mirror.

Plotinus, not Vergil: a significant change toward the Neoplatonic philosopher of light, "Iamblicus' light." And finally, we have the extended view of purgatory in Canto 16, the last in the initial installment of the cantos. It opens with a view of two purgatorial mountains and a vision of Pound's predecessor in the English tradition of poetical prophets: the illustrator of Dante, here seen in the manner of some of his own designs:[12]

> And the running form, naked, Blake,
> Shouting, whirling his arms, the swift limbs,
> Howling against the evil,
>> his eyes rolling,
> Whirling like flaming cart-wheels,
>> and his head held backward to gaze on the evil
> As he ran from it . . .
>> and like him Peire Cardinal.
> And in the west mountain, Il Fiorentino,
> Seeing hell in his mirror,
>> and lo Sordels
> Looking on it in his shield;
> And Augustine, gazing toward the invisible.

This last line offers a reminder of Augustine's Neoplatonic, Plotinian antecedents. Peire Cardinal belongs here because he denounced the evils of the clergy, and Sordello belongs here because of his appearance in the *Purgatorio*. We move then through the purgatorial acid until, as in the *Purgatorio*, we arrive at a pastoral scene, an earthly paradise:

> Then light air, under saplings,
> the blue banded lake under aether,
>> an oasis, the stones, the calm field,

12. The figure of Blake and his setting seem to be a composite vision drawn from numerous prints and drawing by Blake, among them his designs for the *Divine Comedy* (see Appendix, "Pound, Blake, and Dante"). The presentation is not, I think, derogatory to Blake, but rather represents one pole of prophetic utterance, the mode of violent denunciation, which Pound has just demonstrated in the two preceding ("Hell") cantos. The figures on the other mountain seem to represent the other pole of prophecy: the mode that promises redemption (Sordello acts as Dante's guide in the *Purgatorio*). For different views of Blake here see John Glendening, "Ezra Pound and Ezra Pound's Blake: Method in Madness, Madness in Method," and Guy Davenport, *Cities on Hills: A Study of I–XXX of Ezra Pound's Cantos*, 191–93.

the grass quiet . . .
    and by their fountains, the heroes,
Sigismundo, and Malatesta Novello,
    and founders, gazing at the mounts of their cities.

At this point we may realize clearly what has been latent before: that the earlier passages about Sordello and Cunizza da Romano evoke memories of their appearances in the *Purgatorio* and the *Paradiso*, while the allusion to the Malatesta family may suggest that, in the Malatesta Cantos, Pound has been following Dante's example, at much greater length, by dealing with the sort of turmoil in Italian history that plays so large a part in Dante's poem. Indeed, it may well be that Pound's long immersion in the affairs of Sigismundo led the way toward the open imitation of Dante in Cantos 14, 15, and 16.

Now, in this earthly paradise, "one man rose from his fountain / and went off into the plain." This may evoke the disappearance of Vergil in the *Purgatorio*, but more seems to be involved here. Vergil does not go off into the plain; he simply disappears. It is Ezekiel who goes off "into the plain," as we have heard twice in the passage quoted earlier from Ezekiel. It is significant that just before Vergil's disappearance in the *Purgatorio*, Dante recalls the vision of Ezekiel and urges us to read that prophet (29.100).

Then Pound continues: "Prone in that grass, in sleep / et j'entendis des voix." Now follows the Dantesque series of voices and vignettes largely concerned with the hell of World War I and the Russian revolution. Thus Cantos 14, 15, and 16, with their visions of hell, purgatory, and hell again, may be taken to suggest that Dante has shown Pound the kind of poem he was writing.

In accordance with this kind of poem, Canto 17, first in a new volume, turns to a vision of another earthly paradise, Venice raised to the ideal power. The opening landscape suggests the backgrounds seen in many Venetian paintings of the Renaissance, and indeed this part of the canto is a painting in words:

And the boat drawn without sound,
Without odour of ship-work,
Nor bird-cry, nor any noise of wave moving,
Nor splash of porpoise, nor any noise of wave moving . . .

The first half of the poem is a composition in related and repeated colors, with "The light now, not of the sun"; then the colors ripple before us, "Chryso-phrase," a green stone, "And the water green-clear, and blue-clear; / On, to the great cliffs of amber." Then the repeat:

    cliff green-gray in the far,
In the near, the gate-cliffs of amber,
And the wave
    green clear, and blue clear . . .

These are the very colors of Venetian landscape painting, in Giorgione, Titian, or Cima da Conegliano. A visit to the Accademia, where Pound must have gone frequently, will prove the point that Richard Turner has made with regard to Giorgione's *Tempesta:* "Giorgione has conceived the entire picture as a close blend of greens and blues." Except for certain "spots of color" the "rest of the picture is a blend of earths, greens, and blues. The center of the painting is framed by a U of earth colors and olive-greens. . . . The whole comes to life through variations of shade within the blues and greens."[13] Pound's earth color is "amber." The scene is then framed by the reminder, "the light not of the sun"—a supernatural light that may be created by a white pigment.

After a vision of the gods, who often appear in Venetian landscape, we return to the marble forest, the ideal city where heroes assemble: "Borso, Carmagnola, the men of craft, *i vitrei.*" This brings a repeat of the line that had come near the close of the Malatesta cantos, summing up the effect of the Tempio amid the distractions and defeats of the hero's career, an echo placed in quotation marks to remind us of the earlier occurrence and to create the effect of a familiar epigram: "In the gloom the gold / Gathers the light about it." Or "against it," as in Canto 11. In either phrasing the epigram sums up the effect of prophecy, in the Bible, in Dante, and in Pound.

From here on the explicit echoes of Dante are rare, though highly significant. Thus in Pound's Canto 32 the concluding echo of the words with which Dante introduces Sordello—"a guisa di leon quando si posa" (*Pur.* 6.66)—reminds us of the long tirade against tyrants that follows—a parallel with the list of royal "fools" that Pound has placed before this allusion. And the heading for Canto 38, the quotation from the *Paradiso* (19.118–19) relating the woes produced by false coinage, foretells the financial woes of Europe related in that canto. Most important is the translation from Cavalcanti in Canto 36, a canzone bound to remind us that this poet was Dante's close friend; and if we missed this memory, Pound alerts us in the line that immediately follows this translation, a line placed in quotation marks: "Called thrones, balascio or topaze"—a threefold allusion to the *Paradiso.*[14]

As in the Bible and Dante, the various modes of prophetic speech are brought together within the personal presence of the prophet, whom we have seen sitting on the Dogana's steps, or on the steps of the arena at Verona, or going up to Freiburg to talk with old Levy about the meaning of that word *noigandres,* or talking with Yusef in Gibraltar, or, in Canto 46, talking with the "major" and reminding us of how many years he has spent on this case, as his "first part" "draws to a conclusion / of the first phase of this opus." The whole final canto of this group, Canto 51, represents a descent from heaven down to hell, beginning

---

13. A. Richard Turner, *The Vision of Landscape in Renaissance Italy* (Princeton: Princeton University Press, 1966), 89–90; see chaps. 5 and 6, on Giorgione and "Venetian Landscapes."

14. See Terrell, *Companion,* 1:143. Important too are the quotations in Canto 39 from the *Paradiso* (23.129 and 30.62), which stress the "paradisal" nature of this sexual vision.

with the bright lines from Guinicelli: "Shines / in the mind of heaven God / who made it" and concluding with a descent into the depths of hell with Dante's monster of fraud: "I am Geryon twin with usura."

In the next sequence of twenty cantos Pound lays aside the prophetic voice, lays aside Dante, and uses instead the voice of the history teacher: ten cantos relate the history of ancient China; ten cantos relate through John Adams the views of America's founding fathers. Why the change? Perhaps the cause may be found in the darkening political situation that prevailed in 1938 and 1939 while Pound was writing these cantos—omens of war, the alliance with Hitler, the actual outbreak of war in September 1939, only five months before these cantos were published. Under these threats Pound's mind seems to have sought stability in exploring two examples of sustained political wisdom. But I side with those who feel that these twenty cantos are not successful: they go on too long; they become tedious. Then, for five long years, we have no more cantos, until, late in the winter of 1944–1945, in the face of disaster, Pound wrote in the Italian language his cantos 72 and 73 and sent them to Mussolini in the doomed "republic" of Salò. However deeply we may disapprove of the political views set forth in these two cantos, we should read them in their proper sequence, as they appear in Mary de Rachewiltz's edition of 1985 and in the latest printing of the American edition of the *Cantos,* which also includes the recently discovered translation of Canto 72 made by Pound himself.[15]

The importance of these Italian cantos lies in the way in which they make a junction with the first fifty-one cantos, joining with the allusion to Dante at the close of Canto 51 to create the most elaborate imitation of Dante's method to be found in the *Cantos.*[16] Canto 72 uses Dante's method of voice and vision, as Pound speaks with the ghost of Marinetti and hears the violent words of Ezzelino da Romano, inspired by the translation of Mussato's Latin tragedy about Ezzelino made by Pound's friend Manlio Torquato Dazzi. Why Pound thus resurrects a character damned by Dante is perhaps explained by Ezzelino's cry that he has been betrayed by Mussato. It appears that Pound may be trying to do for this tyrant what he has done for Sigismundo: repair his reputation. The main point to be made, though, is that the name of Ezzelino da Romano links with the name of his sister in the earlier cantos, while the mistaken query "Are you Sigismundo?" takes us back to Ixotta and the Tempio. Lastly, the voice of Galla Placidia reminds us of that mausoleum where the gold shines against the gloom or, more sadly, in Canto 21, "Gold fades in the gloom." Similarly, the

---

15. See *I Cantos* and *The Cantos,* 13th printing. Pound's translation of Canto 72 was first published with a commentary by James Laughlin in *Paris Review* 128 (1993): 307–17. Cantos 72 and 73 have been translated, along with fragments of other passages in Italian, by Massimo Bacigalupo, in "Ezra Pound's Cantos 72 and 73: An Annotated Translation."

16. See Bacigalupo, "Pound's Cantos 72 and 73": "Cantos 72 and 73 pick up methods and themes from previous sections, such as the Dantesque form of the vision (see especially Cantos 15–17), and Dantesque characters like Guido Cavalcanti and Ezzelino da Romano, whose sister Cunizza [played] a major role in Cantos early and late" (20).

voice of Cavalcanti in Canto 73 reminds us of the translation of his canzone in Canto 36 and leads the way into the unexpected *Pisan Cantos,* where the key is found in the familiar words of that canzone: "dove sta memoria."[17] "Where memory liveth" Love "takes its state"

> Formed like a diafan from light on shade . . .
> And his strange quality sets sighs to move
> Willing man look into that forméd trace in his mind . . .
> (Canto 36)

So it is with Pound in captivity. In the hell of the prison camp memory brings moments of redemption, as he recalls with affection his "companions" in the creation of the bittersweet new style of modernism. Yeats, Joyce, Williams, H.D., "Fordie," and many others receive their affectionate tributes in memory, as Dante paid his tributes to his poetical friends, while harsh voices from the outside remind us of the prison setting:

> "Hey Snag, what's in the bibl'?
> > what are the books of the bibl'?
> Name 'em! don't bullshit me!"
> (Canto 77)

(Has the guard seen Pound reading his Bible?) And then, only four lines later:

> "Sligo in Heaven" murmured uncle William
> > when the mist finally settled down on Tigullio

Amid these oscillations between light and shade, in the middle of these eleven cantos the prophet reveals his name for the first and only time,[18] as Dante reveals his name in the *Purgatorio* (30.55–63):

> The moon has a swollen cheek
> and when the morning sun lit up the shelves and battalions
> of the West, cloud over cloud
> > Old Ez folded his blankets
> Neither Eos nor Hesperus has suffered wrong at my hands.
> (Canto 79)

Then follows one of Pound's greatest and most sustained prophetic utterances: the lynx hymn that proclaims the presence of the gods in this camp. From here on the power of memory becomes stronger and stronger, until in Canto 81 we

---

17. For the repeated phrase "dove sta memoria" see Canto 76.

18. One is struck by the coincidence with Isaiah's revelation of his mission in the middle of his first eleven chapters.

reach the vision of the eyes in the tent and the prophetic voice that speaks in biblical diction, summing up the meaning of these redemptive memories of old friends, old achievements, beloved places, and sustaining myths:

> What thou lovest well remains,
> the rest is dross
> What thou lov'st well shall not be reft from thee
> What thou lov'st well is thy true heritage

These memories rise to a climax in the splendid Canto 83 (originally designed as the last in the sequence),[19] with its moving tribute to H.D. ("Dryad") and the long, humorous, affectionate tribute to Yeats, "downstairs composing" at Stone Cottage.

In this way Pound is fulfilling, within the context of this painful and involuntary exile, the role of Dante as described by one eminent Dante scholar: "Prophecy is not simply the prediction of events to come. The prophet, for Dante, is one who is engaged in *reading* the signs of the times and who, sustained by faith, bears witness to his own words with the reality of his life."[20] At the same time Pound is also fulfilling the prophecy that he had made long before, when he wrote to his mother in 1909: "But the American who has any suspicion that he may write poetry, will walk very much alone, with his eyes on the beauty of the past of the old world, or on the glory of a spiritual kingdom, or on some earthly new Jerusalem."[21]

19. Ronald Bush, "Modernism, Fascism, and the Composition of Ezra Pound's *Pisan Cantos*," esp. 77–80.
20. Mazzotta, *Dante, Poet of the Desert*, 299.
21. Family Letters.

6.

William Carlos Williams, *Paterson*

The Quest for the Beautiful Thing

MEANWHILE, BACK IN America, Pound's friend from their student days in Philadelphia, Dr. William Carlos Williams, had been brooding bitterly over the success of *The Waste Land,* which he called "the great catastrophe to our letters."[1] In Williams's view *The Waste Land*'s success stopped the progress of truly American poetry for nearly thirty years. In the early 1920s a group of artists and writers in New York City had been attempting to produce what they regarded as truly American art, works that, though thoroughly aware of European traditions, were nevertheless local in their basic inspiration, as independent and boldly original as those of Walt Whitman, or Melville, or Edgar Allan Poe.[2] They were in fact attempting to carry out the aim that D. H. Lawrence had described in an essay published in the *New Republic* in 1920, two years before the appearance of Eliot's *Waste Land:*

> Let Americans turn to America, and to that very America which has been rejected and almost annihilated. Do they want to draw sustenance for the future? They will never draw it from the lovely monuments of our European past [as Ezra Pound had been doing!]. These have an almost fatal narcotic,

1. Williams, *Autobiography,* 146, 174–75.
2. See Bram Dijkstra, *Hieroglyphics of a New Speech;* Dickran Tashjian, *William Carlos Williams and the American Scene, 1920–1940;* William Marling, *William Carlos Williams and the Painters, 1909–1923;* Peter Halter, *The Revolution in the Visual Arts and the Poetry of William Carlos Williams.*

dream-luxurious effect upon the soul. America must turn again to catch the spirit of her own dark, aboriginal continent. . . . Americans must take up life where the Red Indian, the Aztec, the Maya, the Incas left it off. They must pick up the life-thread where the mysterious Red race let it fall. They must catch the pulse of the life which Cortés and Columbus murdered. . . . A great and lovely life-form, unperfected, fell with Montezuma. The responsibility for the producing and the perfecting of this life-form devolves upon the new American. It is time he accepted the full responsibility. It means a surpassing of the old European life-form. It means a departure from the old European morality, ethic. It means even a departure from the old range of emotions and sensibilities. The old emotions are crystallized for ever among the European monuments of beauty. There we can leave them.[3]

This indeed is what William Carlos Williams was soon to recommend in the essays that made up *In the American Grain* (1925), the germ of his own prophetic poem, *Paterson,* deeply influenced by both Lawrence and Whitman.

What does Williams prophesy? For whom does he speak? We begin to learn the answers in the second book of *Paterson,* where the poem's collage of what we call prose and what we call poetry rises to a climax as the prophet-poet, like another Moses on Mount Pisgah, climbs to the top of the mountain in the Park on a Sunday afternoon, observing all the inhabitants, dogs, grasshoppers, and people, and above all, *listening,* like Walt Whitman, to the voices all about him.

> Voices!
> multiple and inarticulate .   voices
> clattering loudly to the sun,
> to the clouds. Voices!
> assaulting the air gaily from all sides.
>
> —among which the ear strains to catch
> the movement of one voice among the rest
> —a reed-like voice
> of peculiar accent[4]

"A reed-like voice": is he seeking the music of poetry, the organ reed that might bring all together? ("The human vocal chords are really free reeds," says the unabridged Webster's dictionary.)

3. Lawrence, "America, Listen to Your Own," in *Phoenix,* ed. Edward D. McDonald, 90–91. For Lawrence's appreciative review of *In the American Grain* see *Phoenix,* 334–36.

4. The relation of Williams to Whitman has been dealt with by many commentators. See especially Stephen Tapscott, *American Beauty: William Carlos Williams and the Modernist Whitman,* and James E. Breslin, *William Carlos Williams: An American Artist.* Tapscott in a long note (249, n. 4) reminds us that we should also be aware of the example of Joyce, particularly in *Finnegans Wake.*

Quotations are taken from *Paterson,* "Revised edition prepared by Christopher Mac-Gowan"; hereafter cited in the text by page reference.

Then "a trumpet sounds fitfully"; he stands "at the rampart," on the summit of the mountain, and looks

> —beyond the gap where the river
> plunges into the narrow gorge, unseen
>
> —and the imagination soars, as a voice
> beckons, a thundrous voice, endless
> —as sleep: the voice that has ineluctably called them—
>   that unmoving roar! (55)

It is the central symbol of the poem—the roar of the Falls, suggesting the voices of all the past and present in the city, "pouring down," in verse of various forms, in letters, newspaper clippings, historical memoirs, advertisements, financial treatises, reports of a rock-drill down through the earth below Paterson—a roar in which he finds "his voice, one among many (unheard) / moving under all" (55).

> So during the early afternoon, from place
> to place he moves,
> his voice mingling with other voices
> —the voice in his voice
> opening his old throat, blowing out his lips,
> kindling his mind (more
> than his mind will kindle)   (56)

"The voice in his voice" is the voice of all the city, its unspoken consciousness, its needs and desires, struggling for words, within the prophet's voice. ("I act as the tongue of you," said Whitman.)

Now, in this central section of Book Two, he comes upon what might seem to be a "reed-like voice / of peculiar accent" and finds the source of the trumpet sound in a meager group with "a cornet, clarinet and trombone," assembled before the Evangelist, a German immigrant who has given away his wealth and now preaches against riches. Then Williams creates, in versified lines, the rambling, prosy sermon of the Evangelist, interrupted, ironically, by prose passages that tell of Alexander Hamilton's financial plans for the new republic, and also by prose quotations from pamphlets denouncing the Federal Reserve System. The sermon is set in verse, but is it poetry? The poet has his doubts, for he remarks:

> —with monotonous insistence
> the falls of his harangue hung featureless
> upon the ear, yet with a certain strangeness
> as if arrested in space   (70)

"Hung featureless": the sermon lacks the concrete poetical detail and subtle pacing that could grip an audience, and yet the fervent sincerity of the speech makes it rise above the ordinary, above the economic and historical prose that interrupts its flow. This Evangelist, like the prophet Ezekiel, has "heard a voice"— "a voice—just / as I am talking to you here today."

> And the voice said,
> Klaus, what's the matter with you? You're not
> happy. I am happy! I shouted back,
> I've got everything I want. No, it said.
> Klaus, that's a lie. You're not happy.
> And I had to admit it was the truth. I wasn't
> happy. That bothered me a lot.
> . . . .
> And the Lord said to me, Klaus, get rid of your
> money. You'll never be happy until you do that. (69)

The flow of the sermon is interrupted here by a prose passage about the importance of manufactured goods for "the young republic" and Hamilton's plans for "a national manufactory" at the Falls; then the voice of the evangelist returns:

> Give away your money, He said, and I
> will make you the richest man in the world!
> And I bowed my head and said to Him, Yea, Lord.
> And His blessed truth descended upon me and filled
> me with joy, such joy and such riches as I
> had never in my life known to that day and I said
> to Him, Master!
> In the Name of the Father
> and the Son and the Holy Ghost.
> Amen.
>
> Amen! Amen! echoed the devout assistants. (70–71)

The poet does not join in this Amen. In stanzas of his own that rise poetically higher than the versified sermon he asks, "Is this the only beauty here?"

> The beauty of holiness,
> if this it be,
>
> is the only beauty
> visible in this place
> other than the view
> and a fresh budding tree. (71)

The poet's mind is not deeply concerned with all these financial issues: immediately after a fierce passage of prose denouncing the Federal Reserve banks as
"a Legalized National Usury System," the poet concludes with a long poetical
meditation and prayer to some higher power that he feels working within the
universe. Here, if anywhere, is the voice he is seeking: that "reed-like voice / of
peculiar accent":

> If there is subtlety,
> you are subtle. I beg your indulgence:
> no prayer should cause you anything
> but tears. I had a friend . . .
> let it pass. I remember when as a child
> I stopped praying and shook with fear
> until sleep—your sleep calmed me—
>
> You also, I am sure, have read
> Frazer's Golden Bough. It does you
> justice—   (74)

The wry allusion to Frazer's study of ancient religious practices sounds like a
crack at Eliot, who says in his notes to *The Waste Land* that the poem is indebted
to Frazer's work. But Williams is addressing and testifying to his belief in the
eternally creative powers of nature:

> You are the eternal bride and
> father—quid pro quo,
> a simple miracle that knows
> the branching sea, to which the oak
> is coral, the coral oak.
> The Himalayas and prairies
> of your features amaze and delight—

Then comes the abrupt question:

> Why should I move from this place
> where I was born? knowing
> how futile would be the search
> for you in the multiplicity
> of your debacle.   (75)

Why *debacle*? I suppose he refers to the loss ("a sudden breaking up") of faith
in these eternal powers that has (Williams implies) led his fellow poets, Eliot,
Pound, and H.D., to go abroad in search of what he has called in Book One

> loveliness and
> authority in the world—

> a sort of springtime
> toward which their minds aspired (35)

Williams must find his answer here, for to him the creative powers are universally present:

> The world spreads
> for me like a flower opening—and
> will close for me as might a rose—
>
> wither and fall to the ground
> and rot and be drawn up
> into a flower again. But
> you never wither—but blossom
> all about me. In that I forget
> myself perpetually—in your
> composition and decomposition
> I find my . . .
>
> despair! (75)

This is the "despair" that sometimes overcomes the constantly striving human creator, in despair of ever matching the eternal creative power in nature. And it is also the peculiar "despair" that Williams describes in a letter to Marianne Moore, where he speaks of "a sort of nameless religious experience" that he had when he was "about twenty,"—"a sudden resignation to existence, a despair—if you wish to call it that, but a despair which made everything a unit and at the same time a part of myself." It was, he says, an experience that made him "feel as much a part of things as trees and stones."[5] As a result of this sense of unity with all creation the poet-prophet here does not lose confidence, as the opening of the next section shows:

> The descent beckons
>   as the ascent beckoned
>   Memory is a kind
>   of accomplishment
>   a sort of renewal   (78)

And so he continues the quest:

> Caught (in mind)
> beside the water he looks down, listens!
> But discovers, still, no syllable in the confused
> uproar: missing the sense (though he tries)

5. *Selected Letters of William Carlos Williams,* ed. John C. Thirlwall, 147. Cited by Paul Mariani, *William Carlos Williams: A New World Naked,* 47–48.

> untaught but listening, shakes with the intensity
> of his listening.   (82)

Meanwhile we note that the word *despair* that concluded the poetry of this book's second section is immediately followed by one of the letters from "Cress" (Marcia Nardi) that express a different and much more dangerous form of despair:

> I have been feeling (with that feeling increasingly stronger) that I shall never again be able to recapture any sense of my own personal identity (without which I cannot write, of course—but in itself far more important than the writing) until I can recapture some faith in the reality of my own thoughts and ideas and problems which were turned into dry sand by your attitude toward those letters and by that note of yours later. (76)

These letters, running throughout Book Two and rising to a flood in the final five-page letter that concludes the book, stand as a constant reproach to the prophetic speaker, who declares his empathetic response to all the voices about him—and yet here, in these poignant and bitter letters, we see a major failure in human sympathy. The very presence of these letters acts as a constant rebuke to the prophet-poet, questioning his wisdom and authority, and suggesting that his adoption of the prophetic stance has divorced him, at least in this one instance, from truly human understanding. Inclusion of the letters in such bulk seems an implicit acceptance of the need for humility and deeper self-understanding in Dr. P.[6]

It is appropriate, then, that Book Three should open in a humbler, chastened mood, turning inward to search the self, as the poet prepares us to watch the fulfillment of all those dozens of allusions to the Falls that have run throughout the first two books:

> Spent from wandering the useless
> streets these months, faces folded against
> him like clover at nightfall, something
> has brought him back to his own
> >   mind.
> >   in which a falls unseen
> tumbles and rights itself

6. Similar interpretations of this reproach implied by the letters have been given by Henry M. Sayre, *The Visual Text of William Carlos Williams* ("The effect of the Nardi letters on *Paterson* is to challenge the authority of Williams' art," 106); and by Theodora R. Graham, "'Her Heigh Compleynte': The Cress Letters of William Carlos Williams' *Paterson*," esp. 182–88. For the problem of Williams's revision of the Nardi letters raised by Graham, see MacGowan's discussion in his edition of *Paterson*, 275–77. For further details see *The Last Word: Letters between Marcia Nardi and William Carlos Williams,* ed. Elizabeth Murrie O'Neil.

and refalls—and does not cease, falling
and refalling with a roar, a reverberation
not of the falls but of its rumor

                                            unabated

                                    Beautiful thing,
          my dove, unable and all who are windblown,
          touched by the fire   (96–97)

Now we meet the inner action of the prophet-poet's mind, as he absorbs and
re-creates the voices of the past and the present, while the roar of the Falls is
heard within the reader of this poem. It is essential to stress the way in which the
opening section of Book Three invites the reader's participation. Dr. P. himself,
reading in the Library, brings these old records to life: "The mind / reels, starts
back amazed from the reading" (98).

                    Awake, he dozes in a fever heat,
          cheeks burning   .   .   loaning blood
          to the past, amazed   .   risking life. (101)

Thus Dr. P. reads, thus he imagines the city's great fire:

                        The person submerged
          in wonder, the fire become the person   .   (122)

The Library, he says in vehement capitals, "IS SILENT BY DEFECT OF
VIRTUE IN THAT IT / CONTAINS NOTHING OF YOU" (123). There
is the point.

                              That which should be
          rare, is trash; because it contains
          nothing of you . . .
                              But you are the dream
          of dead men
                              Beautiful Thing! (123)

Is not the Beautiful Thing the affectionate realization of past and present in the
mind of the living?

                              The pitiful dead
          cry back to us from the fire, cold in
          the fire, crying out—wanting to be chaffed
          and cherished
                              those who have written books (123)

Then, as we "dig in," we find deep within the book

> a nothing, surrounded by
> a surface, an inverted
> bell resounding, a
> white-hot man become
> a book, the emptiness of
> a cavern resounding (124)

This is also the cavern behind the Falls, at the very end of Book One, where

> Thought clambers up,
> snail like, upon the wet rocks
> hidden from sun and sight—
>   hedged in by the pouring torrent—
> and has its birth and death there
> in that moist chamber . . .   (38–39)

The book is nothing until it contains something of you, and then the white-hot man by his reading rescues and renews the white-hot author of the book, "in that cavern, that profound cleft," the living mind of a later day, repairing the old in a new image and idiom. (Eliot and Pound would reply that they too are trying to speak in the present tense, to re-create their myths, their religions, their heroes, within the modern scene—but Williams finds them stricken with too much nostalgia; however much they may speak of and in the present, their longing moves for him too strongly toward the past.)

We have by Book Three moved far away from the "start" that Williams had made "out of particulars" in Book One, which began by repeating the famous phrase from his old poem of 1927: "Say it, no ideas but in things."[7] That phrase, sometimes taken as the essence of Williams's poetic, is only the beginning of the poetic of *Paterson*, which is a poem not simply of beginning, but of "beginning, seeking, achieving . . ."[8] Book One begins with the facts, the things. In Book Two Williams seeks to catch "the movement of one voice among the rest." And in Book Three we have the achievement of a prophetic voice that holds the roar of all contemporary consciousness within the mind. Williams's poetic formula has subtly shifted from ideas found in things to things taken up affectionately within the mind, so that all things are here re-created, as a bottle is given a new glaze by the human apprehension of its shape and form, or as a tin roof is lifted by fire to float down within the human consciousness in a gracefully formed descent, or as a battered, scarred girl is apprehended within the speaker's mind:

7. "Paterson," in *The Collected Poems of William Carlos Williams, Volume I, 1909–1939*, ed. A. Walton Litz and Christopher MacGowan, 263–66.

8. "Author's Note" to Book One, *Paterson*, ed. MacGowan, 253; also p. xiv in paperbook edition.

—for I was overcome
by amazement and could do nothing but admire
and lean to care for you in your quietness—

who looked at me, smiling, and we remained
thus looking, each at the other   .   in silence   .

You lethargic, waiting upon me, waiting for
the fire and I
          attendant upon you, shaken by your beauty

Shaken by your beauty   .
                                   Shaken.   (126)

The Beautiful Thing then is not the girl in herself, but it is the human response, the fire of the imagination, the fire of human affection. One is struck by the emphasis on the word *mind* in Book Three, a word associated with the images of fire, flood, wind, falls, and the phrase "Beautiful thing":

                    a roar of books
          from the wadded library oppresses him
                                                  until
          his mind begins to drift   .
                                   Beautiful thing:

                                   — a dark flame,
          a wind, a flood—counter to all staleness.   (100)

Paterson, Book Three, thus becomes a hymn, a celebration, "a sort of chant, a sort of praise," to the creative power of human consciousness, when it works with affection and wonder to apprehend the "overall beauty" of the world in which it lives. And so in Book Three, Williams places within each section a chant—"So be it. So be it."—his version of the ancient Amen, words of approval and acceptance that he had withheld from the Evangelist's sermon. (Thus *amen* appears in the unabridged Webster's: "So is it; so shall it be; so be it; verily; assuredly;—a term used in solemn ratification of expressions of faith, or of wish in which higher powers are expected to concur.") Book Three is the fulfillment of the poet's vision. Here, at last, after the often sordid and ugly world this poem has presented, the poet-prophet-physician applies his healing benediction:

                              Rain
          falls and surfeits the river's upper reaches,
          gathering slowly. So be it. Draws together,
          runnel by runnel. So be it. A broken oar
          is found by the searching waters. Loosened

it begins to move. So be it. Old timbers
sigh—and yield. The well that gave sweet water
is sullied. So be it. And lilies that floated
quiet in the shallows, anchored, tug as
fish at a line. So be it. And are by their
stems pulled under, drowned in the muddy flux.
The white crane flies into the wood.
So be it. Men stand at the bridge, silent,
watching. So be it. So be it.   (130)

In this chant one has a sense of fulfillment as the wind, fire, and water become symbols of the creative spirit destroying the old and yet creating the new. Then, at the very close of Book Three, Williams once again draws together the first three books of his poem as he sums up the meaning of the symbol with which the poem has begun, the symbol of the great Falls of the Passaic:

The past above, the future below
and the present pouring down: the roar,
the roar of the present, a speech—
is, of necessity, my sole concern .
. . . .
                    I cannot stay here
to spend my life looking into the past:

the future's no answer. I must
find my meaning and lay it, white,
beside the sliding water: myself—
comb out the language—or succumb (144–45)

Like all true prophets his concern lies with "the roar of the present" out of which, through his "redeeming language,"[9] he can discern and present the Beautiful Thing.

9. See the note on the dust jacket of Book Three; *Paterson,* ed. MacGowan, 279. Sayre (*Visual Text,* 109) stresses the essential point here: "*Paterson* embodies a double movement. It is both destructive and ameliorative—and it cannot be one without first having been the other."

7.

William Carlos Williams, *Paterson*

A Local Tapestry

*I*F WE HAD ONLY the first three books of *Paterson*, published together as they were in one volume in 1950, I believe that we would have a sense of almost perfect accomplishment, of a poem that with all its variety holds together with a dominant symbolism and a soaring climax. But clearly, Williams did not wish to end with such an effect. Even as he announced the completion of his poem in 1951, with the news release concerning the fourth book, he described how hard he had to think about "how I was going to end the poem."

> It wouldn't do to have a grand and soul satisfying conclusion because I didn't see any in my subject. Nor was I going to be confused or depressed or evangelical about it. It didn't belong to the subject. It would have been easy to make a great smash up with a "beautiful" sunset at sea, or a flight of pigeons, love's end and the welter of man's fate.
>
> Instead, after the little girl gets herself mixed up at last in the pathetic sophisticate of the great city, no less defeated and understandable, even lovable, than she is herself, we come to the sea at last. Odysseus swims in as man must always do, he doesn't drown, he is too able but, accompanied by his dog, strikes inland again (toward Camden) to begin again.[1]

Camden, of course, evokes Walt Whitman, although there is nothing within the published ending of the fourth book that would indicate Whitman. That allusion

1. See *Paterson*, ed. MacGowan, xiii–xiv.

seems to be a memory of an early draft of the poem's ending, in which Walt Whitman is presented looking out toward the sea.[2] In any case, the important phrase is "to begin again." For Book Four is not so much a conclusion as it is a set of new beginnings. The idyll of Corydon and Phyllis is a complete break with the central images and the city setting of the preceding books. Now it is New York City, not Paterson. It is the East River, not the Passaic, and the parody of a traditional literary form is something not found in the earlier three books.

What is the meaning of this abrupt change? Paul Mariani's biography of Williams helps to show how all this came about.[3] In 1946 Williams had spent some time as a patient in a hospital overlooking the East River, just as his work on *Paterson* was well advanced. This experience at least explains the location and helps with the autobiographical aspects of the poem, though, alas, for me this knowledge does not make the poetry of this episode any better.

Then we learn something more significant. He came home from the hospital by December 22, 1946, "and began at once to assemble his notes for *Paterson* 2 and 3, thinking to write them together in one burst of activity. He thought he might even have them both ready before summer. The fourth book, he could see now, would need particular attention, since it would have to deal in a special way with the sense of ending, especially as the ending of *Paterson* would obviously come to include his own." Thus Books Two and Three flow one out of the other, an inseparable unity, moving toward the Falls: that climactic symbol of poetic achievement at the very end of Book Three. But Book Four, he realized, was a special problem, so difficult a problem that "sustained work" on the poem came to a halt for five months.[4] Williams was busy and bothered with many matters—but from Mariani's account it looks as though he was willing to do almost anything else but work on Book Four. This is what we all do when we are working against the grain. He had promised four books of *Paterson,* had even explained briefly what each book would do. It was a mistake, for a writer like Williams. Mariani shrewdly cites his 1947 letter to Kenneth Burke in which Williams says he simply cannot believe that Vergil would ever have written the *Aeneid* according to some "preliminary plan." "That he set down a primary scheme and followed it I can't for a moment believe." No, as Mariani well says, "the poet had to avoid prior patterns at all costs." Williams "meant to think with the poem and not with a preconceived master plan, going where the poem led him."[5]

Williams had got himself into a situation such as Walter Scott faced with *The Heart of Midlothian.* Scott had promised his publishers a four-volume set, but

2. For the manuscript passage see Benjamin Sankey, *A Companion to William Carlos Williams' Paterson*, 201.

3. *William Carlos Williams*, 533–36.

4. Ibid., 534–35, 603.

5. Williams, *Selected Letters*, 251; Mariani, *William Carlos Williams*, 540.

by the end of the third volume he had finished the story of Jeanie Deans. The novel was really over, but somehow a fourth volume had to be produced: hence the disappointing sequel. So it is with *Paterson*. One can see why Williams felt the need for a long pause in the composition. But when he returned to work on it again, at Yaddo, Mariani notes, "the poem's opening section had suffered a sea change from a meditation on Whitman on the Jersey shore to an anti-pastoral Fellini-like landscape set on New York's fashionable East Side."[6] Going over to the East River is no way of following the Passaic from the hills to the sea.

Williams knew, I think, that Book Four was not a complete success, in spite of his passionate defenses of it. Norman Pearson and I had lunch with him in New Haven not long after Book Four had appeared and very shortly after Marianne Moore had expressed her adverse opinion of the book.[7] Williams was bitterly disappointed and resentful, and he looked to us to tell him how wrong she was. He knew how much I admired the first three books, and I am sure he expected high praise. I did my best, saying I liked the use of Madame Curie and the radium image, liked the pastoral scenes from old Paterson, and especially admired the final beach scene. But he must have realized that I was holding back. "I've decided to write another book of *Paterson*," he said, "to show people what I mean." "But what about your plan," we asked, "the four-book plan?" "I've got to write another book," he said, "the poem isn't finished." (I'm remembering at a distance of more than forty years, and the words may not be exact, but this is the gist of what happened.)

Some admirers of *Paterson* (including myself) were struck with consternation at the thought that a *fifth* book of *Paterson* was contemplated. That four-part design, so carefully announced and explained by the poet—was it to be discarded now? But Williams knew what he was doing. When, in 1958, the threatened Book Five at last appeared, it proved to be an epilogue or coda, considerably shorter than the other books, and written in a reminiscent mode that Williams hoped would bind together all the foregoing poem. As Williams wrote on the dust jacket of Book Five: "I had to take the world of Paterson into a new dimension if I wanted to give it imaginative validity. Yet I wanted to keep it whole, as it is to me."

The leading symbol of this new dimension is one that may seem incongruous with Williams's lifetime dedication to the local, with his persistent refusal to adopt or approve the learned, foreign allusions of Ezra Pound or T. S. Eliot: for in Book Five the organizing symbol is the series of matchless tapestries in The Cloisters representing "The Hunt of the Unicorn." Williams had dealt briefly with these tapestries in the third book of *Paterson:*

6. *William Carlos Williams,* 603.
7. See Williams's letter of June 19, 1951, to Marianne Moore, which is clearly an answer to her adverse criticism and in which he concedes an element of "failure" in book 4; but see also his letter to her on June 23, 1951, in which he defends the pastoral episode (*Selected Letters,* 303–5).

> A tapestry hound
> with his thread teeth drawing crimson
> from the throat of the unicorn   (126)

Here the allusion acts as a reminder of the suffering inflicted upon the Beautiful Thing throughout the ages, as now the girl in her "white lace dress" has been beaten and apparently raped by "the guys from Paterson" or "the guys from Newark" (127–28).

In Book Five Williams is using the tapestries for a different purpose: to defend and explain his own technique by suggesting an analogy with the Unicorn Tapestries, which, like *Paterson,* achieve their success through a peculiar combination of natural beauty, realistic, even brutal details from local life, and a mythical protagonist. As I have noted before,[8] the tapestries display 101 trees, shrubs, herbs, and flowers so realistically that 85 of them have been identified by botanists. The "millefleurs background" is not made up of merely symbolic designs; the brilliant colors burst forth from the actual, recognizable violet, cornflower, daisy, calendula, or dandelion. Meanwhile, amid these beauties of nature, we see the vicious faces of certain hunters, the dog gutted by the unicorn's horn, the dog biting the unicorn's back, the spears stabbing the "milk-white beast," and the slanting, provocative, betraying eyes of the female attendant upon the virgin. In a similar way Williams has composed

> a tapestry
> silk and wool shot with silver threads
> a milk white one horned beast
>   I, Paterson, the King-self
> saw the lady
>   through the rough woods
>   outside the palace walls
> among the stench of sweating horses
> and gored hounds
>   yelping with pain (231)

The mythical beast, so clearly equated with "I, Paterson, the King-self," is the spirit of the imagination, the redeeming presence of art:

> The Unicorn
> has no match
>   or mate   .   the artist
> has no peer
>
> . . . .

8. "The Unicorn in *Paterson*," *Thought* 35 (1960): 537–54. For the botanical details see E. J. Alexander and Carol H. Woodward, *The Flora of the Unicorn Tapestries,* 2d ed. (New York: New York Botanical Garden, 1947). See also the illustrated booklet on the tapestries by Margaret B. Freeman and Linda Sipress (New York: Metropolitan Museum, 1974).

So through art alone, male and female, a field of
flowers, a tapestry, spring flowers unequaled
in loveliness,
>   through this hole
>   at the bottom of the cavern
>   of death, the imagination
>   escapes intact
he bears a collar round his neck
>   hid in the bristling hair.   (209–10)

Thus in the last of the series, the most famous of the tapestries, the Unicorn appears in peaceful resurrection. As "Paterson" now writes "In old age"—the opening line of Book Five—he knows the threat of mortality as well as the reassurance promised by everything that the Unicorn represents.

So Book Five suggests that we should regard *Paterson* as a kind of local tapestry, woven out of memories and observations, composed by one man's imagination, but written in part by his friends, his patients, and all the milling populace of the city and its region, past and present. The poem is a personal testament to the poet's vehement belief, represented throughout *In the American Grain,* "that there is a source in AMERICA for everything we think or do."[9] Why then, he asks, "Why should I move from this place / where I was born?" (75).

In this belief lies the source of the basic disagreement on poetical matters that we can see in the many years of correspondence between Williams and Pound.[10] The nature of that disagreement was shrewdly described by Williams in 1932, at a time when only thirty of Pound's cantos were available; Williams had read them in the handsome first editions, with their imitation of medieval manuscript illuminations:[11]

> So far I believe that Pound's line in his *Cantos*—there is something like what we shall achieve. Pound in his mould, a medieval inspiration, patterned on a substitution of medieval simulacra for a possible, not yet extant modern and living material, has made a precomposition for us. Something which when later (perhaps) packed and realized in living, breathing stuff will (in its changed form) be the thing.[12]

This is a theme developed throughout *Paterson,* beginning on the first page of the poem, with the "local" image of the dog "Sniffing the trees": "The rest

9. *In the American Grain,* 14th printing, 109.
10. See *Pound/Williams: Selected Letters of Ezra Pound and William Carlos Williams,* ed. Hugh Witemeyer.
11. See Donald Gallup, "The William Carlos Williams Collection at Yale"; on p. 56, among the books in Williams's library, we find *A Draft of XVI. Cantos* (Paris, 1925) and *A Draft of the Cantos 17–27* (London, 1928).
12. *Selected Letters,* 135.

have run out—after the rabbits." This shaft at the exiles of his generation is then
reinforced by his wry echo of the opening of Eliot's "East Coker":

> For the beginning is assuredly
> the end—since we know nothing, pure
> and simple, beyond
> our own complexities.   (3)

The theme is then openly enforced near the end of Book One, where the
"Moveless" poet "envies the men that ran / and could run off / toward the
peripheries—"

> a sort of springtime
> toward which their minds aspired
> but which he saw,
> within himself—ice bound
>
> and leaped, "the body, not until
> the following spring, frozen in
> an ice cake."   (35)

The descent into the memory of Paterson—city, poet, physician, and prophet—
must be attempted, though the result may be disaster.

The theme is continued a page later in the conversation between "P" and "I"
based, as we might assume, on a memory of something Pound has said: "Your
interest is in the bloody loam but what / I'm after is the finished product."[13]
The bitter answer reflects upon Pound's own disaster and the disaster of fascist
"empires": "Leadership passes into empire; empire begets insolence; insolence
brings ruin" (37). In the second section of Book Two, however, their disagreement is more gently and more harmoniously treated, in the passage that seems to
evoke Pound's "medieval" incantation of the phrase "with usura" in Canto 45.
Williams similarly repeats the phrase "without invention," using the word in the
meanings described by Webster's: "The mental power or faculty of constructing
or creating; broadly, the power of imagining new relations of ideas . . . also, the
quality of freshness and originality as shown in the choice or treatment of a
theme."

> Without invention nothing is well spaced,
> unless the mind change, unless
> the stars are new measured, according
> to their relative positions, the
> line will not change . . .

---

13. For the origin of the passage see MacGowan's note, *Paterson*, 267, and Tapscott,
American Beauty, 205–6.

> without invention
> nothing lies under the witch-hazel
> bush, the alder does not grow from among
> the hummocks margining the all
> but spent channel of the old swale,
> the small foot-prints
> of the mice under the overhanging
> tufts of the bunch-grass will not
> appear: without invention the line
> will never again take on its ancient
> divisions when the word, a supple word,
> lived in it, crumbled now to chalk .   (50)

Here indeed is a filling-in of Pound's "precomposition" with "living, breathing stuff" derived from the "loam," just as elsewhere Williams adapts Pound's use of letters by bringing in letters from his friends and acquaintances.[14]

Toward the end of Book Three Williams presents one of his major typographical inventions, as he suggests a world in disorder by throwing the lines aslant (137). How can such a world be redeemed? Pound's answer comes first, in stanzas that Williams has wittily arranged from a letter by Pound sent from "S. Liz"—St. Elizabeths hospital:[15]

> reread all the Gk Tragedies in
> Loeb.—plus Frobenius, plus Gesell,
> plus Brooks Adams
> ef you ain't read him all.—
> Then Golding's Ovid is in
> Everyman's lib.   (138)

The classics, anthropology, economics—these will provide the solution. Williams's reply is cleverly tacit. Adding the heading *SUBSTRATUM*, he presents on the facing page (139) a "tabular account of the specimens found" while drilling for an "Artesian Well at the Passaic Rolling Mill, Paterson." And at the end of this page-long table, we find the note: "The fact that the rock salt of England, and of some of the other salt mines of Europe, is found in rocks of the same age as this, raises the question whether it may not also be found here." For Williams the inspiration must be found here, in the local rock, in the bloody loam.[16]

14. See the detailed interpretation of this passage by Joel Conarroe, *William Carlos Williams' Paterson: Language and Landscape,* 34–36.

15. For the original letter of October 13, 1948, see *Pound/Williams,* 253–54.

16. Sankey (*Companion to Paterson,* 158) disagrees with this interpretation, but I still hold by it. Williams's addition of the title "SUBSTRATUM" as though this list were a poem seems to bear out my view of the passage as an answer to Pound's erudition (see MacGowan's note, *Paterson,* 286).

Nevertheless, in certain portions of *Paterson* Williams shows considerable sympathy with Pound's economic views: in the prose passages on economic matters intertwined with the Evangelist's sermon against money, and especially in the second section of Book Four, where the long passage headed "MONEY : JOKE" is prefaced by the full-page "Advertisement" urging a reform in the "present method of financing the national budget" (180). This whole five-page portion of Book Four is composed in a manner quite unusual for Williams. It has some of the tone of a Poundian diatribe against what Williams here calls "the cancer, usury"; and the Poundian quality is stressed by bringing in a paraphrase of Pound's epistolary answer to Williams's rock-drill in Book Two: "just because they ain't no water fit to drink in that spot (or you ain't found none) don't mean there ain't no fresh water to be had NOWHERE" (182).[17] The rest of the section is composed in a manner resembling Pound's multicultural style, with expressions in Hebrew and Spanish, along with allusions to the Parthenon, "Phideas," Pallas Athena, and the Elgin marbles—all this ending with an example of Pound's unmistakable epistolary style:[18]

> IN
> venshun.
> O.KAY
> In venshun (184)

Pound is recognizing Williams's argument for "invention" in Book Two, but he is most interested in the economic passages there, which he hopes may indicate a movement in this direction:

> and seeinz az how yu hv / started. Will you consider
> a remedy of a lot :
>   i.e. LOCAL control of local purchasing
>   power .
>   ? ?
>
> Difference between squalor of spreading slums
> and splendour of renaissance cities.   (185)

But Williams does not continue with this mode of writing, essentially not congenial to him, as Pound recognized back in 1928, when he described the difference between their two temperaments: "If he wants to 'do' anything about what he sees, this desire for action does not rise until he has meditated in full and at leisure. Where I see scoundrels and vandals, he sees a spectacle or an ineluctable process of nature. Where I want to kill at once, he ruminates."[19]

---

17. See MacGowan's note, *Paterson*, 291–92; and *Pound/Williams*, 264.
18. See MacGowan's note, *Paterson*, 292; and *Pound/Williams*, 267–68.
19. Pound, "Dr Williams' Position," *Literary Essays*, 392.

This difference is vividly displayed in Book Five, where a long vituperative letter by Pound on American politics and economics is set between Williams's delicate version of a passionate fragment by Sappho and the long, quiet, ruminative poem addressed to the unknown woman whose appearance "upon the street" "stopped me in my tracks" (215–18). In this context Pound's crude and bitter tirade may be taken to indicate how far Pound has departed from both the ancient and the modern poetry that he has admired, how far he has departed from his true poetical mission.[20]

But Williams himself, as he opens the second section of Book Four, seems to suggest that he too, in the first section of this book, has moved away from the core of his own mission, for he interpolates the significant parenthesis: "(What I miss, said your mother, is the poetry, the pure poem of the first parts .)." And in the very first line of the third section he puts the question: "Haven't you forgot your virgin purpose, / the language?" (186) "What language?" he asks, and answers in words later attributed to his grandmother: "The past is for those who / lived in the past." So much for the "splendour of renaissance cities." We move at once to the first of the series of horrible murders recorded in the history of the city, along with memories of a grandmother and other women in "Paterson's" life, until we come, in muted climax, to the long series of memories of the old town, a pastoral vision:

> In a deep-set valley between hills, almost hid
> by dense foliage lay the little village.
> Dominated by the Falls the surrounding country
> was a beautiful wilderness where mountain pink
> and wood violet throve: a place inhabited only
> by straggling trappers and wandering Indians. (192)

Here is true pastoral, antidote to the false pastoral of the first section. Here remembering the past is appropriate, for this is local, this is part of the city's memory, essential to indicate how drastically industrial development has altered the scene. These are memories that avoid sentimentality, mainly by the concrete precision of detail, and also by the interpolated passages of prose that do not allow us to linger upon the beauties of the past: the news item about the accidental killing of his daughter by Fred Goodell (194–95) and, more important, the letter from Williams's disciple Allen Ginsberg, representing a new generation of poet-prophets, as Ginsberg tells of "walking the streets and discovering the bars" of modern Paterson (193)—that decaying city along the river that, according to Williams, the industrial schemes of Alexander Hamilton have converted into "the vilest swillhole in christendom."[21] But this pastoral is not all past: the Falls

20. See MacGowan's note, *Paterson,* 302; *Pound/Williams,* 302–3.
21. *In the American Grain,* 195.

remains, its "dominant" beauty stressed five times in these memories of old Paterson, even in the final word:

> Just off Gun Mill Yard, on the gully
> was a long rustic winding stairs leading
> to a cliff on the opposite side of the river.
> At the top was Fyfield's tavern—watching
> the birds flutter and bathe in the little
> pools in the rocks formed by the falling
> mist of the Falls   .   .   (197)

No amount of urban degradation can destroy the majesty and beauty of the Falls: it lives, a symbol of the ability of creative minds to apprehend the Beautiful Thing.

Here by the Falls is our home, says the poet, not in the sea, as Williams concludes in the rousing finale of Book Four—originally designed as the ending of the whole poem: "I warn you, the sea is *not* our home. / the sea is not our home" (199). The warning is repeated five more times against the persistent pull of this "nostalgic sea" that "draws us in to drown, of losses / and regrets" (199–200). Is this the sea of Eliot's "Dry Salvages" that "tosses up our losses"? Certainly the classical references here point to a kind of poetry that celebrates the glories of the past:

> Oh that the rocks of the Areopagus had
> kept their sounds, the voices of the law!
> Or that the great theatre of Dionysius
> could be aroused by some modern magic
>
> . . . .
> Thalassa! Thalassa!
>   Drink of it, be drunk!
> Thalassa immaculata:our home, our nostalgic
> mother in whom the dead, enwombed again
> cry out to us to return .   (200–201)

" . . . not our home! It is NOT / our home," cries the prophetic voice.[22]

---

22. Tapscott (*American Beauty,* 181–87) has shown the rich complexity of this final section, where the "sea of blood" suggests the era of the Korean War and the lure of "savage lusts" that Williams describes in a letter of 1950 (*Selected Letters,* 291–92). But, as Tapscott points out, the "seeds" of renewal are also present, floating toward the shore. This interpretation leads well into Book Five, where, as Peter Schmidt has said, "the destructive and creative principles that had been at war throughout the previous books are wrested at last into equilibrium, so that each creative 'upturn' and the decadent 'downturn' are finally held in balance" (*William Carlos Williams, the Arts, and Literary Tradition,* 190). These views are in accord with the "oscillating movement" of prophecy that I have frequently noted in the preceding essays.

Suddenly the scene shifts to the shore, where a swimmer emerges from the water, to be greeted by his dog. He lies down on "the hot sand"; "—must have slept. Got up again" and dresses in the sort of precise detail that Williams at his best draws from the local scene:

> rubbed
> the dry sand off and walking a
> few steps got into a pair of faded
> overalls, slid his shirt on overhand (the
> sleeves were still rolled up) shoes,
> hat where she [the dog] had been watching them under
> the bank and turned again
> to the water's steady roar, as of a distant
> waterfall .   (202)

"What do I do?" asks the prophetic voice in an italicized passage in Book Two, and it answers in a way that sums up the action of this entire poem: "I listen, to the water falling. (No sound of it here but with the wind!) This is my entire occupation" (46).

8.

H.D.
Set Free to Prophesy

H.D. IS THE LAST of the great generation born in the 1880s to receive due recognition. Pound, Joyce, Eliot, Lawrence all received early acclaim—notoriety at least, if not their just due; and William Carlos Williams, after the publication of *Paterson*'s first four books, soon found his poetry admired in terms that equal the acclaim won long before by his bitterly resented rival Eliot. But H.D. had to wait until the 1970s before her true stature could be widely recognized. Why has H.D. thus lagged behind?

It is not simply because after the appearance of her first volume she became fixed, delimited, by the label *Imagiste* that Pound gave her in 1912, when he sent her early poems to Harriet Monroe for publication in *Poetry*. Pound, of course, never meant to trap her in this way; two years later he was publishing her famous "Oread" in the first issue of *Blast* as an example of "Vorticist" poetry. And indeed "H.D. Vorticist" would have been a better description of her early poetry, with its swirling, dynamic power: the sort of turbulent force that Henri Gaudier-Brzeska described in his own sculptural definition of "Vortex": "Plastic Soul is intensity of life bursting the plane."[1] This restless movement, the constant surging of intense vitality, lies at the center of H.D.'s early poetry, and thus the static, lapidary, crystalline implications usually carried by the word *imagism* could never contain the strength of H.D.'s muse.[2]

1. Ezra Pound, *Gaudier-Brzeska*, 21.
2. See Cyrena N. Pondrom, "H.D. and the Origins of Imagism."

Why, then, did the term cling to her poetry? Partly because H.D. continued to support the movement after Pound had given it over to Amy Lowell; partly too because the critical and poetical currents of the 1920s and 1930s, under the influence of Eliot and Pound and T. E. Hulme, were violently reacting against romanticism and were insisting upon the need for terse, compact poetry, rich in imagistic inference but spare in abstraction and exclamation. Thus the concentrated imagery of poems such as "Pear Tree" or "Sea Rose" seemed to represent her essence, and her passionate protest against the "Sheltered Garden" could be overlooked, along with some of the longer poems in her first volume, *Sea Garden* (1916), that show her reaching beyond Imagism toward the development of a prophetic voice more akin to Shelley than to Pound or Eliot. Her stance as prophetess has of course been widely recognized, especially by Susan Stanford Friedman in her classic book of 1981.[3] Here I wish to explore the development of this prophetic voice throughout her career.

Her early poem "Sea Gods," for example, protests against contemporary tendencies to deny the supernatural:

> They say you are twisted by the sea,
> you are cut apart
> by wave-break upon wave-break,
> that you are misshapen by the sharp rocks,
> broken by the rasp and after-rasp.

But in the second section of the poem she pays tribute to the sea gods by gifts of violets of every kind, violets as the symbols of love. And then the third section concludes in a style of ritual, liturgical repetition that foreshadows the style of "The Dancer" in the 1930s:

> For you will come,
> you will yet haunt men in ships,
> you will trail across the fringe of strait
> and circle the jagged rocks.
> You will trail across the rocks
> and wash them with your salt . . .
>
> For you will come,
> you will come,

3. *Psyche Reborn: The Emergence of H.D.*, esp. 74–75. Like everyone who has written on H.D. in recent years, I am deeply indebted to the insights contained in this book, especially with regard to *Trilogy* and *Helen in Egypt*. For an account of H.D. as a poet pursuing a quest for transcendence and redemption throughout her career, see the important but neglected study by Angela DiPace Fritz, *Thought and Vision: A Critical Reading of H.D.'s Poetry*. For H.D. as "a visionary poet" see Alicia Ostriker, "The Poet as Heroine: Learning to Read H.D." At a June 1996 conference in Orono, Maine, Ostriker demonstrated the continuance of the tradition of Hebrew prophecy by drawing a parallel between Allen Ginsberg and the prophet Jeremiah.

you will answer our taut hearts,
you will break the lie of men's thoughts,
and cherish and shelter us.[4]

Such a style is far removed from the terse style recommended by Pound in his famous "Don'ts" for Imagists.[5] Other longer poems in *Sea Garden* seem to defy Pound's demand for "economy of words" and his warning, "Go in fear of abstractions." In poems such as "The Cliff Temple" and the poem that concludes the volume, "Cities," we can feel the poet reaching toward some sort of prophetic vision that needs a style of exhortation and exclamation, where repetition of phrases serves to enforce the expression of a need or a hope:

Is our task the less sweet
that the larvae still sleep in their cells?
Or crawl out to attack our frail strength . . .

Though they sleep or wake to torment
and wish to displace our old cells—
thin rare gold—
that their larvae grow fat—
is our task the less sweet—
Though we wander about,
find no honey of flowers in this waste,
is our task the less sweet—

who recall the old splendour,
await the new beauty of cities?   (*CP*, 41)

This prophetic sense of the decline of civilization along with a mission to re-deem is more strongly enforced in the ten-page poem "The Tribute," published in the *Egoist* in 1916—the same year in which *Sea Garden* appeared. Using a Greek setting, the poem fiercely attacks the decay of values in contemporary society in time of war, using throughout a technique of repeating whole lines and phrases with liturgical, ritual effect:

Squalor spreads its hideous length
through the carts and the asses' feet,
squalor coils and reopens
and creeps under barrow
and heap of refuse . . .

4. H.D., *Collected Poems 1912–1944,* ed. Louis L. Martz, 29–31. Quotations from H.D.'s poetry up through *Trilogy* are taken from this edition, hereafter cited as *CP*.
5. Pound, *Literary Essays,* 3–5.

> Squalor spreads its hideous length
> through the carts and the asses' feet—
> squalor has entered and taken our songs . . .
>
> Squalor spreads its hideous length
> through the carts and the asses' feet,
> squalor coils and draws back . . .
> with no voice to rebuke—
> for the boys have gone out of the city,
> the songs withered black on their lips. (*CP*, 59–60)

All gods have been banished from the city except the war god, as "the people gather to cry for revenge, / to chant their hymns and to praise / the god of the lance." But now the words of rebuke are arising, led by the prophetic speaker, accompanied by the voices of "a few old men" and "a few sad women" and "a few lads" who cry out, praying to the gods of nature to redeem the city from its hate:

> O spirit of simples and roots
> O gods of the plants of the earth—
>
> O god of the simples and grasses,
> we cry to you now from our hearts,
> O heal us—bring balm for our sickness,
> return and soothe us with bark
> and hemlock and feverwort. . . .
>
> Return—look again on our city,
> though the people cry through the streets,
> though they hail another,
> have pity—return to our gates . . . (*CP*, 63–64)

This appeal to the healing powers of nature continues through the ninth strophe of this attempted ode, but then in the last two sections the speaker turns toward a defense of "beauty"—an abstract beauty never defined, though it is something that can never be destroyed despite the violence of wartime emotions:

> Could beauty be caught and hurt
> they had done her to death with their sneers
> in ages and ages past

And then the poem abruptly ends with what seems to be a tribute to the creative achievement of the "boys" before they were sent to their destruction:

> Could beauty be beaten out,—
> O youth the cities have sent
> to strike at each other's strength,
> it is you who have kept her alight. (*CP,* 68)

The poem is hardly successful, although it shows a prophetic spirit struggling for release into larger forms of poetry, such as the choruses from Greek tragedy that H.D. was at this time publishing—examples that encouraged her to pursue this ritual mode of utterance in her own verse.

H.D. was in fact at this very time writing long, much more powerful poems: the sequence that in her typescript she calls "poems of *The Islands* series"— dating from 1916 or 1917.[6] These poems all deal with the anguish of a deserted woman, an Ariadne on Naxos, as in "The Islands":

> What are the islands to me
> if you are lost,
> what is Paros to me
> if your eyes draw back,
> what is Milos
> if you take fright of beauty,
> terrible, tortuous, isolated,
> a barren rock?   (*CP,* 127)

The story is told at length in the triad preserved in her typescript: "Amaranth," "Eros," and "Envy," poems that leave no doubt that the sequence arises from the infidelities of her husband, Richard Aldington. "The Islands" was published in 1920, but the triad was never published complete during H.D.'s lifetime, although in *Heliodora* (1924) she published truncated versions of these poems under the guise of adaptations of fragments from Sappho—but carefully separated and with all references to a male lover removed.[7] In her volume of 1924, following the truncated version of "Eros" she placed a poem that might be taken to conclude "The Islands" series: "Toward the Piraeus." The title, referring to the port of Athens, suggests a poem written or conceived during the curative voyage to Greece in 1920, as the poet ponders the disaster recorded in the "Amaranth" triad. The poem opens with a prologue that fiercely denounces the weakness of modern men, compared with the heroic Greeks:

> *Slay with your eyes, Greek,*
> *men over the face of the earth,*

---

6. The typescript is in the H.D. Archive of the Beinecke Library, Yale University; see the introduction to *CP,* xiv.

7. For an account of these changes see the introduction and notes to *CP,* xiv–xviii, 617–18. An interpretation of these changes has been given by Elizabeth Dodd in *The Veiled Mirror and the Woman Poet: H.D., Louise Bogan, Elizabeth Bishop, and Louise Glück,* 57–70.

slay with your eyes, the host,
puny, passionless, weak.

The first section of the poem proper then conveys a complex view of the destructive yet creative power that her unfaithful lover has exerted upon her:

You would have broken my wings,
but the very fact that you knew
I had wings, set some seal
on my bitter heart, my heart
broke and fluttered and sang.

The second section then shows the source of the inner strength that has enabled her to survive this betrayal: it is her prophetic power, the power displayed by the prophetess at the oracle of Delphi:

I loved you:
men have writ and women have said
they loved,
but as the Pythoness stands by the altar,
intense and may not move,

till the fumes pass over
and may not falter or break,
till the priest has caught the words
that mar or make
a deme or a ravaged town:

so I, though my knees tremble,
my heart break,
must note the rumbling,
heed only the shuddering
down in the fissure beneath the rock
of the temple floor;

must wait and watch
and may not turn nor move,
nor break from my trance to speak
so slight, so sweet,
so simple a word as love.

Something deeper, something more mysterious than this love sustains her: a sense that some greater destiny awaits her. And so at the close she is able to utter a fair and balanced judgment of their troubles, with the perception that the cause of the disaster might be found in her own nature, which had to guard

her poetical and her sexual qualities against the power of a soldier-husband and
a fellow poet:

> It was not chastity that made me wild, but fear
> that my weapon, tempered in different heat,
> was over-matched by yours, and your hand
> skilled to wield death-blows, might break
>
> With the slightest turn—no ill will meant—
> my own lesser, yet still somewhat fine-wrought,
> fiery-tempered, delicate, over-passionate steel. (*CP*, 175–79)

The prophetic stance of the Pythoness is not often found again in the poems
that H.D. published during the 1920s, though sometimes, as in "Demeter" or
"Cassandra," it powerfully appears. It is not until *Red Roses for Bronze* (1931)
that H.D. showed persistent attempts to strike the prophetic stance, in poems
that carry the technique of repetition to an extreme, first in translations from the
choruses of Greek tragedy, as in this version from *The Bacchae:*

> O which of the gifts of the gods
> is the best gift?
>
> this,
> this,
> this,
> this;
> escape from the power of the hunting pack,
> and to know that wisdom is best
> and beauty
> sheer holiness.
>
> Hard,
> hard it is to wake the gods,
> but once awake,
> hard,
> hard,
> hard is the lot
> of the ignorant man . . .   (*CP*, 227)

This effort to achieve something like the ritual effect of a Greek chorus apparently
led to the same technique in her own independent "Choros Sequence: from
Morpheus":

> I live,
> I live,
> I live,

you give me that:
this gift of ecstasy
is rarer,
dearer
than any monstrous pearl
from tropic water;
I live,
I live,
I live . . .   (*CP*, 263)

In an earlier essay I said, "This is pitiful, grasping for a response the words cannot command." But I agree with Gary Burnett's view that this "pattern is so pervasive and so carefully pursued" that the above "characterization of it seems inadequate."[8] It would be better to say that this pervasive technique is a manifestation of H.D.'s effort to create the effect of "the Pythoness" standing by the altar, intense and trembling, waiting for a message from below the temple floor. The technique is not successful in many poems in this volume because it is simply too obvious; but where it is restrained, as in "In the Rain," "Chance Meeting," or, significantly, "Trance," the poems work. Perhaps it was H.D.'s own dissatisfaction with *Red Roses for Bronze* that led her to include near the close her "Epitaph"; but we must note that this is immediately followed by a concluding poem, "The Mysteries: Renaissance Choros," a controlled and successful poem, with the word *Renaissance* suggesting both a new era of culture and a time for personal rebirth under the power of the religious faith and figure represented in the "voice" that speaks out of the dark turbulence of the opening section: "peace / be still"—the words of Christ that calm the storm at sea (Mark 4:39). The poem continues with allusions to the Gospels, especially to the parables, combining these with allusions to the pagan mystery cults as the "voice" concludes:

The mysteries remain,
I keep the same
cycle of seed-time
and of sun and rain;
Demeter in the grass
I multiply,
renew and bless
Iacchus in the vine. . . .

I keep the law,
I hold the mysteries true,
I am the vine,

8. Introduction to *CP*, xxiii; Burnett, *H.D. between Image and Epic: The Mysteries of Her Poetics*, 104.

the branches, you
and you.   (*CP,* 305)

This concluding poem of 1931 is closely linked, both in style and in subject, with the poem "Magician" (Christ is called a "magician" in the second section of "The Mysteries"), published in an obscure magazine (*Seed*) in January 1933, two months before H.D. began her treatments with Freud. This poem is spoken in the person of a disciple of Christ who has heard his words and witnessed his miracles, and who now places reliance, not upon the symbols of the Crucifixion, but upon the images of nature that appear in the parables: nature as a channel toward the divine. Both the ending of *Red Roses for Bronze* and "Magician" show that H.D. had not utterly lost her creative powers when she sought help from Freud. She was capable of writing well, and Freud seems to have realized that her condition did not require the sort of deep analysis that would occupy years. A few months of advice would, and did, suffice to bring forth an immense surge of creative power, represented in "The Dancer" triad and in the completion of her long-contemplated version of the *Ion* of Euripides, published in 1937.

What was it that Freud helped her to discover? The first part of her *Tribute to Freud, Writing on the Wall,* provides the clue in the vision, or hallucination, that gives this part its title. The vision consists of three pictures.

> The first was head and shoulders, three-quarter face, no marked features, a stencil or stamp of a soldier or airman. . . . It was a silhouette cut of light, not shadow, and so impersonal it might have been anyone, of almost any country. And yet there was a distinctly familiar line about the head with the visored cap; immediately it was *somebody* unidentified indeed, yet suggesting a question—dead brother? lost friend?[9]

One thinks at once of Aldington, a soldier at the time of her anguish at his infidelity. The second picture is "the conventional outline of a goblet or cup"— symbol of the female. Do these two images suggest her bisexuality, the "two loves separate" that she describes in her poem about Freud?

The third picture is the most important and given the longest description. It is a "three-legged" image in perspective: "none other than our old friend, the tripod of classic Delphi . . . this venerated object of the cult of the sun god, symbol of poetry and prophecy" (*TTF,* 46). Delphi is then emphasized a few pages later, as she concentrates her attention on these pictures, saying, "it seems now possible that the mechanism of their projection (from within or from without) had something to do with, or in some way was related to, my feelings for the shrine at Delphi" (*TTF,* 49). The "idea of Delphi has always

---

9. *Tribute to Freud: Writing on the Wall, Advent,* 45–46; hereafter cited as *TTF.*

touched me very deeply," she adds, recalling that she had said to her friend Bryher (Winifred Ellerman), while recovering from her 1919 illness, "If I could only feel that I could walk the sacred way to Delphi, I know I would get well." In section 36 she clarifies the meaning of this picture, beginning with the thought that "all through time, there had been a tradition of warnings or messages from another world or another state of being." Delphi, she reminds us, "was the shrine of the Prophet and Musician, the inspiration of artists and the patron of physicians." Then she applies the meaning of Delphi to her own situation. "Religion, art, and medicine, through the later ages, became separated; they grow further apart from day to day." But now for herself, under the ministrations of this "blameless physician," Sigmund Freud, the three are growing together, as her third picture indicates: "These three working together, to form a new vehicle of expression or a new form of thinking or of living, might be symbolized by the tripod, the third of the images on the wall before me" (*TTF*, 50–51).

The tripod, she explains, "was the symbol of prophecy, prophetic utterance of occult or hidden knowledge; the Priestess or Pythoness of Delphi sat on the tripod while she pronounced her verse couplets, the famous Delphic utterances which it was said could be read two ways." ("Verse couplets": is this perhaps one reason for adopting the form of couplets for her wartime *Trilogy*, a form not at all characteristic of her earlier poems? "The Pythian pronounces," she declares in the opening poem of the *Trilogy*, the prologue written in tercets, after which all is written in couplets.)[10]

Now in section 36 we come to the most revealing utterance:

> We can read my writing,[11] the fact that there was writing, in two ways or in more than two ways. We can read or translate it as a suppressed desire for forbidden 'signs and wonders,' breaking bounds, a suppressed desire to be a Prophetess, to be important anyway, megalomania they call it—a hidden desire to 'found a new religion' which the Professor ferreted out in the later Moses picture. Or this writing-on-the-wall is merely an extension of the artist's mind, a *picture* or an illustrated poem, taken out of the actual dream or daydream content and projected from within . . . (*TTF*, 51)

The "Moses picture" is the vision dealt with in section 25, the dream of "the Princess" who descends the stairs to find a baby "in the water beside me," in a "shallow basket or ark or box or boat." It is an image drawn from the Doré Bible, an illustration of the finding of Moses.

---

10. The relation of H.D.'s couplets (a "marked divergence from the style of H.D.'s earlier verse") to the couplets of the Pythian has been noted by Sandra M. Gilbert and Susan Gubar in *No Man's Land: The Place of the Woman Writer in the Twentieth Century*, 3:192.

11. The phrase "my writing" refers directly to the "writing on the wall," but it may well be taken to describe H.D.'s own writing.

> The Professor and I discuss this picture. He asks if it is I, the Dreamer, who am the baby in the reed basket? I don't think I am. . . . The Professor thinks there is a child Miriam, half concealed in the rushes; do I remember? I half remember. Am I, perhaps, the child Miriam? Or am I, after all, in my fantasy, the baby? Do I wish myself, in the deepest unconscious or subconscious layers of my being, to be the founder of a new religion? (*TTF*, 37)

Is it this "new religion" that, as she says in her poem to "The Master," Freud has "set me free / to prophesy?" If so, of what does this "religion" consist? It would include, first of all, the Greek elements represented in her earlier poems and also in some of the poems that apparently derive from the 1930s, "Delphi" and "Dodona," where she seeks the elusive presences of Apollo and Zeus. It would include, eminently, the declaration of female equality and power represented in her eloquent poem "The Dancer," published in 1935 and perhaps based on her memories of a performance by Isadora Duncan, whose Greek and erotic modes of dancing seem to lie behind the poem. The use of the Greek term for "rose" or "red"—*rhodo*—in repeated addresses to "Rhododendron" and "Rhodocleia" may relate to the well-known reputation of Isadora as a "Red" after her stay in Moscow in 1920. In American performances after this visit, in defiance of those who denounced her "Red" sympathies, she wore a red tunic and flourished a red scarf.[12] It was perhaps her return from Moscow that led H.D. to open the poem thus:

> I came far,
> you came far,
> both from strange cities,
> I from the west,
> You from the east . . . (*CP*, 440)[13]

12. For an account of her notorious performance as a "Red" in Boston see Irma Duncan and Allan Ross Macdougall, *Isadora Duncan's Russian Days and Her Last Years in France* (London: Gollancz, 1929), 164–65. The color red pursued Isadora even at her death, when her red shawl became entangled in the wheel of that Bugatti. In "The Dancer" H.D. presents herself as a witness of an actual performance: could this possibly have been the famous "Roses from the South" for which we have detailed choreographical directions? (See the recent volume by Nadia Chilkovsky Nahumck, *Isadora Duncan: The Dances* [Washington, D.C.: National Museum of Women in the Arts, 1994], 391–405). If this were so, the dance might provide another reason for the prefix "rhodo." In the reprise of the Dancer in the next poem of this triad, "The Master," H.D. gives (*CP*, 456) a more precise description of the "rhododendron" dance: "she leaps from rock to rock / (it was only a small circle for her dance) / and the hills dance, / she conjures the hills; / rhododendrons / awake." In this reprise the Dancer is three times addressed as "Rhodocleia" at the close; the name is evidently derived from the Greek κλέος, meaning "fame" or "glory": "red fame," "rose glory." To see the Dancer as Isadora would complete the triad with another famous figure, to match the allusions to Freud and Lawrence in the two subsequent poems. In *CP* I suggested that the Dancer might be the actress-ballerina Anny Ahlers (*CP*, xxviii, 614 n. 15). But I now think this identification is unlikely, except as the early death of Anny Ahlers in 1933 may have precipitated a memory of Isadora.

13. In this opening H.D. seems to be using the word *strange* in the old sense of "foreign," "situated outside one's own land" (*OED*). These two Americans have come together (in

Fig. 4. The Dancer (?), Isadora Duncan. Photograph by
Arnold Genthe. Beinecke Library, Yale University.

Isadora's revolutionary spirit and her free forms of dancing ("I worship nature, /
you are nature" H.D. says at the end of the poem's first strophe) seem to express
what H.D. celebrates in this poem, seeing the dancer as a true messenger of
Apollo, who says to her:

Paris?) from "strange cities" (London, Moscow). Then at the outset of the second section
she adds: "I am now from the city / of thinkers, of wisdom-makers." Is this the "Miletus" in
which she met with Freud? The whole poem sounds like a backward projection, an experience
relived in the present. For H.D.'s powers of projection see Adalaide Morris, "The Concept
of Projection: H.D.'s Visionary Powers." In *Feminist Studies* 7 (1981): 407–16, Rachel Blau
DuPlessis and Susan Stanford Friedman published "The Master," followed by their essay,
" 'Woman Is Perfect': H.D.'s Debate with Freud."

"you are my arrow,
my flame;
I have sent you into the world;
beside you,
men may name
no other;
you will never die;

nor this one,
whom you see not,
sitting, sullen and silent,
this poet."   (*CP*, 445)

But the poet does not remain silent: in the next strophe she flings forth her plea:

O chaste Aphrodite,

let us be wild and free.
let us retain integrity,
intensity,
taut as the bow
the Pythian strings
to slay sorrow. (*CP*, 446)

The assertion of female integrity is closely related to her sessions with Freud, as she makes clear by including an even more fervent celebration of the Dancer in the middle of her poem to "The Master," with its erotic allusion to "red" and "rose":

there is purple flower
between her marble, her birch-tree white
thighs,
or there is a red flower

there is a rose flower
parted wide,
as her limbs fling wide in dance
ecstatic
Aphrodite,
there is a frail lavender flower
hidden in grass;

O God, what is it,
this flower
that in itself had power over the whole earth?
for she needs no man,

> herself
> is that dart and pulse of the male,
> hands, feet, thighs,
> herself perfect.   (*CP*, 456)

This, then, is yet another element in her "new religion." But there is a more inclusive message in her prophecy, as set forth in the one volume of poetry that H.D. published between 1931 and 1944: her version of the *Ion* of Euripides, published at last in 1937, after years of pondering the play. Here the poetry is constantly interspersed with a prose commentary that is indeed inseparable from the verse, for the prose makes plain the prophetic purpose behind her choice of this particular drama—one she had worked with even during the years of World War I.

Ion is a drama that deals with the reconciliation of Apollo with Athene: the god of poetry and the goddess of wisdom combine to ensure the future of Athens, city of Ion, son of Kreousa by Apollo, and thus ensure the beginning of a great new era, Ionian culture, after a time of sterility, doubt, hatred, and attempted murder. The message to the modern world is this: it can happen again, as H.D. explains when she writes here of "the woman who is queen [Kreousa] and almost goddess, who now in her joy wishes to be nothing but the mother of Ion; the mother, if she but knew it, of a new culture, of an aesthetic drive and concentrated spiritual force, not to be reckoned with, in terms of any then known values; hardly, even to-day, to be estimated at its true worth."[14] She then makes explicit the application to the world of the present time, 1937:

> Let not our hearts break before the beauty of Pallas Athené. No; she makes all things possible for us. The human mind today pleads for all; nothing is misplaced that in the end may be illuminated by the inner fire of abstract understanding; hate, love, degradation, humiliation, all, all may be examined, given due proportion and dismissed finally, in the light of the mind's vision. Today, again at a turning-point in the history of the world, the mind stands, to plead, to condone, to explain, to clarify, to illuminate; and, in the name of our magnificent heritage of that Hellenic past, each one of us is responsible to that abstract reality; silver and unattainable yet always present, that spirit again stands holding the balance between the past and the future. What now will we make of it? (*Ion*, 113)

She adds a parable: the story of how, after the Persians had burned Athene's temple on the Acropolis and reduced her sacred olive tree to a charred stump, one devotee had climbed the Acropolis and found this:

> Close to the root of the blackened, ancient stump, a frail silver shoot was clearly discernible, chiselled as it were, against that blackened wood;

14. *Ion: A Play after Euripides*, rev. John Walsh, 112; hereafter cited as *Ion*.

incredibly frail, incredibly silver, it reached toward the light. Pallas Athené, then, was not dead. Her spirit spoke quietly, a very simple message. . . .

Today? Yesterday? Greek time is like all Greek miracles. Years gain no permanence nor impermanence by a line of curious numbers; numerically 1920, 1922 and again (each time, spring) 1932, we touched the stem of a frail sapling, an olive-tree, growing against the egg-shell marble walls of the Erechtheum. (*Ion*, 115)

That she had indeed touched the olive tree is proved by the eloquent poetical finale that follows. Thus the voice of the prophet, though often bitter in denunciation, is ultimately optimistic: the prophet believes that her people, at least part of her people, can be saved—a remnant that can lead to a great renewal.

The prophetic voice in *Ion*, released by Freud's ministrations, may be closely related to another remarkable poem that seems to come from this same era: "A Dead Priestess Speaks," the title poem of a collection of pieces mostly datable from the 1930s, which H.D. arranged and sent over to Norman Pearson, with a letter that helps to explain their meaning. On March 16, 1949, she wrote to Pearson: "Now I have had typed, a series of poems. I do not 'place' them, except as milestones on my way. . . . I call this series, *A Dead Priestess Speaks*. That is the title of the first poem and rather describes my own feelings."[15]

The title poem is the most significant and the richest of this group. Exactly when it was written we cannot say. Since most of the other poems are datable from the 1930s, one might assume that this one also comes from that era, but its range and depth, and one reference to "a new war" after she has spoken of an older war, would seem to suggest that the poem may at least have been retouched as it became the title piece for this series. In any case the reference to the Priestess as Delia of Miletus associates the poem closely with H.D. in person, for Delia Alton was a favorite pen name, while Miletus is the place where she came to be cured by the Master in her poem addressed to Freud:

> when I travelled to Miletus
> to get wisdom,
> I left all else behind . . .
> "every gesture is wisdom,"
> he taught;
> "nothing is lost,"
> he said;
> I went late to bed
> or early,

15. H.D.–Pearson Correspondence, H.D. Archive, Beinecke Library, Yale University. *CP* (367–439) gives the whole group in H.D.'s arrangement. It is a series that moves from Greek themes through overtly personal poems of love and friendship to the final poem, "Magician" (originally entitled "Master"). (See introduction to *CP*, xxiv–xxvi.)

Fig. 5. Freud in his study at Berggasse 19, Vienna, 1937. Freud Museum, London.

> I caught the dream
> and rose dreaming,
> and we wrought philosophy on the dream content,
> I was content. . . .   (*CP*, 451)

(Note the rich pun on "content.") Delia of Miletus: why Miletus? It was the greatest of all Greek cities at one time, standing on the Turkish shore of the Aegean Sea, home of the earliest Greek philosophers, the pre-Socratics: where else would one go to seek the sources of wisdom? It was also a city famous for poets, one of which claimed to be a direct disciple of Homer. And it was the birthplace of one of the earliest female intellectuals in recorded history— the famous Aspasia, noted for her learning, her wit, and her beauty. But more important, it was the city that sponsored the nearby temple of Apollo at Didyma, one of the largest shrines ever built in the Greek world, famous for the words of its prophetess. Yes, H.D. knew all the resources of that word *Miletus*.

So Delia of Miletus becomes a priestess who speaks wisdom, but it is a wisdom understood only by her deepest inner self, not by the outside world, which sees her as a pure, beneficent, and dignified figure, but does not know the anguished inner self. Even when they glimpse what they would call her eccentricities, such as her refusal to write about war, they misunderstand:

I answered circumspectly,
claiming no
virtue
that helped the wounded
and no fire
that sung of battle ended,

then they said,
ah she is modest, she is purposeful,
and nominated for the Herald's place,
one
Delia of Miletus.   (*CP*, 372)

And when they learn that she has gone into the wild wood at night to gather strange herbs and fruit, they see only the outward effects of her times of inward anger, bitterness, and despair.

tasting leaf and root,
I thought at times of poison,
hoped that I
might lie deep in the tangle,
tasting the hemlock
blossom,
and so die;

but I came home,
and the last archon saw
me reach the door, at dawn;
I did not even care what he might say . . .

I waited for the crowd to mutter filth
and stone me from the altar,
but the new archon cried,
fresh honour to Miletus,
to Delia of Miletus who has found
a new brew of bay. . . .   (*CP*, 374)

They do not know the anguish and the exaltation of the inner self that lies beneath the Imagist; they do not know *me*,

me, whom no man yet found,
only the forest-god
of the wet moss,
of the deep underground,
or of the dry rock
parching to the moon . . . (*CP*, 370)

They do not know that within her calm demeanor she has been pursued by a god:

> how was it I,
> who walked so circumspectly, yet was caught
> in the arms of an angry lover,
> who said,
> late,
>
> late,
> I waited too long for you, Delia,
> I will devour you,
> love you into flame,
>
> O late
> my love,
> my bride
> Delia of Miletus.   (*CP*, 376)

They do not know the prophet within the priestess, for this lover, though no doubt he had his human counterparts, is surely here the god of poetry and prophecy—Apollo.

Gary Burnett has argued that this poem represents an answer to D. H. Lawrence,[16] and in a sense this may be so, for Lawrence had spoken sarcastically of her "virtue" and her "spiritual" being.[17] But this poem, and others, such as "Eurydice," "Toward the Piraeus," and the "Amaranth" triad, do not derive their power from the identification of any single person who may have been the poem's point of origin. As Sandra Gilbert and Susan Gubar say, such poems as these transcend their local origins by showing how the speakers "struggle with roles to which they have been consigned because of the male poet's 'glance.'" "While H.D. brooded upon Pound's or Lawrence's mastery in the first two decades of her long career, she confronted the empowering glamour and the painful frigidity brought about by her absorption with her male peers and by her dread that artistry itself somehow required ruthless strategies of objectification."[18] The struggle of woman to assert her independent integrity in the face of male misunderstanding, betrayal, or demand for submission underlies her entire career, reaching a climax in *Trilogy* and *Helen in Egypt*.

Freud and her poems of the 1930s thus led the way toward *Trilogy*, her long wartime work completed in December 1944—the best original poetry of her career.[19] *Trilogy* is sometimes called epic, but I wonder whether this is the right

---

16. *H.D. between Image and Epic*, chap. 9.
17. See below, p. 118–19.
18. Gilbert and Gubar, *No Man's Land*, 3:180.
19. The following commentary on *Trilogy* is substantially the same as the commentary that appeared in the introduction to *CP*, but with a stronger emphasis on the prophetic voice.

term. This work, like the later *Helen in Egypt,* seems rather to belong to the genre of prophecy, because it consists of a sequence of short lyric or meditative utterances, presenting a series of voices and visions amid the ruins of bombed London, where H.D. spent those wartime years. The first part, *The Walls Do Not Fall* (composed in 1942, published in 1944), presents a series of experiments in responding to the danger and the bravery of the scene, a sequence firmly grounded at beginning and end in the actual experience of the bombing:

> pressure on heart, lungs, the brain
> about to burst its brittle case . . .
>
> the bone-frame was made for
> no such shock knit within terror,
> yet the skeleton stood up to it . . .

But the question remains: "we passed the flame: we wonder / what saved us? what for?" (*CP,* 510–11).

Already the opening section has begun its tacit answer to that question, as, in accord with the dedication, "for Karnack 1923 / from London 1942," the poem equates the opening of an Egyptian tomb with the "opening" of churches and other buildings by the bombs:

> there, as here, ruin opens
> the tomb, the temple; enter,
> there as here, there are no doors:
>
> the shrine lies open to the sky . . . (*CP,* 509)

So too an opening happens in the mind, under the impact of disaster:

> ruin everywhere, yet as the fallen roof
> leaves the sealed room
> open to the air,
>
> so, through our desolation,
> thoughts stir, inspiration stalks us
> through gloom:

With this theme the commentary is distinct from, though related to, the many important interpretations of *Trilogy* that have appeared in the last two decades, many of them written from the standpoint of psychiatric theory, as in the studies of Dianne Chisholm, Susan Edmunds, Claire Buck, and Deborah Kelly Kloepfer listed in the bibliography. For a study of *Trilogy* from a related point of view see Donna Krolik Hollenberg, *H.D.: The Poetics of Childbirth and Creativity.* For a reading of *Trilogy* in the context of Pre-Raphaelite and Decadent views of woman, see Cassandra Laity, *H.D. and the Victorian Fin de Siècle,* chap. 7. See also the studies by Albert Gelpi and Adalaide Morris listed in the bibliography.

unaware, Spirit announces the Presence;
shivering overtakes us,
as of old, Samuel:

trembling at a known street-corner,
we know not nor are known;
the Pythian pronounces— (*CP*, 509–10)

(The body of the poem is written in "Pythian" couplets, as I noted earlier, but of course H.D. was well aware that biblical poetry was also composed in couplets; as with Samuel and the Pythian, two traditions merge.)

The fourth section presents this opening in yet another way: reverting to her old Imagist technique, she picks up the image of "that craftsman, / the shell-fish" and makes it represent the tough integrity of the artist, saying, "I sense my own limit"—and yet know "the pull / of the tide."

be firm in your own small, static, limited

orbit and the shark-jaws
of outer circumstance

will spit you forth:
be indigestible, hard, ungiving,

so that, living within,
you beget, self-out-of-self,

selfless,

that pearl-of-great-price.

This is only a beginning. From here she moves out to remember the meaning of "Mercury, Hermes, Thoth," inventors and patrons of the Word. And then, "when the shingles hissed / in the rain of incendiary," a voice speaks louder than the "whirr and roar in the high air" (*CP*, 520), and she has her vision and dream where "Ra, Osiris, *Amen* appeared / in a spacious, bare meetinghouse"—in Philadelphia or in Bethlehem, Pennsylvania:

yet he was not out of place
but perfectly at home

in that eighteenth-century
simplicity and grace . . . (*CP*, 523)

As in Freud's study, all religions are blending into one in her mind, though critics, she knows, will complain that "Depth of the sub-conscious spews forth

/ too many incongruent monsters" (*CP*, 534). Nevertheless, through wordplay and all her other poetic devices, like them or not, her aim is to

> recover the secret of Isis,
> which is: there was One
>
> in the beginning, Creator,
> Fosterer, Begetter, the Same-forever
>
> in the papyrus-swamp
> in the Judean meadow.   (*CP*, 541)

This is all preliminary: the secret is not yet found; the quest must continue, as the wordplay upon the name *Osiris* in sections 40–42 makes plain. "Osiris equates O-sir-is or O Sire is":

> O Sire, is this the path?
> over sedge, over dune grass,
>
> silently
> sledge-runners pass.
>
> O Sire, is this the waste? . . .
>
> drawn to the temple gate, O, Sire,
> is this union at last? (*CP*, 540, 542)

The answer now comes in the second part, *Tribute to the Angels* (composed in 1944, published in 1945), a sequence wholly unified and sustained, moving forward confidently under the guidance of Hermes Trismegistus, inventor of language, father of alchemy, founder of Egyptian culture; and with the support of the Book of Revelation, in which she boldly and wittily finds her role as prophet justified:

> *I John saw. I testify;*
> *if any man shall add*
> *God shall add unto him the plagues,*
> *but he that sat upon the throne* said,
>
> *I make all things new.* (*CP*, 548–49)

H.D. is remembering how the author of the Book of Revelation emerges in his own voice at the very end: "For I testify unto every man that heareth the words of the prophecy of this book, If any man shall add unto these things, God shall add unto him the plagues that are written in this book"—thus denying future prophets any function. But the poet prefers to take her stand upon the words of Jesus himself, earlier in the book: "And he that sat upon the throne said, Behold, I make all things new. And he said unto me, Write: for these words are true and faithful" (Rev. 21:5). And so, with this encouragement, she writes her own prophecy. But, as Susan Gubar points out, her prophecy of hope and redemption is utterly different from "the severity and punishing cruelty of John's apocalypse." "While John sings the praises of seven angels whose seven golden bowls pour out the wrath of God upon the earth, H.D. calls on seven angels whose presence in war-torn London is a testament to the promise of rebirth that her bowl holds."[20]

She writes because she has been privileged to witness an apocalyptic scene of war in the heavens such as no earlier generation had seen, and more than this, she has watched with all the others who

> with unbowed head, watched
> and though unaware, worshipped
>
> and knew not that they worshipped
> and that they were
>
> that which they worshipped . . . (CP, 551)

That is, the very spirit "of strength, endurance, anger / in their hearts." Out of all this her visions appear: "where the red-death fell / . . . the lane is empty but the levelled wall / is purple as with purple spread / upon an altar"—but this is not the sacrifice of blood: "this is the flowering of the rood, / this is the flowering of the reed" (CP, 551). Thus in her wordplay the rod of Aaron and the cross of Christ are merged; the reed that struck Christ merges with the reed of the Nile earlier mentioned, with overtones of music and of poetry. Now the poetry shows an alchemical change, as "a word most bitter, *marah*," changes into "mer, mere, mère, mater, Maia, Mary, / Star of the Sea, / Mother," and this star changes into "Venus, Aphrodite, Astarte, / star of the east, / star of the west" (CP, 552–53), as the crucible of the mind creates a jewel

> green-white, opalescent,
>
> with under-layer of changing blue,
> with rose-vein; a white agate
>
> with a pulse uncooled that beats yet,
> faint blue-violet;
>
> it lives, it breathes,
> it gives off—fragrance?   (CP, 554)

20. Susan Gubar, "The Echoing Spell of H.D.'s *Trilogy*," *Signets*, 307.

It is an image that suggests a concentration of creative power in a mind prepared to realize the miracle happening in the outer world, which now in May (Maia) is re-creating itself in the same subtle hues:

> tell me, in what other place
>
> will you find the may flowering
> mulberry and rose-purple?
>
> tell me, in what other city
> will you find the may-tree
>
> so delicate, green-white, opalescent
> like our jewel in the crucible?
> . . . .
> the outer precincts and the squares
> are fragrant . . .   (*CP*, 557)

Thus inner world and outer world share in this power of re-creation.

In this spirit of discovery the first half of the sequence reaches a climax as she crosses a "charred portico," enters "a house through a wall," and then sees "the tree flowering; / it was an ordinary tree / in an old garden-square"—a tree "burnt and stricken to the heart," yet flowering. This was actual, "it was not a dream / yet it was vision, / it was a sign":

> a half-burnt-out apple-tree
> blossoming;
>
> this is the flowering of the rood,
> this is the flowering of the wood . . . (*CP*, 558–61)

But now the dream follows, to create a higher climax, out of a dream interpreted in ways that she had learned from Freud to trust. Instead of one of the seven angels of the poem, "the Lady herself" has appeared (*CP*, 564). But who was this Lady? Was she the Virgin Mary, as painted in the Renaissance with all her grace and glory and "damask and figured brocade"?

> We have seen her
> the world over
>
> Our Lady of the Goldfinch,
> Our Lady of the Candelabra,
>
> Our Lady of the Pomegranate,
> Our Lady of the Chair . . . (*CP*, 564)

And so on for twenty-three couplets of affectionate detail, only to conclude: "But none of these, none of these / suggest her as I saw her," though she had something of the pagan and "gracious friendliness" of the "marble sea-maids in Venice / who climb the altar-stair / at *Santa Maria dei Miracoli*" (*CP*, 566). This joyous, teasing mood is something rare in H.D., and it continues in its tantalizing way. Her "veils were *white as snow*," to use the language of Christ's transfiguration, but in fact she bore "none of her usual attributes; / the Child was not with her" (*CP*, 566–67). So then it was not Mary. But who then?

> she must have been pleased with us,
> for she looked so kindly at us
>
> under her drift of veils,
> and she carried a book.

This is a trap for the academic interpreter, whom she now proceeds to parody:

> Ah (you say), this is Holy Wisdom,
> *Santa Sophia*, the SS of the *Sanctus Spiritus* . . .
>
> she brings the Book of Life, obviously. (*CP*, 568–69)

And so on and so on. But now the poet intervenes.

> she is the Vestal
> from the days of Numa,
>
> she carries over the cult
> of the *Bona Dea* . . .

This is a cult of which the Virgin Mary is perhaps a descendant, in her beneficent and redemptive function. But she has another dimension:

> she carries a book but it is not
> the tome of the ancient wisdom,
>
> the pages, I imagine, are the blank pages
> of the unwritten volume of the new . . .
>
> she is Psyche, the butterfly,
> out of the cocoon. (*CP*, 570)

She is the creative consciousness of the prophetic voice, represented by this poet, writing amid ruin, but reaching out toward the future, predicting its redemption, exulting in the victory of life over death.

The redemptive quality of the female presence is continued in the third part, *The Flowering of the Rod* (composed in 1944, published in 1945), where the poet creates a new fable of redemption by her story of how Mary Magdalen gained from Kaspar, one of the Magi, the alabaster jar from which she anointed the feet of Christ. The fable places great emphasis upon the radiance of "her extraordinary hair," which, the reader knows, she used to dry the feet of Christ. Thus the Magdalen stands forth as a figure that is both sensuous and spiritual, with the fragrance from the ointment in the jar suggesting the same combination of sensuous and spiritual experience.[21] This is a tale, as the opening sections make clear, that reaches out now to cover all the "smouldering cities" of Europe—not only London, but other "broken" cities that need renewal, in other lands. It is a universal myth of forgiveness and healing, a parable like that of the grain of mustard seed:

> *the least of all seeds*
> that grows branches
>
> where the birds rest;
> it is that flowering balm,
>
> it is heal-all,
> everlasting;
>
> *it is the greatest among herbs*
> *and becometh a tree.* (*CP*, 585)

This is told in a manner that in places resembles a children's story—but then one remembers that it is a Christmas tale, as the date at the end reminds us: "December 18–31, 1944."

Her use of the myth of Isis in the *Trilogy* leads on to the central image (or *Eidolon,* as she calls it) of her longest and most difficult poem, *Helen in Egypt,* published in the year of her death, 1961, but completed during the early 1950s. It is a work of intermingled prose and poetry, like her version of the *Ion* of Euripides. But here the prose sometimes presents a special problem, for it often does not so much interpret the action of the poetry as question and trouble it.

Feeling this effect, I once searched in H.D.'s manuscripts and correspondence to find some evidence that the placing of these prose "captions" at the head of each poem was not H.D.'s conception. But it was. After the poetical sequence was complete, H.D. deliberately composed them to go with each poem, and she directed their placement. In a letter to Norman Pearson from Lugano on November 26, 1955, she says:

---

21. Susan Schweik, in *A Gulf So Deeply Cut: American Women Poets and the Second World War,* has given an eloquent account of the imagery of myrrh and the figure of the Magdalen in the third part of *Trilogy;* see her chap. 9, "Myrrh to Myrrh: H.D., War, and Biblical Narrative."

I have the captions, the captions for the recording gave me this idea—and I think you will find that this whole set (no repeats from recording-captions) does hold the poems together, explain the at-times difficult 'philosophy' and put some of the mythological matter on the map. I am sure that you will like the set. I have asked Miss Woolford to leave broad white space between each numbered caption, so that the pages can be cut and each caption mounted BEFORE the poem, on a page facing the same, as for later printer.[22]

So there the captions are, and their presence creates a different work from the purely poetical sequence that she originally composed. We are not at liberty to ignore them. The question is: how do they function?

We may find an answer by remembering how often the prophetic writings of the Bible, as in the Books of Isaiah or Jeremiah, intermingle poetry and prose, with the effect that the prose creates a setting, or an explanation, for the poem that follows. I do not mean to say that H.D. consciously modeled her work on the writings of the biblical prophets, although she knew those writings well. I mean only to suggest that this analogy offers perhaps a key to the *kind* of work she was writing, and thus a key to the way in which we might deal with her intermingling of poetry and prose, here as well as in *Ion.*

First of all, we might regard *Helen in Egypt* as belonging to the genre of prophecy. If we grant this we can perhaps see more clearly how the various voices in the poem work—including the prose voices. As the example of the Hebrew prophets indicates, it is the role of the prophet to hear voices and to speak forth the words of those voices. The very word *prophet,* in Greek (as I have noted earlier), means "one who speaks for another"—for God, for the gods, or for other human beings.

From the opening poem in *Helen in Egypt,* H.D.'s Helen speaks with the voice of a prophet, saying "in this Amen-temple" (the temple of Amen-Ra, or Zeus-Ammon, in Egypt) she hears the "voices" of "the hosts / surging beneath the Walls" of Troy, voices that cry

O Helen, Helen, Daemon that thou art,

we will be done forever
with this charm, this evil philtre,
this curse of Aphrodite;

so they fought, forgetting women,
hero to hero, sworn brother and lover,
and cursing Helen through eternity[23]

But the next poem presents a voice of redemption, as Helen says,

22. H.D.–Pearson Correspondence, H.D. Archive.
23. *Helen in Egypt,* 4; hereafter cited as *H.*

Alas, my brothers,
Helen did not walk
upon the ramparts,

she whom you cursed
was but the phantom and the shadow thrown
of a reflection;

you are forgiven for I know my own,
and God for his own purpose
wills it so, that I

stricken, forsaken draw to me,
through magic greater than the trial of arms,
your own invincible, unchallenged Sire . . . (*H*, 5)

The poem is based on the alternate myth of Helen that Euripides used in his play on this subject and that Richard Strauss used for his opera *The Egyptian Helen,* which H.D. may have seen. Here the story says that Helen never was in Troy, but that the gods sent there a phantom of Helen, while the true Helen was transported by Zeus to Egypt, where, after the war, she was reunited with Menelaus, or in H.D.'s version, with Achilles:

Had they met before? Perhaps. Achilles was one of the princely suitors for her hand, at the court of her earthly father, Tyndareus of Sparta. But this Helen is not to be recognized by earthly splendour nor this Achilles by accoutrements of valour. It is the lost legions that have conditioned their encounter, and "the sea-enchantment in his eyes."

How did we know each other?
was it the sea-enchantment in his eyes
of Thetis, his sea-mother?   (*H*, 7)

In that phrase "the sea-enchantment in his eyes" we meet in both the prose and the poetry the leading phrase and symbol of the work, for Thetis will, as the sequence proceeds, be merged with Aphrodite, also born of the sea, and with Isis, called in the prose "the Egyptian Aphrodite" (*H*, 15). Helen herself is in the latter part of the work transformed into a living symbol of all these goddesses: the love of Achilles for Helen, then, suggests a way of redeeming the war-torn world, as the voice of Helen has said very early in the poem:

it was God's plan
to melt the icy fortress of the soul,
and free the man;

God's plan is other than the priests disclose;
I did not know why
(in dream or in trance)

God had summoned me hither,
until I saw the dim outline
grown clearer,

as the new Mortal,
shedding his glory,
limped slowly across the sand.   (*H*, 10)

All this is quite in accord with the dual meaning of the work that H.D. suggested later on in the letter to Norman Pearson just cited. There she says that her poem has both "exoteric" meaning related to "all war-problems . . . as well as being strictly INNER and esoteric and personal." That is to say, the imagery of war suggests the problems raised by war for all mankind down through the ages, along with the personal problems that such wars inevitably cause for individual lives, and caused, as we know, for H.D. herself, witness of two wars. Helen has taken within herself the sufferings of the whole war-stricken world:

mine, the great spread of wings,
the thousand sails,
the thousand feathered darts

that sped them home,
mine, the one dart in the Achilles-heel,
the thousand-and-one, mine.   (*H*, 25)

To say that Helen speaks throughout as the prophet or priestess of Isis would be to sum up the meaning of the work; for Isis, that benevolent, creative goddess, was known throughout the Mediterranean world as the "Goddess of many names." For H.D., in this poem, her name is Helen.[24]

---

24. For detailed interpretations of the poem see the studies by Albert Gelpi, Dianne Chisholm, Susan Edmunds, Susan Stanford Friedman, Donna Krolik Hollenberg, and Deborah Kelly Kloepfer listed in the bibliography.

Fig. 6. H.D. at Mecklenburgh Square, London, ca. 1917. Beinecke Library, Yale University.

9.

H.D. and D. H.

H.D.'S USE OF THE myth of Isis and Osiris in her later poems may serve, finally, to introduce another result of her conferences with Freud: her ability to remember and face the consequences of her friendship and break with D. H. Lawrence during the years 1914–1918. In *Advent*, the second part of her *Tribute to Freud*, H.D. has given us selections from the diary of her treatment by Freud, "taken direct from the old notebooks of 1933, though it was not assembled until December 1948, Lausanne," as H.D. says in a prefatory note (*TTF*, xiv). The materials have been selected and "assembled" so as to create a growing awareness, both in the writer and in the reader, that the memory of Lawrence, whether repressed or resurrected, remained a crucial factor in her creative consciousness. She talked at length with Freud about Lawrence, though she says, significantly, "I am certain that I never mentioned Lawrence in my three months' preliminary work with Mary Chadwick at Tavistock Square, in Bloomsbury. I felt that Miss Chadwick could not follow the workings of my creative mind" (*TTF*, 150). Lawrence, then, has something to do with her "creative mind." *Advent*, in its selection and arrangement, suggests how and why her remembrance of and reconciliation with Lawrence played an essential role in the recovery of her creative and prophetic powers.

The crucial revelation comes in her entry for March 5, where she speaks of Lawrence's last novel, which deals with Jesus as he arises from his tomb, never having suffered actual death:

The Man Who Died?
I don't remember it, I don't think of it. Only it was a restatement of his philosophy, but it came too late.
I don't mean that.
I have carefully avoided coming to terms with Lawrence, the Lawrence of *Women in Love* and *Lady Chatterley.*

(Note that these are the two novels in which Lawrence deals most openly and provocatively with issues of sexual love.) "But," she continues, "there was this last Lawrence."

He did not accept Sigmund Freud, or implied it in his essay.
I don't want to think of Lawrence.
'I hope never to see you again,' he wrote in that last letter.
Then after the death of Lawrence, Stephen Guest brought me the book and said, 'Lawrence wrote this for you.'
Lawrence was imprisoned in his tomb; like the print hanging in the waiting room, he was 'Buried Alive.'
We are all buried alive.
The story comes back automatically when I switch off the bed-lamp.
I do not seem to be able to face the story in the daytime. (*TTF*, 134)

Five pages later she returns to this theme:

Yes, I was 'Buried Alive.'
Is this why my thoughts return to Lawrence?
I can only remember that last book he wrote. *The Man Who Died* was buried alive. (*TTF*, 139)

This leads into the first of her extended memories of Lawrence, the entry for March 8, where varied memories of Lawrence occupy two and a half pages (*TTF*, 140–42), beginning with a passage in which she associates Lawrence with her father:

I dream of a photograph of an unbearded D. H. Lawrence. I had such a photograph of my father . . .
I first met Lawrence in August 1914 at the time of the actual outbreak of war; he looked taller in evening-dress. It was the only time I saw this unbearded manifestation of Lawrence.

Her dream continues with a memory of "a neat 'professional woman'" with Lawrence, along with "a group of children." Is this woman, she asks, "a sort of secretary?" And again she associates Lawrence with her father: "I acted for a short time as secretary to my father." This association carries on from the

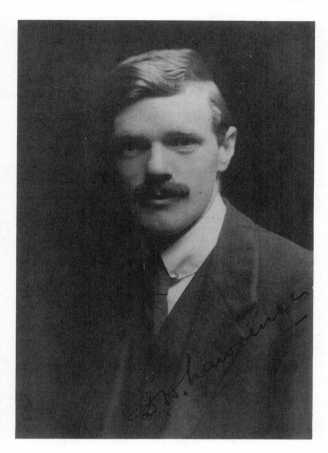

Fig. 7. The "unbearded" Lawrence, ca. 1913. Photograph by W. G. Parker. Department of Special Collections, University Research Library, University of California, Los Angeles.

earlier mix-up of dates, when she discovers that she has "substituted my father's birthday for the death-day of D. H. Lawrence" (*TTF,* 131).

　　She then proceeds to associate Lawrence with her mother:

> Lawrence at one time was a school-master and I always had a longing to teach. The children in this dream 'class' or family are of assorted sizes; they stand back of Lawrence and the young woman, grouped round a piano.
> My mother taught music and painting at one time, at the old Seminary. (*TTF,* 140)

This association of Lawrence with her family shows him living at the deep center of her memory.

But in my dream, I take out a volume from a shelf of Lawrence novels. I open it; disappointed, I say, 'But his psychology is nonsense.'

I envied these women who have written memoirs of D. H. Lawrence, feeling that they had found him some sort of guide or master. I envied Bryher her hero-worship of the psychoanalyst Dr. Hanns Sachs. I cannot be disappointed in Sigmund Freud, only I have this constant obsession that the analysis will be broken by death. I cannot discuss this with the Professor. When he first greeted me, he reminded me of Lawrence. (*TTF*, 140–41)

So we have learned on the second page of *Advent:* "he is like D. H. Lawrence, grown old but matured and with astute perception" (*TTF*, 116). And again, a dozen pages later: "he smiled a charming, wrinkled smile that reminded me of D. H. Lawrence. . . . I spoke of the last war-year" (*TTF*, 128). Does this imply that during their years of friendship H.D. had sought to find in Lawrence "some sort of guide or master"? And now, with this new guide, will she recover what Lawrence had earlier meant to her?

These conjectures may be borne out by the resentment that H.D. has earlier expressed for "these women" who have written about Lawrence: "There it is on my table, that last volume that I disliked so. It was sent to me from London, another fanatical woman writing her story of D. H. Lawrence" (*TTF*, 131). This is probably Mabel Dodge Luhan's *Lorenzo in Taos,*[1] or it may be the less eccentric book by Catherine Carswell, *The Savage Pilgrimage;* both books appeared in 1932, not long before H.D. undertook her treatment by Freud. The resentment continues:

I wasn't fair but I could hardly cope with his enormous novels. They didn't seem to ring true. That is, I was not susceptible to the frenzy in them. In them? Or in the choros of Maenads ["these women"]? I do not like that last book. I have not liked any of these books that have come out since his death. What do they know of Lawrence? (*TTF*, 133)

Rebecca West, Carswell, Luhan, John Middleton Murry—they have all, she believes, missed the essential Lawrence known to her, as they exchanged letters

---

1. *Lorenzo in Taos* is the only book on Lawrence by a woman mentioned in H.D.'s letters to Bryher during her treatment by Freud. The main problem, though, is that, far from disliking this book, she was delighted with it; thus she wrote on May 23, 1933, "I stayed up too late reading Taos. It is marvelous." "Nothing I have read has amused me so, she is a wonderful recorder." "But Fido, no more books . . . these are wonderful and Taos saved my whole life" (Bryher Papers, Beinecke Library, Yale University). Another problem lies in the fact that the above references to "this last book" occur in the section dated March 4, whereas H.D. did not receive Luhan's book until late in May. All this may be a prime example of H.D.'s way of editing the past. Rebecca West's moving tribute to Lawrence (forty pages) was published by Secker in 1930, not long after Lawrence's death. Dorothy Brett's *Lawrence and Brett* (Philadelphia: Lippincott) appeared in the week of May 6, 1933; it seems unlikely that the book would have reached H.D. before she left Vienna in mid-June, but while she was "assembling" her notes for *Advent,* she may well have thought of Brett as "another fanatical woman writing her story of D. H. Lawrence."

and poems throughout those wartime years—letters apparently destroyed by Richard Aldington as part of a general destruction of her letters.

Aside from *Advent,* the most fruitful view of this relationship is given in her novel *Bid Me to Live,* written under advice from Freud that she should write history, as we learn from several of her unpublished letters to Bryher. "I have been soaking in D. H. L. letters," she wrote on May 15, 1933 (Aldous Huxley's selection had just appeared in 1932); "not too good for me, but Freud seems to agree with me for once. Evidently I blocked the whole of the 'period' and if I can skeleton-in a vol. about it, it will break the clutch . . . the 'cure' will be, I fear me, writing that damn vol. straight, as history." And again, after she had been reading Middleton Murry's book on Lawrence, *Son of Woman* (1931), she wrote that Freud "seems to believe explicitly that it would be best for me to make this vol. of mine about 1913–1920 explicit."[2] Clearly H.D. had been "soaking in" a good many writings by and about Lawrence during these conferences— a sign of her determination to master the problem of what Lawrence meant to her.

In *Bid Me to Live* Lawrence appears, very thinly disguised, along with Frieda, in the setting of the Mecklenburgh Square apartment where H.D. had offered them sanctuary after their expulsion from Cornwall as suspected German spies. Lawrence appears under the name Rico and H.D. under the name Julia, the name that Lawrence had given to his caricature of her in his novel of 1922, *Aaron's Rod.* But that name Rico itself contains a sharp retort, for Rico is the name of the contemptible artist-husband who fails the dynamic Lou Witt, heroine of Lawrence's novel *St. Mawr,* published in 1924. Rico is a man who fails so badly to match his wife's strong character that she deserts him and goes off to find her true self in the mountains above Taos, New Mexico, as Lawrence himself had done when he wrote the novel.

During their years of friendship H.D. had written a sequence of poems based on the story of Orpheus and Eurydice, a sequence related in some way to

2. Bryher Papers. The letter about Middleton Murry is dated May 18, 1933. The authenticity of the novel as "history" is borne out by H.D.'s daughter Perdita in her biographical memoir appended to the edition of *Bid Me to Live* published by Black Swan Books in 1983: "The names have been changed. Otherwise, it is straight autobiography, a word-for-word transcript" (186); hereafter cited as *Bid.*

The relation between Lawrence and H.D. in this novel has been frequently studied, notably by Susan Stanford Friedman in her authoritative book on H.D.'s prose: *Penelope's Web: Gender, Modernity, H.D.'s Fiction,* 141–70. Most recently Mark Kinkead-Weekes has given an illuminating account of these events at Mecklenburgh Square in *D. H. Lawrence: Triumph to Exile, 1912–1922,* 416–22. See also Teresa Fulker, "Not-War and the Inspiration of the *Gloire* in H.D.'s *Bid Me to Live*"; Peter E. Firchow, "Rico and Julia: The Hilda Doolittle–D. H. Lawrence Affair Reconsidered"; Joseph Milicia, "*Bid Me to Live:* Within the Storm"; Janice Robinson, *H.D.: The Life and Work of an American Poet,* chap. 15; Rachel Blau DuPlessis, "Romantic Thralldom in H.D.," in *Signets,* 408–13; Helen Sword, "Orpheus and Eurydice in the Twentieth Century: Lawrence, H.D., and the Poetics of the Turn"; Paul Delaney, *D. H. Lawrence's Nightmare: The Writer and His Circle in the Years of the Great War,* chap. 8.

Lawrence. In *Bid Me to Live* Julia quotes or reconstructs a letter to her from Rico-Lawrence in which he says,

> I don't like the second half of the Orpheus sequence as well as the first. Stick to the woman speaking. How can you know what Orpheus feels? It's your part to be woman, the woman vibration, Eurydice should be enough. You can't deal with both. (*Bid,* 51)

Lawrence himself, of course, had no hesitation in trying to imagine the woman's point of view, as Julia realizes a few pages later:

> Rico could write elaborately on the woman mood, describe women to their marrow in his writing; but if she turned round, wrote the Orpheus part of her Orpheus-Eurydice sequence, he snapped back, "Stick to the woman-consciousness, it is the intuitive woman-mood that matters." He was right about that, of course. But if he could enter, so diabolically, into the feelings of women, why should not she enter into the feelings of men? (*Bid,* 62)

Nevertheless, in her poem "Eurydice," published in May 1917 (before the break with Lawrence), she followed his advice: the poem uses the voice of Eurydice to utter a fearsome denunciation of male infidelity and "ruthlessness," reflecting no doubt her anger at Richard Aldington for his flagrant infidelity, along with, perhaps, some resentment of Ezra Pound's defection, and an indication of how condemned to hell she might feel if Lawrence also should now fail her:

> so for your arrogance
> and your ruthlessness
> I am swept back
> where dead lichens drip
> dead cinders upon moss of ash . . .

But she is not destroyed by this treatment; her spirit responds with a counter-attack:

> yet for all your arrogance
> and your glance,
> I tell you this:
>
> such loss is no loss,
> such terror, such coils and strands and pitfalls
> of blackness,
> such terror
> is no loss . . .
>
> my hell is no worse than yours
> though you pass among the flowers and speak
> with the spirits above earth.

And she concludes with a powerful assertion of her independent selfhood:

> At least I have the flowers of myself,
> and my thoughts, no god
> can take that;
> I have the fervour of myself for a presence
> and my own spirit for light . . . (*CP*, 51–55)

The poem was written, it seems, at Corfe Castle (1916), or in London, when Lawrence was writing to her from Cornwall; it is powerful testimony to the inspiration that Lawrence was giving to her in this time of deep discouragement, with the loss of her child and her husband's errant behavior—inspiration that she suggests in a later passage of her novel:

> She groped for the matches and the candle that she kept in readiness by her bed, in case of sudden air-alarm or in case that steady pulse and throb that was in her head, rather than her heart beating, should command her. *Bid me to live and I will live*. It was something in the distance (Rico was in Cornwall) that empowered her, so that in the middle of the night she could strike a match, and crouched over her bed-clothes, run her pencil down a page, or rather let it run for her. She had sent copies of the poems to Rico, she had not to Rafe. (*Bid*, 59)

When Rafe (Aldington) asks her, suspiciously, "What's this Orpheus that you've been writing for old Rico?" she replies, "I wasn't exactly writing it for Rico," then admits to herself: "But she had, she was; it was Rico's pale face and the archaic Greek beard and the fire-blue eyes in the burnt-out face that she had seen, an Orpheus head, severed from its body" (*Bid*, 51). And the "fire blue" of his eyes lives within the words of his letters—"the words that flamed alive, blue serpents on the page that Rico wrote her" (*Bid*, 52). "They were burning in her head, blue-fire, the things he wrote and the things that he didn't write, the way the blue-flame licked out of the paper, whatever it was he wrote" (*Bid*, 54–55).

So, in this period of her husband's "arrogant" affair with "Bella" at Mecklenburgh Square, she turns to Rico. It was, she suggests, "as if Bella had completed" Rafe "in some purely physical way," with the result that it was "as if Rico with his 'We will go away together where the angels come down to earth' had completed her, in her purely emotional-cerebral dimension" (*Bid*, 57). The invitation lingers in her mind, repeated in more general form as she now tells Rafe more about her communications with Rico:

> He sent me a manuscript of one of his novels, but it seemed very long, very confused, I must have written you about it. Then when I was alone—when was it?— maybe last spring after you left—no, it was at Corfe Castle, he wrote, *we must go away where the angels come down to earth*.

"Go away?" asks Rafe. "Well," she answers, "not go away—you know what he's like. He talks of going away. I suppose he wrote a dozen people. Maybe he didn't. Maybe he wrote just me. Anyhow that is what he wrote" (*Bid,* 66). Rafe continues his inquisition: "What did you write him?" "I don't know," she replies, "I sent him some poems. That's how we began really to write." Then he asks her plainly whether she loves Rico. "No, not at this minute," she evasively replies. "He is part of the cerebral burning, part of the inspiration. He takes but he gives" (*Bid,* 67).

What does Lawrence mean by saying they should go away? The invitation seems to be part of Lawrence's campaign, then at its height, to persuade his friends to join him in the colony of "Rananim" to be founded in South America: his letters of 1917 are filled with these plans, including one specific reference saying that "Hilda Aldington" will "probably" join the group that is "going away."[3] But H.D. chooses to take the invitation personally, and no wonder, for Lawrence pursues this "courtship" intensely, telling her during the stay in Mecklenburgh Square, "You are there for all eternity, our love is written in blood for all eternity" (*Bid,* 78)—words that also linger in her mind. This was rash of Lawrence, dealing with a woman as sensitive as H.D. With these words in mind, she now provokes the painful movement of rejection:

> She got up; as if at a certain signal, she moved toward him; she edged the small chair toward his chair. She sat at his elbow, a child waiting for instruction. Now was the moment to answer his amazing proposal of last night, his "for all eternity." She put out her hand. Her hand touched his sleeve. He shivered, he seemed to move back, move away, like a hurt animal, there was something untamed, even the slight touch of her hand on his sleeve seemed to have annoyed him. Yet, last night, sitting there, with Elsa [Frieda] sitting opposite, he had blazed at her; those words had cut blood and lava-trail on this air. Last night, with the coffee-cups beside them on the little table, he had said, "It is written in blood and fire for all eternity." Yet only a touch on his arm made him shiver away, hurt, like a hurt jaguar.
>
> He was leopard, jaguar. It was not she who had started out to lure him. It was himself with his letters, and last night his open request for this relationship. (*Bid,* 81)

But Lawrence's moving away from her touch was his way of saying what Prufrock feared one of his ladies would say: "That is not what I meant at all. / That is not it, at all." The sort of relationship that Lawrence had in mind (though it was "ruthless" of him to pursue it so passionately) was fully explained by him in the letter he wrote to Cecil Gray from H.D.'s apartment at Mecklenburgh Square on

---

3. From Mecklenburgh Square, October 27, 1917, in *The Letters of D. H. Lawrence,* vol. 3, ed. James T. Boulton and Andrew Robertson (Cambridge: Cambridge University Press, 1984), 173.

November 7, 1917, in answer to a letter from Gray in which, as Gray recalls, "I accused him . . . of allowing himself to become the object of a kind of esoteric female cult, an Adonis, Atthis, Dionysos religion of which he was the central figure, a Jesus Christ to a regiment of Mary Magdalenes."[4] Lawrence replied in a letter that reveals a rather callous and condescending attitude toward this "regiment": "As for me and my 'women,' I know what they are and aren't and though there is a certain messiness, there is a further reality." The "messiness," I suppose, was caused by the way in which these women, like H.D., tended to develop more than a religious interest in Lawrence. But, he continued, "Take away the subservience and feet-washing, and the pure understanding between the Magdalene and Jesus went deeper than the understanding between the disciples and Jesus, or Jesus and the Bethany woman." "And my 'women,'" he added in an unpleasant tone, "Esther Andrews, Hilda Aldington etc. represent, in an impure, and unproud, subservient, cringing, bad fashion, I admit—but represent none the less the threshold of a new world, or underworld, of knowledge and being."

> The old world must burst, the underworld must be open and whole, new world.—You want an emotional sensuous underworld . . . my 'women' want an ecstatic subtly-intellectual underworld, like the Greeks—Orphicism—like Magdalen at her foot-washing—and there you are.[5]

This letter was published in the Huxley edition that H.D. was reading during her consultations with Freud, with the names of the two women deleted.[6] But her reading of the letter did not affect her record of the "history" that she was writing: she recorded her own misunderstanding of what Lawrence wanted,

4. Ibid., 3:179, n. 2.
5. Ibid., 3:179–80. In "Orpheus and Eurydice in the Twentieth Century," Sword argues effectively that Lawrence played some part in the resistance to male domination expressed by H.D. in "Eurydice"; Lawrence had set forth his views on "gender ideology" in his "Study of Thomas Hardy," written in 1914 but not published until 1936. It is conceivable that Lawrence may have sent her portions of this work, or expressed similar views in his letters to her in 1916. On the other hand, the "rejection" by Lawrence recorded in *Bid Me to Live* played no part in the composition of "Eurydice," since the poem was published in May 1917, some six months before the Lawrences sought refuge in Mecklenburgh Square, where they arrived October 20. As Kinkead-Weekes points out (*D. H. Lawrence,* 421) Lawrence's description of his "women" as inhabiting an "underworld" is not meant to be derogatory: "The essential distinction he draws is between a mode of relation between the sexes which is merely sexual, and one that is sexual/religious in that its essence . . . has to do with transforming the self through its 'death' and 'resurrection.' The first kind is secretive, sensual, remaining underground, between selves that will not change. The other sheds old selves in the 'underworld' of the unconscious in order to emerge in new and open life." This seems to be the meaning of the concluding stanzas of "Eurydice."
6. *The Letters of D. H. Lawrence,* ed. Aldous Huxley, 422–23. Writing to Bryher on March 11, 1933, H.D. said that she had borrowed the Huxley edition from a circulating library; she noted the letters from Mecklenburgh Square and concluded: "All this has come up, made a violent purple-patch in my analysis" (Bryher Papers).

along with her own temptation to ascend the stairs at night to join Lawrence in his room, an action she did not perform, held back by Lawrence's shivering away from her touch.

All this lies behind her poignant recognition in *Advent* that her troubled state of mind was perhaps "partly due to the fact that I lost the early companions of my first writing-period in London," where "the two chief companions" were "Richard Aldington and D. H. Lawrence [who] had both seemed to like my writing." But, she adds, "I was unhappily separated from Aldington and it was impossible at that time to continue my friendship with Lawrence" (*TTF*, 149). Why was it impossible? H.D. tells us why in the tensely understated scene of *Bid Me to Live* where she records her last meeting with Rico-Lawrence. Rejected, as she feels, by both Aldington and Lawrence, she has without much enthusiasm decided to go off with Cecil Gray ("Vane") and live with him for a while in the house in Cornwall that he was renting, close to the house where Lawrence and Frieda had lived. Hearing of her plan, Lawrence comes to see H.D. in her Mecklenburgh apartment (the Lawrences had by this time moved to Berkshire).

> What problem was there? Rico was saying something that seemed unrelated, he was speaking, almost as if he were concerned. What was he thinking?
> "You are really going to Cornwall?"
> "Why, yes. Why, I thought it was understood, you brought Vane in, you said 'You and Vane are made for one another.' "
> "Yes," he said.
> He said, "Why don't you take our cottage? You see everything is there. We did up some elderberry jam. There are some books." He was offering her his cottage. "It's not so very far from Vane's. He could come in every day to see you." What was all this? (*Bid*, 136–37)

Obviously Lawrence is trying to suggest that she should not live with Vane, should not get involved in sexual relations with him. " 'It would make a difference,' he said, 'don't you realise?' "

> He was correct, almost puritanical. Julia wondered if he hadn't meant what he said [about sexual relations in general or about her and Vane's being so well matched]—or meant it in another dimension. When it came to the actual fact of her going down to Cornwall to stay in Vane's house, he seemed surprised, shocked even. She did not understand this. (*Bid*, 137)

What she does not understand is that Lawrence's view of human sexuality does not approve of such casual relationships, and that in accepting such a relationship she is shattering his view of her as an essentially spiritual being. She repeats his sardonic remarks of the past:

> "Kick over your tiresome house of life," he had said, he had jeered, "frozen lily of virtue," he had said, "our languid lily of virtue nods perilously near the

pit," he had written, "come away where the angels come down to earth";
"crucible" he had called her, "burning slightly blue of flame"; "love-adept"
he had written, "you are a living spirit in a living spirit city." (*Bid*, 138–39)

Two things seem to be confused here. One is the invitation to leave her present
tiresome circumstances and go away with the group to Rananim; the other is
his opinion of her poetry, that it is too abstract: "You jeered at my making
abstractions of people—graven images, you called them" (*Bid*, 164). His jeering
at her "virtue" is probably a reaction to her view of the poems in *Look! We Have
Come Through,* which he had sent to her in manuscript. He received this response:
"Hilda Aldington says they won't do at all; they are not *eternal,* not sublimated:
too much body and emotions."[7] In his letters Lawrence was apparently urging
her to come down closer to actual life in her poetry—but without implying any
such liaison as she was planning with Vane. Most important, by this action she
was breaking away from the role that Lawrence had established for her in his
own mind—her role in that "ecstatic subtly-intellectual underworld" described
in the letter to Gray about his "women."

> "Do you realise," he said, "what you are doing?"
> "Why—yes, I am going away with Vane, Or he is going first. I want to
> go over the books, pack."
> "But—but—do you realise?" (*Bid*, 138)

"What did he mean? She simply did not understand him." But she remembers
that he had used the same phrasing at their very first meeting, in 1914, in Amy
Lowell's rooms "overlooking Green Park."

> It was early August. The war was not a week old. "Don't you know, don't you
> realise, that this is poetry," said Frederick [Rico], edging her away toward the
> far end of the room. He held the pages that she had brought Mary Dowell
> for her anthology.
> "Don't you realise that this is poetry?" (*Bid*, 140)

Now Lawrence is using the same words:

> "Don't you realise," he said now, "that this—" he spoke quietly—he was not
> spitting like a wild-cat. He was burnt out, Dis, Death. "This—" he said, and
> didn't say anything. "I am not happy about this," he said . . . "You realise
> that," he said quietly. (*Bid*, 141)

Then Vane comes in and the conversation ends abruptly. But what did it mean?
It meant that Lawrence saw, in her choosing this physical relation, an end to the
kind of follower that he desired.

7. *Letters*, 3:102, from Cornwall, March 9, 1917.

But in letters written after H.D. had left Cornwall it is clear that he bore no such resentment as might seem to be implied in the sentence from *Advent:* " 'I hope never to see you again,' he wrote in that last letter." This appears to be H.D.'s memory of the last letter that he wrote to her, in 1929, when he was on the verge of death, a grim letter in which he discourages her apparent hope that they might meet again sometime.[8] His letters of 1918 and 1919 speak of her in a friendly way, hoping that the birth of her baby "will soothe her and steady her," though in another letter, speaking of H.D.'s marital problems, he says, "Poor Hilda. Feeling sorry for her, one almost melts." Then he adds: "But I *don't* trust her—other people's lives, indeed!" She has not proved to be a reliable disciple, yet he has not cut himself off from her. In another letter he says, "We shall be going up to London soon, and may see her."[9] He may well have sent to her his next volume of poetry, *Bay,* published in 1919.

In *Advent,* immediately after the sentence in which she says that it was "impossible" to continue their friendship, she adds: "But Lawrence returns after his death, though I have not had the courage or the strength to realize this fully" (*TTF,* 149). And indeed he does return, in the climactic nine-page narration of her dream about "the Man who was not Mr. Van Eck" (*TTF,* 154–62). Janice Robinson has given the right interpretation of this scene, finding the clue in Lawrence's volume of poetry, *Bay,* published just before H.D. left for the voyage to Greece during which this mysterious dream occurred.[10]

In this dream about "the Man who was not Mr. Van Eck" H.D. comes up on deck and sees a man who seems at first to be her shipboard acquaintance, Van Eck (actually Peter Rodeck, for whom she developed an erotic fixation), but this man is taller than Van Eck, he does not have the prominent scar that Van Eck bears, he does not wear glasses, as Van Eck does, and, most significant, in a sentence that has its own paragraph: "His eyes are more blue than I had thought, it is mist blue, sea-blue" (*TTF,* 157). We know how H.D. was affected by Lawrence's blue eyes. Then she notes that Van Eck "had told me he was forty-four or would be on the 10th of March." Lawrence was forty-four when he died in March—a month that she has mentioned earlier in connection with Lawrence's death. The

8. From Baden Baden, August 10, 1929, in *The Letters of D. H. Lawrence,* vol. 7, ed. Keith Sagar and James T. Boulton (Cambridge: Cambridge University Press, 1993), 414–15. Lawrence sent H.D. a group of poems that she had requested for inclusion in the *Imagist Anthology* of 1930. She had apparently asked where Lawrence might be in the autumn and expressed the hope that they might meet again. After complaining, "My cough is a great nuisance," he added: "Where we shall be in the autumn I don't know—but probably somewhere in Italy.—But now it's more than ten years since we met, and what should we have to say? God knows! nothing, really. It's no use saying anything. That's my last conviction. Least said soonest mended: which assumes that the breakage has already happened." Seven months later Lawrence died.

9. *Letters,* 3:314, 308, 347.

10. *H.D.,* 238–41. It is unfortunate that Robinson's unfounded conjectures about Perdita's parentage and the heroine of *Lady Chatterley's Lover* have apparently diverted attention from this and other valid evidence of Lawrence's relation to H.D. presented by Robinson.

clinching point in the identification with Lawrence lies in her vision of dolphins as she is meeting this man on the deck. No one else has seen dolphins, not even the wireless operator, who is an expert on dolphins. But indeed these are not realistic dolphins: "The dolphins are joined by other dolphins. They make a curiously unconvincing pattern, leaping in rhythmic order like crescent moons or half-moons out of the water, a flight or a dance of dolphins" (*TTF*, 158).

Sometimes, she says, "Mr. Van Eck was the Man on the boat but he was not the Man on the boat that I met the first time in the Bay" (*TTF*, 160). "The Bay"—the word has occurred near the outset of this narration, where she says, "I had not heard the Bay of Biscay referred to as the Bay before" (*TTF*, 155). In her dream she is "coasting along in the Bay," with a curious seascape:

> I should have known. I did know, though I could not yet admit it, that not only were the dolphins unconvincing but the sea itself was impossible. That is, it was all right at the time but you do not have a quiet sea and a boat moving with no tremor, with no quiver or pulse of engine, on a sea that is level yet broken in a thousand perfectly peaked wavelets like the waves in the background of a Botticelli. (*TTF*, 160)

A few lines later she refers to "the frieze of flying dolphins." This is exactly the effect of the flying dolphins that appear on the cover of Lawrence's volume *Bay*, as Robinson points out, and as the illustration here should make plain. Where else would she meet a "lost friend" but in the poetry that first brought them together? Lawrence has returned in this guarded way, though she has "not had the courage or the strength to realize this fully."[11]

But she has carefully prepared the way for her readers to realize this fully, for after the words just quoted she adds: "Lawrence came back with *The Man Who Died*. Whether or not he meant me as the priestess of Isis in that book does not

11. When I first read in typescript H.D.'s then unpublished poem "Priest," I felt that this poem had something to do with Lawrence, because of its regret that a man should be so utterly devoted to a dead woman, as in Lawrence's early poems to his mother. But after reading H.D.'s accounts of her relation with Peter Rodeck (see *CP*, xxvi, and *TTF*, 182–84) I discarded this idea, for Rodeck is clearly the frontal figure in the poem. But now, in view of the fusion of Rodeck and Lawrence in *Advent*, I think that perhaps Lawrence does in some way fuse with Rodeck here as well: "you prefer a woman under the earth, / you heap roses above a grave"; here seems to be a memory of Lawrence's poem "On That Day," which he apparently sent to H.D. at Corfe Castle (see Kinkead-Weekes, *D. H. Lawrence*, 418, and H.D.'s *Compassionate Friendship*, first draft, 39 [ms. in H.D. Archive, Beinecke Library]). "Priest" is a poem apparently stimulated by H.D.'s interviews with Freud; in one of her manuscript arrangements it is grouped with the Dancer triad (see *CP*, xxxvi). When she was "soaking" in Aldous Huxley's edition of Lawrence's letters, she would very early in her reading have come upon the letter to Sally Hopkin written on Christmas Day 1912, where, after speaking of his "book of poems" that will be coming out "next month" (*Love Poems and Others*, 1913), he adds: "But I shall always be a priest of love, and now a glad one—and I'll preach my heart out, Lord bless you" (*Letters*, ed. Huxley, 88; *Letters*, 1:493). Have two quite different "priests" fused in this poem?

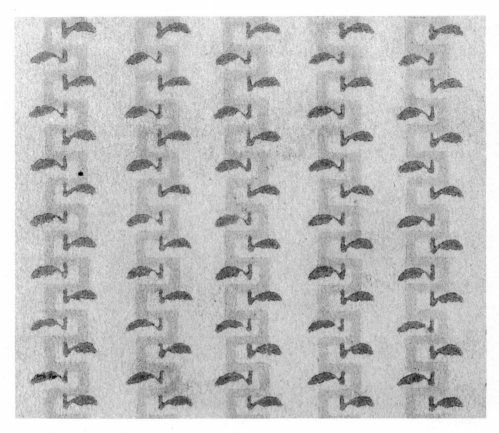

Fig. 8. Cover of Lawrence's *Bay*, 1919. Beinecke Library, Yale University. (Detail, enlarged.)

alter the fact that his last book reconciled me to him. Isis is incomplete without Osiris" (*TTF*, 149–50). Then she adds, thinking of their estrangement: "Judy is meaningless without Punch." Isis and Osiris were twins; H.D. and D. H. were also twins, in a sense, as she has pointed out earlier:

> For one day in the year, H.D. and D. H. Lawrence were twins. But I had not actually realized this until after his death. He was born September 11, 1885: I was born September 10, 1886.
> Stephen Guest brought me a copy of *The Man Who Died*. He said, 'Did you know that you are the priestess of Isis in this book?'
> Perhaps I would never have read the book if Stephen had not brought it to me. Actually, I might have had at first a slight feeling of annoyance. I had told friends of a book that I wanted to write, actually did write. I called it *Pilate's Wife*. It is the story of the wounded but living Christ, waking up in his rock-tomb. I was certain that my friends had told Lawrence that I was

at work on this theme. My first sudden reaction was, 'Now he has taken my story.'

But then she realizes that the story was an "old myth or tradition" (*TTF*, 142–43).

The myth of Isis and Osiris occurs in the second part of *The Man Who Died*, written in June and early July 1928 while Lawrence was living at Chexbres-sur-Vevey, on the shores of Lake Geneva, not far from where H.D. was living, at Territet. They did not meet, but it seems fair to assume that Lawrence knew she was nearby. It is risky to conjecture—but I will conjecture that some memory of H.D. may help to explain the immense difference in style and subject that the second part of this work displays, in contrast with the original part, finished a year earlier, in May 1927, and published in *Forum* in February 1928. This first part is done primarily in a naturalistic style, down-to-earth, in accord with the manner of a once-upon-a-time folktale with which the story opens: "There was a peasant near Jerusalem. . . . This peasant was poor, he lived in a cottage of mud-brick, and had only a dirty little inner courtyard with a tough fig-tree for all his territory."[12] This simple language dominates the story, infiltrated with many echoes of biblical style, along with a few instances of more abstract wording. This paragraph represents the norm of the style of the first part:

> When at dawn on the third morning the man went to the garden, he was absorbed, thinking of the greater life of the body, beyond the little, narrow, personal life. So he came through the thick screen of laurel and myrtle bushes, near the rock, suddenly, and he saw three women near the tomb. One was Madeleine, and one was the woman who had been his mother, and the third was a woman he knew, called Joan. He looked up, and saw them all, and they saw him, and they were all afraid. (*Man*, 35)

In the *Forum* version the story ends with one of Lawrence's open endings, as the Man asks himself "a last question": "From what, and to what, could this infinite whirl be saved?"[13] To connect with the second part Lawrence added an elaborate paragraph denouncing those who would "put a compulsion" on Jesus "and violate his intrinsic solitude" (*Man*, 46).

The second part moves away from the naturalistic mode to tell of how the wounded "man who had died," in the garb of a pilgrim, comes to a temple of Isis on the shores of Lebanon, a temple tended by a young priestess.

> It was Isis; but not Isis, Mother of Horus. It was Isis Bereaved, Isis in Search. The goddess, in painted marble, lifted her face and strode, one thigh

12. *The Man Who Died* (New York: Knopf, 1931), 3; hereafter cited as *Man*.
13. The *Forum* version is republished in *The Escaped Cock* [Lawrence's own title], ed. Gerald M. Lacy, 103–20.

forward through the frail fluting of her robe, in the anguish of bereavement and of search. She was looking for the fragments of the dead Osiris, dead and scattered asunder. . . . And through the years she found him bit by bit, heart and head and limbs and body. And yet she had not found the last reality, the final clue to him, that alone could bring him really back to her. For she was Isis of the subtle lotus, the womb which waits submerged and in bud, waits for the touch of that other inward sun that streams its rays from the loins of the male Osiris. (*Man,* 56)

This phallic theme reaches its climax as the priestess bathes his wounds and chafes "all his lower body with oil," until "he felt the stir of something coming. A dawn, a new sun. A new sun was coming up in him" (*Man,* 93).

He crouched to her, and he felt the blaze of his manhood and his power rise up in his loins, magnificent.

"I am risen!"

Magnificent, blazing indomitable in the depths of his loins, his own sun dawned, and sent its fire running along his limbs, so that his face shone unconsciously. (*Man,* 94)

Whenever I have taught this story the class at this point has erupted in a gale of laughter. Here again, as with his own title for this story, *The Escaped Cock,* Lawrence has carried his phallic campaign beyond the bounds of sympathy for many readers. This whole episode is written in an inflated style that in places reminds one of what H.D. reported about her novel of 1928: "Someone spoke of *Hedylus* as being 'hallucinated writing' " (*TTF,* 149). Is it possible that in creating this fable in such a style Lawrence was in some strange way making amends for the break in their friendship?

In any case, H.D. accepted the analogy of the "twins" and goes on in *Advent* to stress the point, as she describes the famous statues in Freud's study:

We have other minutiae, the images on his table, Osiris the sun in his twelve manifestations, as he journeys through the sky, as well as the bronze Isis that he showed me—his companion.

Those two were twins in the old fairy story. (*TTF,* 143)

And then, a page later, her thoughts move to "those statues in the cottage in Cornwall":

There was a row of them along the mantelpiece of an empty room. The house was only partly furnished. I went there in March 1918. It was D. H. Lawrence who had told me of the old house. It was called Rosigran [Bosigran]. Lawrence said it was haunted. Was I afraid of ghosts? I said I had never met one.

Fig. 9. Freud's desk with "the gods" at 20 Maresfield Gardens, London. Freud Museum, London.

> Here in the semicircle on the table in the other room, is the same or somewhat the same array of images, Osiris, Isis. Perhaps I am afraid of ghosts. But when the Professor said, 'Perhaps you are not happy,' I had no words with which to explain. . . . It is not a question of happiness, in the usual sense of the word. It is happiness of the quest. (*TTF*, 144–45)

"Isis in Search": H.D. had read Lawrence's story. On the deck of the boat she had met his ghost.

Her final reconciliation with Lawrence followed immediately after her poem to Freud in the "Dancer" triad (*CP*, 440–66); or should we say triptych—with "The Master" in the central panel and the tributes to the female and the male artist on either side? In an earlier essay I have said that "The Poet" is "almost certainly" about Lawrence;[14] "almost" because I could find nothing in the poetical or personal relationship with Lawrence that could account for the long opening part of the poem, with its setting by the sea:

14. Introduction to H.D., *Selected Poems,* ed. Louis L. Martz, xiv. See also *CP,* xxviii.

> There were sea-horses and mer-men
> and a flat tide-shelf,
> there was a sand-dune,
> turned moon-ward,
> and a trail of wet weed
> beyond it,
> another of weed,
> burnt another colour,
> and scattered seed-pods
> from the sea-weed . . .

This is reminiscent of the seaside settings of some of the poems in *Sea Garden* (1916); but there is also an inland pond

> filled with water lilies;
> they opened in fresh-water
> but the sea was so near,
> one was afraid some inland tide,
> some sudden squall,
> would sweep up,
> sweep in,
> over the fresh-waterpond,
> down the lilies . . .

This accords well with a setting near Corfe Castle, where H.D. was living in 1916 and where she first truly "met" Lawrence, through their letters and the exchange of their writings.[15] The rest of the poem follows naturally from this memory:

> I look at you,
> I think of your song,
> I see the long trail of your coming,
> (your nerves are almost gone)
> your song is the wail
> of something intangible
> that I almost
> but not-quite feel.

"But you are my brother," she continues, "it is an odd thing that we meet here." Meet where? In memory:

15. Corfe Castle is less than three miles from the Dorset Coast Path, along which one may assume that H.D. frequently walked. At one point along this path the Ordnance Survey map of the region shows a small pond close to the water, near the Kimmeridge Ledges.

> there is this year
> and that year,
>
> my lover,
> your lover,
> there is death
> and the dead past:
>
> but you were not living at all,
> and I was half living . . .

The allusion is to the time after Lawrence's death in 1930 when she found her creative powers partly blocked. But now her powers are renewed, and she can imagine herself in the presence of this poet (for to her his important achievement was poetry, not those long novels that she says she did not understand):

> almost, as you pause,
> in reply to some extravagance
> on my part,
> I believe that I have failed,
> because I got out of the husk that was my husk,
>
> and was butterfly . . .

But she has not failed, nor has he, though now his "shell is a temple":

> I see it at night-fall;
> your small coptic temple
> is left inland,
> in spite of wind,
> not yet buried
> in sand-storm . . .

This seems certainly to be a reference to the "shrine" that Frieda had built for his ashes in New Mexico:

> everyone has heard of the small coptic temple,
> but who knows you,
> who dwell there?
> . . . .
> I say,
> "I don't grasp his philosophy,
> And I don't understand,"

> But I put out a hand, touch a cold door,
> (we have both come from so far);
> I touch something imperishable;
> I think,
> why should he stay there?
> why should he guard a shrine so alone,
> so apart,
> on a path that leads nowhere? . . .
> he couldn't live alone in the desert,
> without vision to comfort him.
>
> there must be voices somewhere.

And so she provides the voice, joining her prophet in the desert:

> I am almost afraid to speak,
> certainly won't cry out, "hail,"
> or "farewell" or the things people do shout:
>
> I am almost afraid to think to myself,
> *why*
> *he is there.*   (*CP,* 461–66)

Fig. 10. Interior of Lawrence's Memorial Chapel ("shrine"), Kiowa Ranch, New Mexico. Photograph by Warren Roberts. Photography Collection, Harry Ransom Humanities Research Center, University of Texas at Austin.

10.

Conclusion
Prophets in Exile

*S*O EVEN Lawrence's ashes had to be preserved in exile from his native land, after all his wanderings and sojourns in Germany, Italy, Sicily, Ceylon, Australia, New Mexico, Old Mexico, and, penultimately, France, where he was buried at Vence in 1930—only, five years later, to have his body exhumed, cremated, and the ashes transported to New Mexico. It is worth remembering that, except for Williams, all the writers considered in the foregoing pages were writing in exile: Pound in England, France, Italy, the prison camp at Pisa, and St. Elizabeths Hospital; Eliot in England; H.D. in England and Switzerland; Joyce in Paris, Trieste, and Zurich, pursuing the plan of "exile and cunning" projected in his *Portrait of the Artist.* All of these exiles, in addition to their geographical situation, were also living in the sort of "theological exile" described by Walter Brueggemann, where writing becomes "an act of polemical theological imagination that guards against cultural assimilation" into the dominant "empire" that seems to be pursuing materialistic goals without regard for the higher values known to an earlier society.[1]

The sound that Matthew Arnold had heard in the 1840s—"the melancholy, long withdrawing roar" of the sea of faith—had not reached these writers in

---

1. *Hopeful Imagination: Prophetic Voices in Exile* (Philadelphia: Fortress, 1978), 110–11. This is part of Brueggemann's view of what he calls "the metaphor of exile" (92)—representing a state of mind that lives in opposition to the surrounding culture and finds that "only memory allows possibility" of return to "home." Thus memory of past achievements, beliefs, and traditions becomes an imaginative action that liberates the mind, with the result that the poetry of 2 Isaiah "proceeds as an act of passion, an act of obedience, an act of hope, an act of subversion" (113). See all of pt. 3 in Brueggemann's book.

their early years, writers all born within a six-year period in the 1880s (Joyce in 1882, Williams in 1883, Lawrence and Pound in 1885, H.D. in 1886, Eliot in 1888). They were all reared in an atmosphere of firm, even devout, religious faith: Eliot in the Unitarianism inherited from his New England roots; Pound in a Presbyterian household; Williams in the atmosphere of a small Unitarian Sunday school; and H.D. in the semimystical religion of the Moravians. To these we should add D. H. Lawrence, reared in the strict beliefs of the English Dissenters, and Joyce, educated in the Roman Catholic school so vividly described in his *Portrait*. I am not of course including *Ulysses* among the works of prophecy, for its epic pattern and dramatized episodes place this work beyond any generic category. But one may say that Leopold Bloom is, in his compassionate way, a sort of failed prophet—and not altogether failed, for, as Pound said in a famous sentence, "On almost every page of Joyce you will find just such swift alternation of subjective beauty and external shabbiness, squalor and sordidness."[2] These are the oscillations of a prophetic consciousness, aware of the degradation of society, but recognizing also, through the consciousness of Bloom, the existence of higher values, of beauty and love.

The situation of all these writers, then, may be seen as symbolized in a famous sculpture by Alberto Giacometti completed in the early 1930s, at just the time when H.D. was experiencing her treatment by Freud. The sculpture is known by two titles: *The Invisible Object* or *Hands Holding the Void*. Here is a female figure kneeling upon a prie-dieu and folding within her hands a vacant space. By her side is the image of a bird, the sacred ibis of ancient Egypt; she seems, then, to be seeking some sort of ancient faith; perhaps she is a priestess, a prophetess, in the sort of guise adopted by H.D. For her that space within her hands may contain the invisible object of her prayer; or perhaps she is praying anxiously for some transcendent presence to occupy that space. The whole sculpture seems to be summed up in the words of a poem that Giacometti wrote in 1933, a year before he completed the cast of the work, shown in the illustration here: "I seek gropingly to grasp in the void / the invisible white thread of the marvellous."[3]

In the void of belief accentuated by and demonstrated in the slaughter of World War I, Eliot, Pound, Lawrence, H.D., and Williams attempted to show ways to grasp, however fleetingly, however gropingly, "the invisible white thread of the marvellous." "I want the wonder back again," cries Lou, the heroine of Lawrence's *St. Mawr* (1924), amid the human wreckage of World War I.[4] "Wonder" is what the heroes of *In the American Grain* (1925) feel as they first glimpse the New World. Columbus, as presented by Williams, on October 12

2. *Pound/Joyce*, 135: "It is the bass and treble of his method." See also p. 139: "There is no perception of beauty without a corresponding disgust."
3. See Valerie J. Fletcher, *Alberto Giacometti* (Washington, D.C.: Smithsonian Institution Press, 1988), 104.
4. *St. Mawr and Other Stories*, ed. Brian Finney, 62.

Fig. 11. Alberto Giacometti, *Hands Holding the
Void*. Plaster sculpture, original cast, 1934. Yale
University Art Gallery. Anonymous Gift.

discovered a world filled with things that were "wonderful," "handsome,"
"marvellous," "beautiful." "During that time I walked among the trees which
was the most beautiful thing which I had ever seen."[5] These are the words
that twenty-five years later Williams brought into the fourth book of *Paterson*
(177), echoing the phrase "beautiful thing" that provided the theme of the
poem's third book. Then we have Cortés, Ponce de Leon, de Soto, Raleigh, and

5. *In the American Grain*, 14th printing, 26. Detailed studies of this book have been given
by Bryce Conrad, *Refiguring America: A Study of William Carlos Williams;* and by Breslin,
William Carlos Williams, chap 4.

Champlain, Williams's favorite, "a man after my own heart"—"like no one else about him, watching, keeping the thing whole within him with almost a woman's tenderness—but such an energy for detail—a love of the exact detail—" (69–70).

Here is a kind of wonder quite unlike the peculiar sort of wonder found in Cotton Mather's *Wonders of the Invisible World,* his account of the witchcraft trials, from which Williams gives shrewdly selected extracts that show how observation can be perverted by ideology, humanity betrayed by false witness. For Mather does not admire the beauty of the land all about him: he feels that he and his people have "embraced a voluntary Exile in a squallid, horrid American Desert" (82). Williams then turns abruptly away from these tales of witchcraft to the chapter headed "Père Sebastian Rasles," which bridges the exact center of the book, with 104 pages preceding and 104 pages following. But we do not meet this Jesuit missionary to the Indians of Maine until sixteen pages have passed. Instead, we are shifted suddenly to Paris in 1924, where Williams is surrounded by artistic and literary exiles: Picasso, Gertrude Stein, the Prince of Dahomi, James and Norah Joyce, Bryher, Mina Loy, H.D., "dear Ezra," and other expatriates. Soon Williams is discussing with Valéry Larbaud the problem of the American writer and arguing fiercely that "what has been morally, aesthetically worthwhile in America has rested upon peculiar and discoverable ground" (109). The trouble with the Puritans, he argues, is that, with their restrictive creed, they could see nothing of interest in their locality, "with a ground all blossoming about them" (114). And on the other hand we have Sebastian Rasles, a symbol of a way of life maintained by what Williams elsewhere calls "the animate touch." For thirty-four years, Williams records, this French priest lived with the Indians, "touching them every day." Rasles displays "a spirit, rich, blossoming, generous, able to give and to receive, full of taste, a nose, a tongue, a laugh" (120). Rasles's view of life, as described by Williams, foreshadows the life of *Paterson:* "Nothing shall be ignored. All shall be included. The world is parcel of the Church so that every leaf, every vein in every leaf, the throbbing of the temples is of that mysterious flower. Here is richness, here is color, here is form" (120–21).

We can see what all this means, set in Paris, in the midst of exiles gathered together from Spain, Romania, Africa, England, Ireland, and especially America. They, like the Puritans, have felt themselves living in a "squallid, horrid American Desert" or in other lands equally offensive to their sensibilities, and so they have fled to Paris for spiritual and cultural sustenance. Williams in the next chapter turns to Daniel Boone, who, says Williams, "lived to enjoy ecstasy through his single devotion to the wilderness with which he was surrounded"; like Rasles, Boone sought "to explore always more deeply, to see, to feel, to touch" (136–37). Here is the deep center of the kinship between Lawrence and Williams, the devotion to "touch" that Lawrence advocates in the second version of *Lady Chatterley's Lover* and also in *The Man Who Died.* For both writers, "touch" means a vivid, "animate" apprehension of the life all about them, not only in sexual relations, but in appreciative response to nature and all human life, whether in the urban wilderness of Paterson or in the many places described by Lawrence in his travel books, his letters, his novels, and his poems. True, Lawrence reacted adversely to many aspects of these places and their people, but his own search for the beautiful thing glows through his adverse commentaries. Even in such a sardonic novel as *Aaron's Rod,* the beauty of the Italian landscape, the natural grace of the Italian people, and the cultural splendor of Florence glow through the rancid comments of the flute player and his friends. In *The Plumed Serpent* and its early version, *Quetzalcoatl,* the magnificence of the landscape never fades, while Lawrence's attitude toward the local populace fluctuates between disgust and admiration.

All these writers "craved the miraculous," as Williams says in the first book of *Paterson,* speaking of the populace of his city, past and present, those who saw in the deformed dwarf "A wonder! A wonder!" (10). But it is the Falls of the Passaic that represents the greatest wonder, as this image of nature's power and beauty becomes the symbol of poetical creation, the imaginative leap:

> There's no mistake in Sam Patch!
>
> 　The water pouring still
> from the edge of the rocks, filling
> his ears with its sound, hard to interpret.
> A wonder!　　　　　　　　　　　　　(16)

Williams refuses to understand the wonder that Eliot and Pound felt in the presence of ancient cultures, and so he regrets

> 　　　That the poem,
> the most perfect rock and temple, the highest
> falls, in clouds of gauzy spray, should be
> so rivaled　　　.　　　that the poet,
> in disgrace, should borrow from erudition . . . (80)

But they are all seeking, in their varied ways, to find "the invisible white thread of the marvellous."

Lawrence and H.D. were both overtly seeking a new religion to replace what they regarded as the outworn pieties of traditional religion: both were syncretists, feeling that true belief in transcendent forces cannot be restricted to any single creed, but that such belief is, in various ways, shared by many creeds. Williams would have none of this. He was the eternal Pelagian, feeling that humankind is not corrupted by any original sin, but may with its own internal powers find a mode of redemption by descending within the self and reaching out from that self to discover and celebrate the Beautiful Thing that may be found even in the most dismal circumstances.

Eliot of course went in the opposite direction and attempted to assimilate himself to a foreign culture—and succeeded to the extent that three of the *Four Quartets* have their composition of place in England. This sort of exile is the basic source of Williams's frequently expressed dislike of Eliot and his works, and explains why, in its original four-book division, *Paterson* represents the eternal Pelagian's answer to the traditional doctrine accepted and implicitly advocated by Eliot in the *Quartets*. For World War II, Eliot did not offer a prophetic voice. He returned to his normal introspective mode, in what he called the "meditative" voice,[6] a quite different poetical voice explored here in the two following essays, on "Burnt Norton" and *Ash-Wednesday*.

But what of Pound? Did not he attempt to assimilate himself to Italy and its fascist politics? Not altogether. Pound's mind was always looking toward America, sending out his messages to America, in the messianic hope of redeeming American culture with the infiltration of cultural treasures from other lands, Chinese, Italian, Greek. In his wartime broadcasts, he desperately attempted to oppose war between his two best-loved countries. Indeed it is possible that this split between two warring loyalties lies behind the mental collapse that one can see occurring even within these broadcasts.[7]

Exile, then, is a complex state of mind that need not involve geographical change of place,[8] and may in fact include some degree of assimilation to the culture of another land. Wherever the location of the writer, "exile" describes a state of mind always searching for "home." In the literal meaning of "home" it is clear that the land of birth is always present in the writer's mind. Wherever Joyce lived on the Continent, Dublin was also there. However deeply Eliot may have become assimilated to English culture and the Church of England, he never forgot the landscapes of his youth: the ailanthus tree, the Mississippi, the granite coast of Massachusetts. H.D., as her *Tribute to Freud* reveals, held intimately to the memories of her Moravian childhood in Pennsylvania and the memories of her friends and family in Philadelphia. Pound, as I have said, never ceased sending messages to America, as his publications and his private correspondence with his mother and father make plain. And Lawrence, in his last important novel, returned to the countryside of his childhood.

But "home" has a deeper meaning for the exile, a meaning related to the literal homeland, but extending far beyond these memories into the deepest recesses

---

6. See "The Three Voices of Poetry," in *On Poetry and Poets*, 97–98.

7. *"Ezra Pound Speaking": Radio Speeches of World War II*, ed. Leonard W. Doob. In many of the speeches Pound seems utterly unable to follow a train of thought; this is confusion far beyond his usual erratic style in prose essays.

8. The point is implicit in Luigi Ballerini's "Exile From and To, and Williams' Sense of Belonging." Ballerini does not deal with *Paterson* and thus does not discuss the complex sense of exile that Williams expresses amid an "empire" of materialistic striving. Many aspects of "exile" are discussed in the illuminating essays in *Women's Writing in Exile*, ed. Mary Lynn Broe and Angela Ingram (Chapel Hill and London: University of North Carolina Press, 1989); see especially Susan Stanford Friedman, "Exile in the American Grain: H.D.'s Diaspora."

of the self, in search of abiding values that will redeem the troubled present. In this sense, all of these exiles, even Joyce, might have agreed with the theme of Lawrence's "Song of a Man Who Has Come Through," where he feels a prophetic inspiration coming from the transcendental world:

> Not I, not I, but the wind that blows through me!
> A fine wind is blowing the new direction of Time.
> If only I let it bear me, carry me, if only it carry me!

The wonder of inspiration rises in him as he senses a religious presence "knocking at the door," the same sort of presence that once came to Abraham, foretelling the child of Sarah and the founding of "a great and mighty nation" in which "all the nations of the earth shall be blessed" (Gen. 18:1–18).

> Oh, for the wonder that bubbles into my soul,
> I would be a good fountain, a good well-head,
> Would blur no whisper, spoil no expression.
>
> What is the knocking?
> What is knocking at the door in the night?
> It is somebody wants to do us harm.
>
> No, no, it is the three strange angels.
> Admit them, admit them.[9]

---

9. *The Complete Poems of D. H. Lawrence,* ed. Vivian de Sola Pinto and Warren Roberts, 250.

Part II

Eliot and Lawrence

Meditation and Prophecy

11.

T. S. Eliot, *The Waste Land* and "Burnt Norton"
Origins of Form in *Four Quartets*

*B*URNT NORTON'' may be read in two contexts: as the first of the *Four Quartets,* or as the last of the poems in Eliot's collected volume of 1936.[1] My own tattered copy of that volume bears the date of purchase, "Oct. 1936," and I well remember the astonishment and puzzlement that the final poem of that book aroused—a poem published there for the first time, without warning, without preparation. That autumn I met on the street Donald Gallup, whose great collection of Eliot's writings was already well advanced (he had shown me his rare copy of the book mistitled *Ara Vus Prec*). I stopped him, crying, "Donald!—I've just been reading the new collected Eliot." "Yes," he said, "and what, *what,* do you make of 'Burnt Norton'?" "Nothing," I said. "My eyes failed, and I knew nothing." "It's the same with me," he said. And then, with the blowing of a horn, he turned and walked away, shaking his head.

That anecdote may not be precisely accurate in detail, but it does, I think, represent the response of early readers to "Burnt Norton." And now, after so many years of explication and annotation, we are still shaking our heads at this, the most elusive of all Eliot's poems. What did it mean in 1936? Certainly not the beginning of a sequence, for Eliot had no thought then of any sequel to this poem. It

1. This essay is reprinted, with revisions, from *Words in Time: New Essays on Eliot's Four Quartets,* ed. Edward Lobb (London: Athlone Press, 1993), 189–204.

seemed to stand in stark isolation at the end of the book, an isolation created by the contrast it offered with the long sequence immediately preceding it, Eliot's unsteady experiment in public, didactic verse, the choruses from *The Rock,* with their deliberately simplified, declarative style. Those choruses, indeed, seemed to have the effect of cutting off "Burnt Norton" from Eliot's earlier writing.

Yet it was evident, even in 1936, that "Burnt Norton" was adapting the five-part structure of *The Waste Land,* for that structure was signaled by the use of a short lyric as the fourth part of the sequence. But what did it mean, what does it mean, to feel the five-part structure of *The Waste Land* working within so different a poem? To answer this question it may help to review the process by which *The Waste Land* gained its peculiar structure, emerging from the hands of Ezra Pound, as Eliot says, reduced to half its manuscript length.

First of all, without Pound's editorial intervention, we would not have the short lyric "Phlebas the Phoenician," appearing by itself as part IV of *The Waste Land,* and thus, presumably, we would not have the short lyrics constituting the fourth sections of all the *Four Quartets*—the short movement that helps to create analogies with Beethoven's late quartets. Indeed we might not have the Phlebas lyric at all, without Pound's advice, for Eliot, upset by Pound's slashing away at the eighty-two lines preceding this lyric in the manuscript, wrote to Pound, "Perhaps better omit Phlebas also???" Pound was horrified: Eliot seemed not to understand the central principle of the poem's operation. "I DO advise keeping Phlebas," Pound replied. "In fact I more'n advise. Phlebas is an integral part of the poem; the card pack introduces him, the drowned phoen. sailor, and he is needed ABSoloootly where he is. Must stay in."[2]

What Pound describes in that vehement answer is the sort of organization that Eliot later called musical, in his lecture "The Music of Poetry," delivered in 1942, just as he was completing *Four Quartets:* "The use of recurrent themes is as natural to poetry as to music," Eliot says. "There are possibilities for verse which bear some analogy to the development of a theme by different groups of instruments ['different voices,' we might say]; there are possibilities of transitions in a poem comparable to the different movements of a symphony or a quartet; there are possibilities of contrapuntal arrangement of subject-matter."[3]

So, in *The Waste Land,* after the embers of lust have smoldered in "The Fire Sermon"—"Burning burning burning"—the death of Phlebas by water provides a moment of serenity, quiet, poise, as Phlebas enters the whirlpool in whispers to a death not to be feared, but foreseen and accepted. The lyric acts as the lines about the still point act in the two poems of "Coriolan," where, first, amid the turmoil of the crowd at the parade, the people think they find their answer in the military leader: "O hidden under the dove's wing, hidden in the turtle's breast, / Under the palmtree at noon, under the running water / At the

2. Eliot, *Letters,* 1:505.
3. *On Poetry and Poets,* 38.

still point of the turning world. O hidden." But then, ironically, it appears in the second poem that the difficulties of a statesman have led him also to seek the still point: "O hidden under the . . . Hidden under the . . . Where the dove's foot rested and locked for a moment. / A still moment, repose of noon."[4] The lyric of Phlebas acts as such a moment of repose, a nodal moment, tying together the strands of the poem, as Pound explained. And the fourth part, the short lyric, in all the *Four Quartets,* performs a similar function of poise and knotting, as the poem finds a temporary rest where themes and images and voices merge for a moment.

One voice of great importance speaks at the close of the Phlebas lyric, which is not simply a translation from Eliot's poem in French, *Dans le Restaurant,* for the closing lines are quite different. The French poem ends in an offhand, conversational tone: "Figurez-vous donc, c'était un sort pénible; Cependant ce fut jadis un bel homme, de haut taille" (Imagine then, it was a distressing fate; / Nevertheless, he was once a handsome man, of tall stature). In *The Waste Land* Eliot has changed the tone from conversational to prophetic by evoking the voice of Saint Paul addressing "both Jew and Gentile" in his epistle to the Romans (Rom. 2, 3): "Gentile or Jew / O you who turn the wheel and look to windward / Consider Phlebas, who was once handsome and tall as you."

A similar effect is created by Pound's critical slashing away of all those weak and in part offensive Popeian couplets at the outset of part III of *The Waste Land* manuscript. "Do something different," Pound advised.[5] So Eliot did: he penciled on the back of the manuscript page a new opening passage, "The river's tent is broken . . ."—lines that stress the eternal presence of the river within the waste land, culminating in the line that echoes the voice of the psalmist in exile: "By the waters of Leman I sat down and wept," with its attendant question, "How shall we sing the Lord's song in a strange land?" (Ps. 137:4).

A similar concentration on the emergence of the prophetic voice is created by the removal of the monologue that opened *The Waste Land* manuscript, the monologue of the rowdy Irishman telling of a night on the town in Boston. This was excised by Eliot himself, perhaps under Pound's influence, perhaps because Eliot himself saw that the rowdy vitality of those singing, drinking men who stage a footrace in the dawn's early light does not accord with the voice that follows, the voice of one who is so reluctant to live that April becomes the cruelest month. That excision brings us quickly to the voice of a modern Ezekiel, speaking the famous lines:

> What are the roots that clutch, what branches grow
> Out of this stony rubbish? Son of man,

---

4. Quotations from Eliot's poetry are taken from his *Collected Poems, 1909–1935* and from his *Collected Poems, 1909–1962.*

5. T. S. Eliot, *The Waste Land: A Facsimile and Transcript of the Original Drafts, Including the Annotations of Ezra Pound,* ed. Valerie Eliot, 127.

> You cannot say, or guess, for you know only
> A heap of broken images.

Then these lines of true prophecy play their contrapuntal music against the voice of the false prophet, Madame Sosostris.

In dealing with the prophetic voice, as I have argued in the opening essay, we should remember the example of the biblical prophets, whose eye is upon the evils of the present, and whose writings display the most remarkable oscillation between virulent denunciation and exalted lyrics, between the actual and the ideal. This is exactly the effect that we find in Pound's *Cantos* and in *The Waste Land*. At the same time, as I have said, the true prophet is never one who speaks for himself; he is one "who speaks for another," as Walt Whitman did in those famous lines:

> Through me many long dumb voices,
> Voices of the interminable generations of slaves,
> Voices of prostitutes and of deformed persons,
> Voices of the diseased and despairing . . .

Voices of past and present, of life and death, oscillating together—this is the method invented by Pound in his early cantos and brought to perfection by Eliot in *The Waste Land*. Pound could see what Eliot was doing because *The Waste Land* represented the fulfillment of his own prophetic impulse, gradually revealed in the seven cantos that he had written by the end of 1919. In "Burnt Norton," Eliot's reprise of the five-part form of *The Waste Land* pays tribute to the outline discovered by Pound in that "sprawling" manuscript, and he proceeds to use its musical form toward other ends. The form of "Burnt Norton" recognizes the existence of an earlier self—that collaborative self of different voices—but proceeds to explore the creation of another self. Or, to adapt Eliot's own words about *The Golden Bough*, "Burnt Norton" remembers that vanished mind of which the present mind is a continuation.[6] The result is that the poem's place at the end of Eliot's volume of 1936 serves to indicate another way of writing and another attitude toward life, an attitude implied in the reluctant recovery of joy in sensory life at the close of *Ash-Wednesday*, where

> the lost heart stiffens and rejoices
> In the lost lilac and the lost sea voices

6. T. S. Eliot, "London Letter," *Dial* 71 (1921): 453: "Even *The Golden Bough* can be read in two ways: as a collection of entertaining myths, or as a revelation of that vanished mind of which our mind is a continuation." This was written in regard to Stravinsky's *Sacre du Printemps*, of which Eliot here remarks (significantly, when one thinks of *The Waste Land* and "Burnt Norton"): "It did seem to transform the rhythm of the steppes into the scream of the motor horn, the rattle of machinery, the grind of wheels, the beating of iron and steel, the roar of the underground railway, and the other barbaric cries of modern life; and to transform these despairing noises into music."

> And the weak spirit quickens to rebel
> For the bent golden-rod and the lost sea smell
> Quickens to recover
> The cry of quail and the whirling plover

Such a recovery is implied as well in "Marina," where the renewed man prays, "let me / Resign my life for this life, my speech for that unspoken, / The awakened, lips parted, the hope, the new ships." These poems serve as preludes to the rose garden of "Burnt Norton."

That garden, like *The Waste Land*, is inhabited by echoes, but they no longer function in the way of *The Waste Land*. The prophetic oscillation between degraded images from modern life and brighter images of past belief is no longer needed, for—"Quick now, here, now, always"—all images of the past are eternally present. The many echoes in the rose garden have been carefully pointed out over the years: intimations of Augustine and Bergson on the problem of time; an echo of *Alice in Wonderland*—a favorite echo of Eliot's, since he took such pleasure in pointing it out to readers who had not noticed it; echoes of Kipling's "They"; echoes of Lawrence's poignant and to Eliot cruel story "The Shadow in the Rose Garden"; above all, though briefest of all, an echo of Dante's *Paradiso* in the phrase "heart of light," evoking the passage where Dante, encircled by "the two garlands of those sempiternal roses," hears a voice speaking "del cor de l'una de le luci nove"—"from the heart of one of the new lights" (*Par.* 12.28).[7]

The last echo leads back to the ecstatic experience of the speaker after his return, late, from the hyacinth garden of *The Waste Land*:

> Your arms full, and your hair wet, I could not
> Speak, and my eyes failed, I was neither
> Living nor dead, and I knew nothing,
> Looking into the heart of light, the silence.

Sexual and religious implications are here blended, as they are in the rose garden of "Burnt Norton," with its image of the "lotus." But the passionate experience of the *Waste Land* garden is overwhelmed by that poem's pervasive theme of sexual failure and degradation, whereas in "Burnt Norton" the experience becomes the central theme, as a different voice ponders the meaning of such a glimpse into the "heart of light"—the meditative voice that Eliot describes in his essay "The Three Voices of Poetry." It is a voice that springs from an "obscure impulse." The poet "does not know what he has to say until he has said it, and in the effort to say it he is not concerned with making other people understand anything."

> He is not concerned, at this stage, with other people at all: only with finding the right words or, anyhow, the least wrong words. He is not concerned

---

7. *Paradiso*, trans. Singleton, 131.

whether anybody else will ever listen to them or not, or whether anybody
else will ever understand them if he does. He is oppressed by a burden which
he must bring to birth in order to obtain relief. . . . and when the words are
finally arranged in the right way—or in what he comes to accept as the best
arrangement he can find—he may experience a moment of exhaustion, of
appeasement, of absolution, and of something very near annihilation, which
is in itself indescribable.[8]

Indescribable, except in the lyrics that constitute the fourth movement of each
quartet.

The change in voice is signaled in the second line of "Burnt Norton" by one
word, "perhaps": "Time present and time past / Are both perhaps present in time
future, / And time future contained in time past." One remembers how Pound
twice queried Eliot's use of the word "perhaps" in part III of *The Waste Land*
manuscript, writing "dam per'apsez" and "Perhaps be damned" in the margin,
and then canceling the word "may" with an annotation that Hugh Kenner calls
"almost a free-verse stanza":[9]

> make up
> yr. mind
> you Tiresias
> if you know
> know damn well
> or
> else you
> don't.[10]

Ezekiel would never say perhaps.

In "Burnt Norton" the note of uncertainty continues: "But to what purpose /
Disturbing the dust on a bowl of rose-leaves / I do not know." Here the
speaker works within a cloud of unknowing: he gropes toward the meaning
of his experience of momentary reconciliation between the worlds of sense
and spirit, a reconciliation celebrated in the formal lyric that opens part II
(matching the formal verse that opens the second part of *The Waste Land*):
"The trilling wire in the blood / Sings below inveterate scars / And reconciles
forgotten wars." Eliot later changed the last line here to read "Appeasing long
forgotten wars"—apparently to avoid the repetition of "reconciled" in the lyric's
concluding lines:

---

8. *On Poetry and Poets*, 98.
9. *The Waste Land: A Facsimile*, 31, 45; Kenner, "The Urban Apocalypse," in *Eliot in his
Time: Essays on the Occasion of the Fiftieth Anniversary of "The Waste Land,"* ed. A. Walton
Litz, 32.
10. *The Waste Land: A Facsimile*, 47.

> We move above the moving tree
> In light upon the figured leaf
> And hear upon the sodden floor
> Below, the boarhound and the boar
> Pursue their pattern as before
> But reconciled among the stars.

I think the original repetition is better, because the lyric deals with a double reconciliation: one within the human body and the other within the outer universe—to say nothing of the unfortunate implications of "appeasing" under the wartime circumstances.

Then follows, as in *The Waste Land,* a section of broken utterances, clipped sentences, cut apart by periods or semicolons, but of course not expressing the hysteria of the frenzied woman in *The Waste Land:*

> "My nerves are bad tonight. Yes, bad. Stay with me.
> Speak to me. Why do you never speak. Speak.
>   What are you thinking of? What thinking? What?
> I never know what you are thinking. Think."

In "Burnt Norton" these broken words are converted into the thinking, probing voice of the meditative seeker, the sort of philosophic probing that one might feel in the fragments of Heraclitus or the other pre-Socratic searchers after the Logos:

> At the still point of the turning world. Neither flesh nor
>   fleshless;
> Neither from nor towards; at the still point, there the dance
>   is,
> But neither arrest nor movement. And do not call it fixity,
> Where past and future are gathered. Neither movement from nor
>   towards,
> Neither ascent nor decline. Except for the point, the still
>   point,
> There would be no dance, and there is only the dance.

Then comes a rounded cogitation, quite unlike the pub scene of *The Waste Land,* but retaining, perhaps, a distant echo of "HURRY UP PLEASE ITS TIME" in the concluding lines:

> Time past and time future
> Allow but a little consciousness.
> To be conscious is not to be in time
> But only in time can the moment in the rose-garden,
> The moment in the arbour where the rain beat,

> The moment in the draughty church at smokefall
> Be remembered; involved with past and future.
> Only through time time is conquered.

But what does that closing aphorism mean? Part III attempts to tell us, in the mode of rational discourse—what was called the working of the intellect in the old meditative procedures. The voice now ponders two ways of using the world of time to conquer time. First, through the sort of sunlit transcendence represented by the rose garden:

> daylight
> Investing form with lucid stillness
> Turning shadow into transient beauty
> With slow rotation suggesting permanence

Second, by "darkness to purify the soul / Emptying the sensual with deprivation," after the manner of the Spanish mystics.

All these cogitations are then blended into the short lyric that is part IV, a lyric that is highly formed within an appearance of informality suggested by the way the line lengths vary from one syllable to fourteen. The words are subtly woven together by rhyme, assonance, alliteration, and repetition, moving toward the one word "Chill" that stands by itself in the sixth line; but this word of fear and death is countered by the hopeful word "still" ambiguously repeated in the succeeding lines. Thus linkages of sound reinforce linkages of imagery ("curled," "world," "cling," "king-," "wing"):

> Time and the bell have buried the day,
> The black cloud carries the sun away.
> Will the sunflower turn to us, will the clematis
> Stray down, bend to us; tendril and spray
> Clutch and cling?
> Chill
> Fingers of yew be curled
> Down on us? After the kingfisher's wing
> Has answered light to light, and is silent, the light is still
> At the still point of the turning world.

The lyric moves around the word "Chill" by a slow rotation suggesting permanence within the transient movement of life from day to darkness, from abundance of natural life to death. The kingfisher's flashing wing is an image of natural beauty and vigor in a transient world, but the light that the wing briefly reflects is an image drawn from the "heart of light." So, through this shaping, "Burnt Norton" moves to its retrospective conclusion, summing up in many different ways the effort of the poem to achieve a goal beyond the reach of the sad time of *The Waste Land:*

> Only by the form, the pattern,
> Can words or music reach
> The stillness, as a Chinese jar still
> Moves perpetually in its stillness. . . .
>
> Sudden in a shaft of sunlight
> Even while the dust moves
> There rises the hidden laughter
> Of children in the foliage
> Quick now, here, now, always—
> Ridiculous the waste sad time
> Stretching before and after.

Thus the prophetic mode of *The Waste Land* has been absorbed and tran-scended by the probing, inward, meditative voice. The five-part structure, re-newed and transformed, now stands ready to serve the poet's need as wartime unexpectedly calls forth the further exploration of that "burden which he must bring to birth in order to obtain relief."

In that exploration "East Coker" also finds its "moment of exhaustion, of appeasement, of absolution," in the lyric that constitutes its fourth part. This is a lyric deliberately performed in the "metaphysical" style that Eliot admired in his essays and echoed in his stanzaic poems around the year 1920:

> The wounded surgeon plies the steel
> That questions the distempered part;
> Beneath the bleeding hands we feel
> The sharp compassion of the healer's art
> Resolving the enigma of the fever chart.

Now, in 1940, the lines that open part V discard that style, adopting a relaxed, conversational, intimate manner of speech:

> So here I am, in the middle way, having had twenty years—
> Twenty years largely wasted, the years of *l'entre deux
>   guerres*—
> Trying to learn to use words, and every attempt
> Is a wholly new start, and a different kind of failure . . .

This "metaphysical" lyric, then, as Eliot has said of the rhetorically inflated lyric that opened part II, is a "study in a worn-out poetical fashion, / Leaving one still with the intolerable wrestle / With words and meanings." It is self-consciously "witty," "conceited," paradoxical, while its strict stanza form of five lines rhyming *ababb* suggests a variation on some of George Herbert's stanzas. At the same time the use of hexameter in the final line evokes a reminiscence of Milton's Nativity Ode, while the stress on "blood" may carry connotations of eucharistic celebrations by Herbert and Crashaw, along with implications of a world now concentrated upon the prosecution of bloody warfare:

> The dripping blood our only drink,
> The bloody flesh our only food:
> In spite of which we like to think
> That we are sound, substantial flesh and blood—
> Again, in spite of that, we call this Friday good.

The lyric thus brings to a climax the Christian implications that have emerged in part III, with its opening echoes of Milton's *Samson Agonistes,* its central meditation on faith, hope, and love, and its closing quotation from Saint John of the Cross. The traditional significance of Good Friday has, in the past, provided surcease from the flux and turmoil imaged in the first three sections of this quartet. Will its meaning still prevail in this world at war?

The conversational, intimate style that ends "East Coker" continues at the beginning of "The Dry Salvages," as Eliot further disclaims the prophetic mode: "I do not know much about gods; but I think that the river / Is a strong brown god." Here is the mode of quiet pondering that dominates this quartet and is especially evident in part III ("I sometimes wonder if that is what Krishna meant—") as Eliot renews his memories of Hindu religion and poetry. "The Dry Salvages," with its prevalent imagery of the ocean, is broad and deep enough to include "Many gods and many voices," but all is controlled by the quiet voice that hears the clanging of the bell and knows "the hardly, barely prayable / Prayer of the one Annunciation" ("Be it unto me according to thy word").

So the lyric of the fourth part binds this quartet together in its quiet prayer to the Virgin, remembering the dangerous voyages of wartime convoys, while the closing allusion to the sea bell and the angelus brings together the bell and Annunciation of the poem's first two parts:

> Lady, whose shrine stands on the promontory,
> Pray for all those who are in ships, those
> Whose business has to do with fish, and
> Those concerned with every lawful traffic
> And those who conduct them.

The flexible, easy, natural movement of these five-line stanzas marks the poet's renunciation of the prophetic mode and the metaphysical style.

Finally, in "Little Gidding," Eliot is able to create a blending of the formal and the intimate: in the rhymed stanzas of the lyric that opens part II, in the modified terza rima of the air-raid warden's communication with the dead, and, climactically, in the Herbertian lyric of part IV that blends the wartime bomber with the tongues of fire at Pentecost:

> The dove descending breaks the air
> With flame of incandescent terror
> Of which the tongues declare
> The one discharge from sin and error.
> The only hope, or else despair
> Lies in the choice of pyre or pyre—
> To be redeemed from fire by fire.

The imagery returns to the imagery at the close of the opening part: "the communication / Of the dead is tongued with fire beyond the language of the living." Thus "The Fire Sermon" of *The Waste Land* has been transformed, while the five-part structure remains, implicit recognition of an earlier self met in this poem's second part:

> And as I fixed upon the down-turned face
> That pointed scrutiny with which we challenge
> The first-met stranger in the waning dusk
> I caught the sudden look of some dead master
> Whom I had known, forgotten, half recalled
> Both one and many; in the brown baked features
> The eyes of a familiar compound ghost
> Both intimate and unidentifiable.

That compound ghost includes the many voices of *The Waste Land* that were drawn together in "I Tiresias"; but, as the ghost here says, "last year's words belong to last year's language / And next year's words await another voice." That voice has been emerging throughout *Four Quartets*, interrupted by moments of high rhetoric or low-key didacticism; but in the last two quartets the truly meditative voice, concentrated in its quest, grows more and more confident, until, in the middle of "Little Gidding," the voice can say: "See, now they vanish, / The faces and places, with the self which, as it could, loved them, / To become renewed, transfigured, in another pattern." This is the "pattern / Of timeless moments" that the meditative voice has sought to discover, and now discovers in this place of the "secluded chapel," "A symbol perfected in death."[11]

11. Commentaries on *Four Quartets* are legion, but I should note especially the books by Helen Gardner and D. A. Traversi, the essays in the books on Eliot by A. D. Moody, Hugh Kenner, Ronald Bush, Grover Smith, and Leonard Unger, along with the more recent books by Steve Ellis and John Xiros Cooper, all listed in the bibliography.

12.

T. S. Eliot, *Ash-Wednesday*
Voices for the Veiled Lady

*I*N THE EDITION of 1930, *Ash-Wednesday* is dedicated "To my Wife," a dedication that gives particular
poignancy to the well-known echo of the opening line of
Cavalcanti's lament for his separation by exile from his beloved lady: "Perch'io
non spero di tornar già mai":[1]

> Because I do not hope to turn again
> Because I do not hope
> Because I do not hope to turn
> Desiring this man's gift and that man's scope

But Shakespeare's line in Sonnet 29 reads "Desiring this man's *art*." Eliot is not
limiting the lost desire to art; *gift* is a larger word: it includes the gift of poetical
creation, along with the gift of religious grace and the gift of human love—that
"power of the usual reign" that most men and women seem to possess, even
though it may be "the infirm glory of the positive hour" or "the one veritable
transitory power." For this speaker the gifts of love and grace and poetry seem

---

1. Cavalcanti, Ballata XI; see *The Translations of Ezra Pound*, with an introduction by
Hugh Kenner, 120–23. I am throughout this essay indebted to the detailed commentary on
this poem by Kimon Friar and John Malcolm Brinnin in their anthology *Modern Poetry* (New
York: Appleton-Century-Crofts, 1951), 465–72. See also the essays on *Ash-Wednesday* in the
books on Eliot by A. D. Moody, Ronald Bush, Hugh Kenner, Helen Gardner, Grover Smith,
and Leonard Unger listed in the bibliography. This essay is reprinted, with minor revisions,
from *T. S. Eliot, Man and Poet*, ed. Laura Cowan, 1:189–96.

to have vanished, for he feels that he has lost the power to "drink / There, where trees flower, and springs flow." He has lost touch with the things of earth and therefore feels that "place is always and only place" without the resonance of memory and the delight of sensory response. Therefore, he chooses to renounce "the blessèd face" that lovers such as Cavalcanti and Dante and Petrarch saw in their beloved ladies. And he renounces too the voice of the beloved, along with the voice of the prophet that had sounded so strongly as the dominant voice of *The Waste Land* (after Pound had performed his drastic excisions in such a way as to allow that voice to dominate): the voice that cried "Son of man," like Ezekiel; the voice that cried so insistently, "HURRY UP PLEASE ITS TIME"; the voice of "I Tiresias"; the voices of Buddha and Augustine; the voice that, like Saint Paul, addresses "Gentile or Jew"; and finally, transcending all, the voice of the Thunder, commanding, "Da / *Datta*," "Da / *Dayadhvam*," "Da / *Damyata*."

All these powerful voices are renounced in this dry voice of penitence and self-analysis:

> And I pray that I may forget
> These matters that with myself I too much discuss
> Too much explain

What those matters have been, at their worst, we may see by reading the excised Fresca passage of *The Waste Land,* or the truly horrifying "Ode: To you particularly, and to all the Volscians, Great hurt and mischief"—a poem of sexual self-laceration that appeared only in *Ara Vos Prec* (1920).[2] *Ash-Wednesday* is, in part, an act of contrition and amendment for such thoughts as these.

> Because I do not hope to turn again
> Let these words answer
> For what is done, not to be done again
> May the judgement not be too heavy upon us

Upon *us.* In this context the prayer does not sound general: it is intimate, personal, *us,* the two of us. But at the close of this section the prayer becomes more general, echoing the liturgy of the Virgin:

> Pray for us sinners now and at the hour of our death
> Pray for us now and at the hour of our death.

One may wonder why Eliot, recently converted to the Church of England, should so insistently in this poem echo the Roman liturgy rather than the Book of

---

2. *The Waste Land: A Facsimile,* 23–27; the ode has recently been reprinted in T. S. Eliot, *Inventions of the March Hare: Poems, 1909–1917,* ed. Christopher Ricks, 383–84.

Common Prayer. But this choice is not ecclesiastical: it is thematic and poetical, a part of the decorum created by the love poetry of Cavalcanti, Dante, and Petrarch. One may think of Petrarch's words in the final poem of his sequence to his beloved, a hymn to the Virgin:

> Tre dolci et cari nomi ài in te raccolti,
> madre, figliuola et sposa,
> Vergine gloriosa,
> donna del Re ché nostri lacci à sciolti
> et fatto 'l mondo libero et felice . . .

> You have gathered into yourself three sweet names: mother, daughter, and bride, O glorious Virgin, Lady of that King who has loosed our bonds and made the world free and happy . . . [3]

Donna del Re. The lady now addressed in the first word of the next poem in Eliot's sequence is primarily the lady of this king—but of course she includes, after the manner of the *dolce stil nuovo,* the beloved earthly lady, transfigured. It is to this composite lady, then, that the "dissembled" speaker tells here, indeed, celebrates here, the story of his redemption. For the three white leopards are the agents of grace who bring to the speaker the message of God, as it came to despairing Elijah "under a juniper-tree," and as it came, in a different way, to Adam and Eve after the Fall "in the cool of the day." What he hears now is a voice that he has just renounced—the voice of the prophet Ezekiel, repeating the words of the Lord that came to him in the valley of dry bones: "God said / Shall these bones live? shall these / Bones live? / . . . And God said / Prophesy to the wind"—words that evoke the redemptive message of Ezekiel:

> Prophesy unto the wind, prophesy, son of man, and say to the wind, Thus saith the Lord God; Come from the four winds, O breath, and breathe upon these slain, that they may live. So I prophesied as he commanded me, and the breath came into them, and they lived, and stood up upon their feet, an exceeding great army. (Ezek. 37:9–10)

Eliot's lines, however, continue with words that imply a state of doubt: "Prophesy to the wind, to the wind only for only / The wind will listen." But the bones seem to know more, for they now sing ("chirping") a long litany to the "Lady of silences":

---

3. *Petrarch's Lyric Poems,* trans. Robert M. Durling (Cambridge: Harvard University Press, 1976), 578–79.

> Terminate torment
> Of love unsatisfied
> The greater torment
> Of love satisfied . . .
> Grace to the Mother
> For the Garden
> Where all love ends.

The conclusion of this section alludes to the later words of Ezekiel: "This is the land which ye / Shall divide by lot" (see Ezek. 47:22). The desert setting may seem to give an ironical twist to the prophet's words as Eliot adds: "This is the land. We have our inheritance." Yet this conclusion is subtly optimistic, for the words from the forty-seventh chapter of Ezekiel are preceded by the long and lyrical description of the bountiful and fertilizing river:

> And by the river upon the bank thereof, on this side and on that side, shall grow all trees for meat, whose leaf shall not fade, neither shall the fruit thereof be consumed: it shall bring forth new fruit according to his months, because their waters they issued out of the sanctuary: and the fruit thereof shall be for meat, and the leaf thereof for medicine. (Ezek. 47:12)

The witty wordplay on "dissembled" and "burden," the "brightness" and singing of the bones, the bland, serene enumeration of what might have been the macabre details of physical disintegration—all combine to support the optimistic tone. These bones will live and the desert will bloom like a garden. It is a land of promise.

The second poem in the sequence thus foretells the goal and progress of the entire group—an interpretation helped by the title and epigraph that Eliot gave this section at its separate publication in 1927: "Salutation. *e vo significando.*"[4] The epigraph points to the passage in the twenty-fourth canto of the *Purgatorio* where Dante acknowledges himself as author of *le nove rime* beginning "Donne ch'avete intelletto d'amore"—"Ladies that have understanding of love."[5] This is the opening line of the canzone (number 19) that marks the turning point of the *Vita Nuova:* the turning away from sickly yearnings of the physical self for the physical lady, and a turning toward the celebration of her redeeming virtue, her heavenly quality:

> My lady is desired in highest Heaven.
> Now let me tell you something of her power.

4. *Saturday Review of Literature* 4:20 (December 10, 1927): 429; also *Criterion* 7 (January 1928): 31–32.
5. *Purgatorio,* trans. Singleton, 261.

> . . . if she finds one worthy to behold her,
> that man will feel her power for salvation
> when she accords to him her salutation
> [ché li avvien, ciò che li dona, in salute]
> which humbles him till he forgets all wrongs.[6]

In the *Purgatorio* Dante tacitly accepts and explains the newness of *le nove rime* by saying: "I am one who, when Love inspires me, takes note, and goes setting it forth [*vo significando*] after the fashion which he [Love] dictates within me." One may wish that Eliot had preserved the early heading for this second section, since it implies that, for the speaker, a turning point is being celebrated, a turning that, as with Dante, marks the regeneration of the poetic voice and the regeneration of the self.

Section 2, in its proleptic action, thus intermingles past, present, and future: memory, present resolution, and the recovery to come. Section 3 is almost wholly memory: of temptations and distractions overcome, especially the distractions offered by sensuous landscape, sensuous music, and sexual love:

> Blown hair is sweet, brown hair over the mouth blown,
> Lilac and brown hair;
> Distraction, music of the flute, stops and steps of the mind
>   over the third stair,
> Fading, fading; strength beyond hope and despair
> Climbing the third stair.

These are distractions overcome by the faith demonstrated in the closing lines that echo again the Roman liturgy, with the words of the faithful centurion to Christ (Matt. 8:5–10):

> Lord, I am not worthy
> Lord, I am not worthy
>
>   but speak the word only.

The speaker no longer renounces the desire to hear the voice: he prays for the healing word to be spoken.

In section 4 the healing word comes, mysteriously, "The token of the word unheard, unspoken." It is unspoken by the Lady

> Who walked between the violet and the violet
> Who walked between

6. *Dante's Vita Nuova*, trans. Mark Musa, 32–33.

> The various ranks of varied green
> Going in white and blue, in Mary's colour . . .
> Who then made strong the fountains and made fresh the springs

Religious and poetic inspiration are mingled in the presence of this Lady who, like another Beatrice or Laura, wears "White light folded, sheathed about her, folded."

> The new years walk, restoring . . .
> With a new verse the ancient rhyme. Redeem
> The time.

It seems inevitable that one should recall that in the fifth chapter of Ephesians, where Saint Paul speaks of "Redeeming the time, because the days are evil," these words are followed by the verses traditionally taken as a justification for writing religious poetry: "be filled with the Spirit; Speaking to yourselves in psalms and hymns and spiritual songs, singing and making melody in your heart to the Lord." And then this passage is immediately followed by Paul's lengthy advice about the proper relationship between husbands and wives. Not only does he give the now (and perhaps then) unpopular advice, "Wives, submit yourselves unto your own husbands, as unto the Lord"; he follows this with the much longer and much more eloquent advice: "Husbands, love your wives, even as Christ also loved the church. . . . So ought men to love their wives as their own bodies. He that loveth his wife loveth himself." In a poem dedicated "To my Wife" I do not see how this context can be forgotten.

But if we hear these marginal grace notes, what do they mean? The "new verse" (*le nove rime*) of religious song is a way of redeeming the time when a failure in love threatens the vital center of being. The speaker here is seeking, in Stevens's terms, the One of Fictive Music who can give back the imagination that he spurned and craves. By following in the mode of ancient rhyme where the "*bella donna*" became the "Lady of all grace,"[7] the speaker here has found a way of creating what modern theory would call a "textual self," a fictional self that can transcend the absence of the beloved, as Cavalcanti did at the close of his ballata, when he cried out to his poem (in Ezra Pound's translation):

> O smothered voice and weak that tak'st the road
> Out from the weeping heart and dolorous,
> Go, crying out my shatter'd mind's alarm,
> Forth with my soul and this song piteous

7. See Pound, *Translations,* 120–21.

> Until thou find a lady of such charm,
> So sweetly intelligent
> That e'en thy sorrow is spent.[8]

A complex of all these things is happening here, for now the veiled lady, fictive image of the higher dream, gives her silent word that seems to be the sign of acceptance, understanding, forgiveness, and renewal:

> The silent sister veiled in white and blue
> Between the yews, behind the garden god,
> Whose flute is breathless, bent her head and signed but spoke
>   no word
>
> But the fountain sprang up and the bird sang down
> Redeem the time, redeem the dream
> The token of the word unheard, unspoken. . . .

I find no problem in moving out from the final words of this part, "And after this our exile," into the chatter and the clatter of the whirling world in section 5. For the speaker's exile from the things of earth has ended. Redeem the time because the days are evil. Such concern for the evils of the world, for those who walk in darkness, is a normal movement in the religious life: from contemplation to action, or the thought of action. It is a sign of returning health, returning wholeness. Section 5 is a prayer for all of humanity, not only for the self. The voice of the prophet, "O my people, what have I done unto thee,"[9] returns to still for a moment the whirl and the clatter of modern rhyming.

And so, finally, in section 6, comes the reluctant recognition that things of the world, things of the flesh, things of the earth are not necessarily distractions:

> Although I do not hope to turn again
> Although I do not hope
> Although I do not hope to turn

the self is already turning, has been turning since the second section dramatized the song of the bones. And now, although he feels it is a backward step, a sign of weakness, and "though I do not wish to wish these things,"

> From the wide window towards the granite shore
> The white sails still fly seaward, seaward flying
> Unbroken wings

8. Ibid., 123.
9. The words are taken from Mic. 6:3; but the phrase "O my people" is also used by Isaiah (3:12, 10:24), and the phrase "my people" constantly occurs in Isaiah and Jeremiah.

This is imagery of release: the wide window looks out toward the granite shore (of New England), and beyond the shore he sees the sails in liberated action, flying seaward. And soon his heart rejoices in what he had thought were "the lost lilac and the lost sea voices":

> And the weak spirit quickens to rebel
> For the bent golden-rod and the lost sea smell
> Quickens to recover
> The cry of quail and the whirling plover

The whirling plover is part of the unstilled world that "whirled / About the centre of the silent Word" in the previous section; but now the rhyming is not a senseless clatter. This is not weakness, it is not rebellion, it is a natural movement in which the redeemed spirit quickens to recover its love of human life. The speaker misapprehends the action of grace upon his whole being, thinks these revived responses to the things of earth are "empty forms between the ivory gates" of a false dream world; nevertheless the process of recovery continues: "And smell renews the salt savour of the sandy earth."

All this is very close to the feeling and attitude conveyed by Dante at the end of the twenty-fourth canto of his *Purgatorio:*

> And as, heralding the dawn, the breeze of May stirs and smells sweet, all impregnate with grass and with flowers, such a wind I felt strike full on my brow, and right well I felt the pinions move, which wafted ambrosial fragrance to my senses; and I heard say, "Blessed are they who are so illumined by grace that the love of taste kindles not too great desire in their breasts, and who hunger always so far as is just."[10]

The senses, then, have their just and proper place in human experience. So Eliot concludes:

> And even among these rocks
> Sister, mother
> And spirit of the river, spirit of the sea,
> Suffer me not to be separated
>
> And let my cry come unto Thee.

By thus truncating the traditional cry, "Suffer me not to be separated from thee," Eliot has created a peculiar effect—a plea not to be separated from the love of woman, not to be separated from love of the river and the sea and the lilac, the goldenrod, the cry of quail, the sea smell, the salt savor of the sandy

10. *Purgatorio,* trans. Singleton, 267.

earth: all the things and beings of earth that make the whole man live and make poetry possible.

But in one respect, at least, the plea could not be answered. In 1936 Eliot removed the dedication to this poem.[11]

11. Lyndall Gordon has made a convincing argument for her view that Eliot's guarded love for Emily Hale lies behind the "veiled sister" of the poem. (*Eliot's New Life,* esp. 12–13, 158–59.) But if so, what shall we make of the dedication in 1930? Eliot seems to invite his wife to read the poem, knowing that she was a perceptive reader of his poetry. What would she make of the "veiled sister"? Is the image herself transfigured, with a mysterious distance between them? Gordon sees the dedication as a "placating gesture" (68). But more than this seems to be involved. Eliot has allowed the wife to see herself as she might have been to him: "Here are the years that walk between, bearing / Away the fiddles and flutes, restoring / One who moves in the time between sleeping and waking." A poignant sadness, "a bright cloud of tears," pervades the fourth section of the poem. This complex tone may be regarded as an expression of regret for the failure of the marriage, along with a regret that this failure has made a later love impossible of fulfillment.

13.

D. H. Lawrence, *Quetzalcoatl* (*The Plumed Serpent*)

Two Versions, Two Novels

QUETZALCOATL was the title Lawrence wanted to give to his Mexican novel, but his new publisher, Knopf, objected to the strange name of the Aztec god. "I did so want to call it 'Quetzalcoatl,'" Lawrence wrote, "but they all went into a panic—and they want the translation—*The Plumed Serpent*—I suppose they'll have to have it—but sounds to me rather millinery." In presenting the early version of this novel the recent edition has returned to Lawrence's own title, which strongly accords with the rich local texture of the book.[1]

When Lawrence wrote from Chapala to his German mother-in-law, he spoke of the work that he was writing as "*die erste volle Skizze*"—"the first complete sketch."[2] The word *sketch* is appropriate, for this revised early manuscript is truly analogous to an artist's careful and detailed drawing made as a design for a larger oil painting. Such drawings frequently have integrity and value in their own right; sometimes, through their fluency and grace of line, they come to

---

1. *The Letters of D. H. Lawrence,* vol. 5, ed. James T. Boulton and Lindeth Vasey (Cambridge: Cambridge University Press, 1989), 254. D. H. Lawrence, *Quetzalcoatl: The Early Version of The Plumed Serpent,* ed. Louis L. Martz. The present essay is a revised and expanded version of the introduction to this edition, hereafter cited as *Q.*

2. *The Letters of D. H. Lawrence,* vol. 4, ed. Warren Roberts, James T. Boulton, and Elizabeth Mansfield (Cambridge: Cambridge University Press, 1987), 450–51.

be valued even beyond the contemplated final work. The version of the novel presented as *Quetzalcoatl* certainly has such integrity and value. Although it is rough in places, it creates its own effect of completeness. It presents, in terms as different as crayon is from oil, a closely related, but different work, when compared with *The Plumed Serpent*.

This version is not exactly the "first rough draft" that Lawrence several times described in his letters of May and June 1923, while he was writing the novel at Lake Chapala. It is a partially revised and corrected version of his original draft, with the equivalent of thirty pages totally revised with long passages crossed out and revisions interlined in his typically neat hand. Beyond this extensive rewriting Lawrence made hundreds of smaller but significant revisions, ranging from a single word or phrase to passages of six or seven lines, and even to one long addition of fifteen lines at the end of chapter 18: the symbolic passage on the snake.[3]

It is true that Lawrence in his letters repeats, over and over, that the work is not finished. Writing from the ranch above Taos, a year after he had left Chapala, he said this early version represented a novel that was only "half finished" or "two-thirds done."[4] But Lawrence did not mean that he was planning to add this much as a continuation of the early version; he was planning to expand the whole body of his complete sketch, recasting its emphasis—enlarging it in oils, we might say—thus producing a work almost twice its original size.

Some sixteen months elapsed between the writing at Lake Chapala and the rewriting in Oaxaca, where, after finishing the novel in February 1925, Lawrence suffered a grave illness and hemorrhage from the lungs that brought him close to death. Much had happened—and not only to his health—in the sixteen intervening months, to change Lawrence's attitude toward the world, and toward his wife, Frieda.

They were happy at Chapala, as photographs and letters show. "Chapala paradise. Take evening train," Lawrence had telegraphed Frieda on first arriving there.[5] But Frieda longed for her children in England and for her mother in Germany. She kept on urging Lawrence to go back with her for a visit. Lawrence demurred, hesitated, agreed, hesitated again and again, went up by train with her to New York, with the uncertain intent of taking passage to England with her. But at the last moment he refused to go, and Frieda went off alone. Leaving the manuscript of *Quetzalcoatl* with his prospective publisher, Thomas Seltzer, to be typed, Lawrence made his way to Los Angeles, where he joined his friend the Danish artist Kai Götzsche. Then the two of them went back to Guadalajara

3. For a detailed account of the manuscript and typescript upon which the above edition is based see the "Textual Commentary" at the back of *Q* and my "*Quetzalcoatl:* The Early Version of *The Plumed Serpent.*"

4. *Letters,* 5:75, 128.

5. Ibid., 4:435.

and Chapala, over difficult mountain ways, from the West, partly by muleback. But when Lawrence saw Chapala again, all was changed, utterly changed. The landscape and the people were the same, but one essential element was missing: Frieda. "I went to Chapala for the day yesterday—the lake was *so* beautiful," Lawrence wrote. "And yet the lake I knew was gone—something gone, and it was alien to me." "I was at Chapala yesterday—It felt strange to me, not the same place."[6] But more than Frieda's absence appears to have been involved here. During the two months away from Chapala, Lawrence seems to have developed a different conception of the scene: it was in his imagination no longer "the same place" in which he had written the early version.

He had been planning to finish his novel on this visit. Only a few days earlier he had written to Seltzer: "I must finish 'Quetzalcoatl.' By the way, I want you to read that MS. and tell me just what you think. Because I must go all over it again, and am open to suggestions. This winter I must finish it."[7] But he found himself so unhappy, so unable to concentrate on the book, that he spent most of his free time revising the novel *The Boy in the Bush* by his Australian friend Molly Skinner. So, in November 1923, he booked passage from Vera Cruz to England, where he caught a debilitating "cold" that lasted for weeks. Nevertheless, he and Frieda visited Paris for two weeks and Germany for another two weeks. Finally, in March 1924, they returned to New York and went from there to Taos and the ranch, where they remained for six months before going down to Mexico "in the autumn, to finish 'Quetzalcoatl.' "[8]

During this long stay at Taos and the ranch, Lawrence found himself unable to deal with *Quetzalcoatl;* he seemed to be willing to do almost anything else. He worked hard physically, repairing the buildings on the ranch; he visited ceremonies at Indian reservations; he wrote all of the short and powerful novel *St. Mawr;* he wrote essays and short stories—some of his longest and best. But these were not really evasions; they were ways of preparing his mind to deal with the vast expansion of the Mexican novel in ways that were deeply affected by his "disheartening" winter in Europe.

Lawrence's return to England and the Continent left him with an increased sense of the decline of the West: his letters express, again and again, his somber conviction that Western civilization, as he had known it, was doomed. Europe, he wrote, "seems to me weary and wearying."[9] He had felt some kind of stirring in depressed Germany, exactly what he did not know, but he saw in that stirring some embers of a new energy, to which he gave an optimistic turn (true prophets cannot live without hope). Back in Mexico, at Oaxaca, in the fall of 1924, he was able to work steadily on his novel. But now he felt much more strongly what

6. Ibid., 4:519–20.
7. Ibid., 4:517.
8. Ibid., 5:45.
9. Ibid., 4:597.

he had felt before coming to America: his conviction that only a new religious revival could bring life again to the Western world—a life that might arise from the soil of America and burst through the imported crust of European modes of life and thought, to create a new era of human existence. And so, as he made his final revision, he added the long sermons of Ramón, leader of the new religious movement, prophet and "manifestation" of the Aztec fertility god, Quetzalcoatl—sermons composed in the style of the biblical prophets. He increased the number and length of the songs and hymns of Quetzalcoatl. He expanded the rituals and symbols of this religious movement. He added long conversations and disquisitions on philosophical, theological, political, and even biological themes. Through these additions, and through many paragraphs and pages of his own ruminations, Lawrence attempted to create a complete mythology for his new religion, combining the sensual and the spiritual, the sexual and the divine, the religious and the political, in a mass movement led by an inspired, indomitable religious leader, accompanied by a powerful military figure—the "manifestation" of the Aztec war god, Huitzilopochtli.

This is a movement whose members salute their leader by raising the right arm straight up toward the sky, palm level with the ground: not quite either the fascist or the communist gesture, but close enough to be menacing to readers of our time. Yet Lawrence was writing in 1923–1925; he knew nothing of Hitler. He knew, however, what was happening in Russia, and he knew at first hand what was happening in Italy, for he had been living there in the early 1920s, and he did not like what he saw. In his novel *St. Mawr,* written in the summer of 1924 (*between* the early and the final stages of his Mexican novel), Lawrence stops the action for three pages in which his heroine, Lou Witt, has "a vision of evil . . . rolling in great waves over the earth":

> The evil! The mysterious potency of evil. . . . There it was in socialism and bolshevism: the same evil. But bolshevism made a mess of the outside of life, so turn it down. Try fascism. Fascism would keep the surface of life intact, and carry on the undermining business all the better. . . .
>
> And as soon as fascism makes a break—which it is bound to, because all evil works up to a break—then turn it down. With gusto, turn it down.

"What's to be done?" asks the authorial voice, then answers: "Generally speaking, nothing. The dead will have to bury their dead, while the earth stinks of corpses. The individual can but depart from the mass, and try to cleanse himself." This thought foreshadows Lou Witt's retreat to the ranch above Taos (Lawrence's own ranch), to preserve her individual soul. Such an assertion of individual integrity closely links Lou Witt with the heroine of *Quetzalcoatl.*[10]

10. Lawrence, *St. Mawr and Other Stories,* ed. Finney, 78–80. Officially the heroine's name is "Lady Carrington," but Lawrence introduces her as "Lou Witt" in the opening words,

Why, then, did he create this mass movement under Don Ramón? Lawrence had apparently sensed in Europe a despair that would lead to the acceptance or the welcoming of a hypnotic leader as a last resort. But he saw as well the potential danger in the cult of the Leader accompanied by a General, for he makes both figures express fierce anger, bitter hatred, and an urge toward violent destruction—tendencies that are held under control by the religious faith of Don Ramón, as we can see from their conversations in both versions of the novel.

But *Quetzalcoatl* provides a much more powerful questioning of this mass movement by filtering the account of its rise through the central consciousness of the heroine, Kate Burns, the Irish widow of a failed Irish patriot, a woman of strong individuality who has lost faith in political revolutions. She watches with a mixture of fascination, revulsion, and sympathy as this religious movement takes shape, but she does not agree to do the three things that she does in *The Plumed Serpent*: she does not agree to marry General Cipriano Viedma; she does not agree to become the manifestation of the rain goddess, Malintzi (or "Malinchi," as she is called in chapter 13 of *Quetzalcoatl*);[11] and, most important, she does not agree to stay in Mexico. In the final version, despite her many doubts and disagreements, in the end she reluctantly submits to "manhood": she marries the general, accepts the role of Malintzi, and ends the novel by pleading with the general, "You won't let me go."

The differences between the two versions of the novel become clear in two chapters dealing with the hymns of Quetzalcoatl: chapter 9 of the early version and chapter 15 of the later. In both versions the preceding chapter has closed with the ugly incident in which Kate attempts to rescue a helpless bird in the water from the mischievous attacks of two little "urchins" who are stoning the limp creature. Her failure to save the bird brings to a climax her feelings of revulsion against the ugly, sordid aspects of native life, to the extent that in both versions she declares that she will leave Mexico. In the final version, however, her declaration is restrained and tentative: " 'But the day will come when I shall go away,' she said to herself."[12] In *Quetzalcoatl* she speaks violently, twice: " 'I've

---

and her maiden name seems appropriate for the maintenance of her individual nature and her closeness to her mother.

11. The name is derived from that of the Indian woman who was the interpreter and mistress of Cortés. Her name is recorded in a great variety of spellings—hence Lawrence's uncertainty about it. For a full account of her career in history and literature see Sandra Messinger Cypess, *La Malinche in Mexican Literature: From History to Myth* (Austin: University of Texas Press, 1991).

12. D. H. Lawrence, *The Plumed Serpent*, ed. L. D. Clark, 218; hereafter cited as *PS*. The present essay is indebted to the introduction and notes to this edition, and also to two important studies by L. D. Clark, *Dark Night of the Body* and *The Minoan Distance*. I owe a special debt to Clark for the helpful suggestions that resulted from his careful reading of the introduction and textual commentary for the Black Swan edition. The recent Penguin edition of *The Plumed Serpent*, edited by L. D. Clark and Virginia Crosswhite Hyde, includes

had enough of this,' she said rising, 'I'm going back to Europe.' " And again, in the last words of the chapter: " 'I loathe Mexico. I loathe it. I'm going back to England' " (*Q*, 144).

In the early version the next chapter begins abruptly with a passage that shows why she becomes more sympathetic to the movement of Ramón and indeed comes seriously to consider staying in Mexico as the novel develops. The passage is a complete rendition of the first hymn of Quetzalcoatl, telling of the god's temporary departure from Mexico and his replacement by Jesus and Mary. In the early version this is the first hymn to appear in the novel, although Kate, in an earlier scene at the Plaza (chapter 5), has watched a mysterious group of men listening to an Indian "singing alone in a low voice to the sound of a mellow guitar" (*Q*, 85). She does not hear the words, and she has no idea what the gathering is all about, until her cousin Owen manages to discover that it has something to do with the new religion of Quetzalcoatl. As the hymn now bursts upon us, without singer or prelude, we assume that this must be something related to the singer in the Plaza, and soon we sense that this is so, for we learn that at the housekeeper's end of the house "two men were singing to one guitar." This "was the second or third night that there had been singing, and the same music, the same words" (*Q*, 146). Kate moves toward the singers but does not hear the actual words. The singers are Rafael and Francisco—Rafael being one of the sons of the housekeeper, Felipa, and Francisco a cousin who has recently come to the house with his fourteen-and-a-half-year-old bride—an actual event during Lawrence's stay at Chapala.[13] Lawrence needs Francisco to play the guitar and lead the singing since none of the other members of Felipa's household have such ability.

We can see Lawrence's exploratory way of writing here. He has already had Kate sit down to hear the singing, but now he adds a second setting, without removing the first. "It was Francisco who played the guitar and sang. Kate tried to persuade him to sit on her verandah and sing. But he was too shy. One night, however, when the electric light had given out," Kate hears the singing again, as "the voices of the two men rose in a queer rapid chant, Rafael, in his throaty voice, singing seconds as spasmodic as the wind in the mango trees"[14]— "seconds" being the technical term for an accompanying (usually lower) tone. Now she is listening "alone in her open sala. . . . But she didn't want to go nearer. In the morning, however, she told Felipa that she liked the singing, and asked what the songs were about: if they were love songs." Felipa says, "No-o, No-o," but she is reluctant to say what they are. However, she finally says that they

---

an important introduction and notes that provide a listing of recent and older studies of this novel. Virginia Hyde has commented on *Quetzalcoatl* (in typescript and manuscript) in her book *The Risen Adam: D. H. Lawrence's Revisionist Typology.*

13. See *Letters*, 4:450.
14. For this and subsequent quotations from chapter 9, see *Q*, 147–54.

are "the Mexican hymns. . . . About the two gods." "The second evening of the singing Kate was still too shy to join the group at the far end of the house. She felt they didn't want her. But the third evening she went," and bluntly asked, "Tell me what the words are." Again, we find the reluctance to reveal the mysterious subject of Quetzalcoatl. But finally "the trumpet-like voice of Rafael" begins to recite the hymn we have just read, with prompting from the others when he breaks down. Assuming that readers know the hymn, Lawrence gives only fragments. " 'And is that all?' asked Kate. 'Yes, Señora. Of this hymn, this is all.' " There are more hymns, then, to be heard.

But instead of more singing Lawrence gives now a long and appealing conversation about Jesus and Mary as "gringo" and "gringuita," couched in a childlike language. The conversation includes a passage that indicates, as earlier hints have done, that Kate may be destined for some sort of divinity in Mexico, for a rumor says "Quetzalcoatl has a wife, and they say she is a gringuita from over there." " 'She will be like the Niña,' said Felipa confidently." Kate, embarrassed, turns the attention back to the hymns and asks them to sing another. "Rafael took his mouth-organ . . . and played a queer, sobbing kind of music," while "Francisco struck the same pulsing tune out of his guitar." Then the two men sing as a duet the beginning of a second hymn of Quetzalcoatl concerning the "heavy souls" of the Mexicans. A pause prepares for the entry of a spoken voice "grave and remote," the voice of the Father, the ultimate power that guides the destinies of both Quetzalcoatl and Jesus. This trio tells the tale of angry, disordered Mexico, a land without a god, without a leader. "We could not get to heaven on the wings of love," they sing. "We are angry souls in the world." The grave voice of the Father promises to send Quetzalcoatl and tells Jesus and Mary to "come home." A painful lament by Felipa is interrupted:

> But there was a noise at the gate, and everybody started.
> "Who is it?" cried Rafael.
> "Jesús!"

It is of course Felipa's son, Jesús, who (symbolically) tends the faltering power plant of the village. Lawrence's droll humor here serves to emphasize the way in which the name of the savior is always present with these people, and they need a savior. Now they sing for Kate the short song of "the coming of Quetzalcoatl," as Jesús, son of Felipa, takes the role of Quetzalcoatl. Dead silence follows the abrupt ending of the song; everyone quietly leaves; and Kate ponders the meaning of the scene in the long passage that ends the chapter:

> Kate went down to her room, wondering. What did these people believe, and what didn't they? So queer to talk of Jesus and Mary as if they were the two most important people in the village, living in the biggest house, the church. Was it religion, or wasn't it?

For her "the world seemed to have become bigger, as if she saw through the opening of a tent a vast, unknown night outside." And the chapter closes with the words: "Life had taken on another gesture altogether." From the beginning of this chapter to its end, Kate is the receiver of the songs, the center of the conversation, her mind the focus of the action.

In the corresponding chapter (15) of *The Plumed Serpent*, the situation is utterly different. The chapter heading tells it all: "The *Written* Hymns of Quetzalcoatl." The hymns here no longer create the effect of arising uncertainly and gradually from the local life, accompanied by village instruments. The hymns are now being circulated on printed sheets throughout the land. Kate has already read one of them in the earlier scene at the Plaza (chapter 7), where singers render it in the circle of the men of Quetzalcoatl, after an old Indian sage has delivered a long, lyrical sermon about the coming of Quetzalcoatl. Now the little group at Kate's house is listening to the hymns as they are read by Julio (formerly Francisco), an educated newcomer who reads first the hymn that has been so slowly extracted from the group by Kate's questioning. After a shortened version of the naive conversation about Jesus and Mary (which omits the comic interruption by the entry of "Jesús"), Julio reads the "second" hymn, which now covers two and a half pages. At the end of this the chapter closes with an abrupt sentence: "There was silence as the young man finished reading." Kate's long rumination over the meaning of religion among the Indians is gone: her responses are no longer at the center of the book. Ramón's presence, through the written hymns he has composed, now dominates the scene: he speaks directly to us, without a questioning intermediary.

In *Quetzalcoatl* the atmosphere of song, arising naturally in an oral civilization, has been carefully prepared for by the setting at the close of the long chapter 5, mainly devoted to descriptions of the household in Chapala and life on the village plaza, where singing to the guitar and violin is part of daily life:

> The tall, handsome men, with sarape over one shoulder, proudly, lounged and strolled about, standing to listen to the singers, of whom there were usually two or three groups. A couple of young men, with different-sized guitars, stood facing each other like two fighting cocks, their guitars almost touching, and they strummed rapidly, intensely, singing in restrained voices the eternal ballads, not very musical, endless, intense, not very audible, and really mournful, to a degree, keeping it up for hours, till their throats were scraped! In among the food-booths would be another trio, one with a fiddle, keeping on at a high pitch and full speed, yet not very loud. (*Q*, 84)

The singer of the Quetzalcoatl legend thus forms part of this tradition of "the eternal ballads."

This passage, slightly altered, appears also in *The Plumed Serpent* (113–14), as part of chapter 7, wholly devoted to "The Plaza." But this account of village life, covering the first third of the chapter, is suddenly invaded by "a new sound, the sound of a drum, or tom-tom," toward which the peons are drifting:

> There was a rippling and a pulse-like thudding of the drum, strangely arresting on the night air, then the long note of a flute playing a sort of wild, unemotional melody, with the drum for a syncopated rhythm. Kate, who had listened to the drums and the wild singing of the Red Indians in Arizona and New Mexico, instantly felt that timeless, primeval passion of the prehistoric races, with their intense and complicated religious significance, spreading on the air. (*PS*, 117)

The ritual, then, is not native to Chapala: Ramón and Cipriano, we later learn, have imported the drums from the north, as part of Lawrence's transformation of the scene into the mythical village and lake named Sayula in *The Plumed Serpent* (the actual name of a much smaller lake in the region). Here, as the drum gives forth its "blood-rhythm," Kate notices men "giving little leaflets to the onlookers"; she receives one and finds on it "a sort of ballad, but without rhyme, in Spanish," while "at the top of the leaflet was a rough print of an eagle within the ring of a serpent that had its tail in its mouth" (*PS*, 118). Lawrence then provides the poem, Quetzalcoatl's song of his coming back to replace Jesus in Mexico. Next, as "the drum was beating a slow, regular thud, acting straight on the blood," the crowd assembles in silence to hear the long lyrical sermon of the Indian sage, telling in biblical language and cadences the full legend of the god's return. Various voices then take up the song printed in the leaflet, and finally the whole company moves into a ritual pattern, "dancing the savage bird-tread" (*PS*, 128). Kate cannot resist the invitation of an unknown man to join in the dance, and she does so, gradually losing her sense of individuality:

> She felt her sex and her womanhood caught up and identified in the slowly revolving ocean of nascent life, the dark sky of the men lowering and wheeling above. She was not herself, she was gone, and her own desires were gone in the ocean of the great desire. As the man whose fingers touched hers was gone in the ocean that is male, stooping over the face of the waters. (*PS*, 131)

Already, only a quarter of the way into *The Plumed Serpent*, it is clear that Kate will not be able to resist the spell of the men of Quetzalcoatl.

Equally important, the scene here shows that the religion of the returned god is fully developed, with its costume, symbols, ritual, sermons, and poetry. But in *Quetzalcoatl*, Lawrence tells us in chapter 11, more than halfway through the novel, that the religious movement "was just in its infancy" (*Q*, 173). We watch its growth as it arises gradually from the native soil and enters into Kate's consciousness. Ramón, in the early version, seems almost like an emanation from the scene, a "dark-skinned" man of the native race (*Q*, 49)—whereas in *The Plumed Serpent* he is lighter in hue and to Kate "he feels European" (*PS*, 237).

The difference in Lawrence's treatment of local materials is clear in the scene where the Christian images are removed from the church and taken away to be burned on the Island of Scorpions—the "Isle of the Alacrans"—that actually lies beyond Chapala. In *The Plumed Serpent* (chapter 18), the ritual of removal begins with the powerful beat of a drum, as a "strong, far-carrying male voice" sings "Jesus' Farewell" in rhymed stanzas reminiscent of a protestant hymnal (*PS*, 279–80); but in *Quetzalcoatl* (chapter 11), the atmosphere of traditional music is maintained, as "a guitar began to strum quietly" and a young priest intones Jesus's farewell in free verse reminiscent of biblical cadences (*Q*, 186). Then, as the images are taken away on the water, the treatment of the removal is vastly different. In *Quetzalcoatl*, while the bell tolls, the images are taken away in a series of small boats, led by the priest, who holds the large crucifix, with its image of the bloody Christ, so that it faces the "multitude" on the shore. (Lawrence uses the word *multitude* twice, stressing the analogy with Christ on the shore of the lake of Galilee; the word is not used in the final version.)[15] The effect is poignant, as the boats are rowed away: "The tall crucifix led the way on the smooth water, heaving like a mast to the pull of the oars. Followed the black canoe with the glass case. Then the boats with the other images, the well-known, beloved images of the village, standing erect and small as the boats diminished on the surface of the water" (*Q*, 189).

The whole scene here is given from the standpoint of the spectators on the shore, including Kate. They cannot see the far-off landing of the boats on the island; they see only the smoke and flames of the burning:

> There was an exclamation as a thin thread of smoke mounted in the air. The bells of the church suddenly clashed. And from the low end of the island out in the lake rose a ragged, orange-reddish flame, with a fringe of bluish invisibility and of smoke. The people were all on their feet again, the men crying in blind, strange voices *Señor! Señor!* the women throwing their hands to heaven and murmuring, moaning *Santisima! Santisima! Santisima!* (*Q*, 189)

In *The Plumed Serpent* this poignancy, this recognition that the images were "beloved," is greatly attenuated. To the "remote, fearsome thud" of a drum, not the tolling of a bell, the images are placed in one large sailing boat, with the crucifix at the prow, "facing outwards," soon to be blotted out as the wind catches "the huge, square white sail" bearing "the great sign of Quetzalcoatl, the circling blue snake and the blue eagle upon a yellow field, at the center, like

---

15. See *Q*, 187; Matt. 13:2: "And great multitudes were gathered together unto him, so that he went into a ship, and sat; and the whole multitude stood on the shore." Like the gospels, *Q* recounts the *beginning* of a religious movement, with the gathering of the disciples by a lake.

a great eye" (*PS*, 282–84). The vantage point from the shore is then abandoned, and the narration follows the boat to the island, where Ramón dominates the scene, lighting the fire. We watch the images burn in grim detail, and the young priest reveals his true affiliation by stripping off his cassock and standing forth in the garb of the followers of Quetzalcoatl.

> Then, when only the last bluish flames flickered out of a tumble of red fire, from the eminence above, rockets began to shoot into the air with a swish, exploding high in the sightless hot blue, with a glimmer of bluish showers, and of gold.
>
> The people from the shore had seen the tree of smoke with its trunk of flame. Now they heard the heavy firing of the rockets, they looked again, exclaiming, half in dismay, half in the joyful lust of destruction:
> "*Señor! Señor! La Purísima! La Purísima!*" (*PS*, 286)

Then the narration returns to Ramón, who comes back from the island in a motorboat and locks the doors of the church. And the chapter ends with these words: "The crowd scattered in the wind, rebozos waving wildly, leaves torn, dust racing. Sayula was empty of God, and at heart, they were glad." In the early version, we have no celebratory fireworks, no "joyful lust of destruction." The appearance of Ramón does not interrupt the novel's concentration on the emotions of the multitude watching from the shore. At the close, Lawrence maintains, even increases, the sense of loss:

> And before the fire had yet burned out, a delicate film of shadow was over the earth-white lake. Low on the stony end of the Isle of Scorpions fire still made a reddish mark on the air, and smoke filmed up. But it was getting less and less, less and less.
>
> Jesus, and his mother, and the saints were gone, and Chapala was empty of God. Lost, and deprived of speech, the people drifted away to their mid-day meal. (*Q*, 190)

In *The Plumed Serpent,* the emphasis is thus thrown upon the dominance of the new religion, with its symbols and its leader conquering the old religion, releasing the people from their lethargy: "and at heart, they were glad." But in *Quetzalcoatl,* the narrative is primarily concerned with exploring and revealing the emotions of a people caught in a painful time of transition, with old loyalties and love remaining, while the new religion strives to work its revolution in their hearts.

This difference is evident in the two accounts of Kate's first visit to Ramón's hacienda, given the symbolic name Las Yemas ("the buds") in the early version, but changed to Jamiltepec in the final version, presumably for the more indigenous effect of the name. In *Quetzalcoatl* (chapter 6) Kate climbs up to a balcony, and as she turns "to look out at the water," she hears "the sound of a guitar, and a man singing in a full, rich voice, a curious music." The single voice is succeeded by "the sound of guitars and violins," while "four or five men started singing." Don Ramón, playing on his guitar, is leading his men in what he calls "the music lesson"—they are practicing a song, with laughter and high spirits. Here again, under the influence of the lake, the music of Quetzalcoatl is beginning to arise from a domestic scene with local instruments. These are "the buds" of the movement (*Q,* 90–91).

In *The Plumed Serpent* no such scene occurs. Kate is ushered into the presence of Ramón's wife, Carlota, and offered a place to rest:

> As she lay resting, she heard the dulled thud-thud of the tom-tom drum, but, save the crowing of a cock in the distance, no other sound on the bright, yet curiously hollow Mexican morning. And the drum, thudding with its dulled, black insistence, made her uneasy. It sounded like something coming over the horizon. (*PS,* 163)

Carlota, it soon appears, hates the sound of the drum and all it signifies; when Kate asks, "Is Don Ramón drumming?" Carlota cries out, "No, Oh, no! He is not drumming, himself. He brought down two Indians from the north to do that" (*PS,* 164). And she proceeds to denounce bitterly her husband's efforts to revive the old gods. With the focus thus shifted to Don Ramón's enterprise, the next three chapters (11–13) are dominated by the words and actions of Ramón and his followers.

In chapter 11 of the final version, "Lords of the Day and Night," Kate is removed from the action, as we watch Ramón praying alone in his room, then visiting the workmen on his estate, as they forge in iron the symbol of Quetzalcoatl: "The bird within the sun" (*PS,* 171). Kate and Ramón's wife briefly come upon the scene, but only to get the key to the boat that will take them away for a row upon the lake. Ramón now visits the artist who is carving his head in wood, and here, as Ramón sits for the sculptor, we are given the fully developed features of the religion of Quetzalcoatl: the prophetic leader, the ritual gestures, the transfer of power from master to disciple:

> The artist gazed with wonder, and with an appreciation touched with fear. The other man, large and intense, with big dark eyes staring with intense pride, yet prayerful, beyond the natural horizons, sent a thrill of dread and of joy through the artist. He bowed his head as he looked.
> Don Ramón turned to him.
> "Now you!" he said.
> The artist was afraid. He seemed to quail. But he met Ramón's eyes. And instantly, that stillness of concentration came over him, like a trance. And then suddenly, out of the trance, he shot his arm aloft, and his fat, pale face took on an expression of peace, a noble, motionless transfiguration,

the blue-grey eyes calm, proud, reaching into the beyond, with prayer. (*PS*, 173)

Then Ramón visits the shed where his people are weaving a sarape that presents a more elaborate symbol of the movement: "a snake with his tail in his mouth, the black triangles on his back being the outside of the circle: and in the middle, a blue eagle standing erect, with slim wings touching the belly of the snake with their tips, and slim feet upon the snake, within the hoop" (*PS*, 174). So the way is prepared for Ramón to call his disciples together and begin the service of Quetzalcoatl.

> They sat in silence for a time, only the monotonous, hypnotic sound of the drum pulsing, touching the inner air. Then the drummer began to sing, in the curious, small, inner voice, that hardly emerges from the circle, singing in the ancient falsetto of the Indians:
> "Who sleeps—shall wake! Who sleeps—shall wake! Who treads down the path of the snake shall arrive at the place; in the path of the dust shall arrive at the place and be dressed in the skin of the snake—"
> One by one the voices of the men joined in, till they were all singing in the strange, blind infallible rhythm of the ancient barbaric world. And all in the small, inward voices, as if they were singing from the oldest, darkest recess of the soul, not outwards, but inwards, the soul singing back to herself. (*PS*, 175)

In the next chapter Kate, too, feels the powerful spell of Ramón, standing and sitting there "naked to the waist," in a passage that further diminishes her individual being:

> "Ah!" she said to herself. "Let me close my eyes to him, and open only my soul. Let me close my prying, *seeing* eyes, and sit in dark stillness along with these two men. They have got more than I, they have a richness that I haven't got. They have got rid of that itching of the eye, and the desire that works through the eye. The itching, prurient, *knowing,* imagining eye, I am cursed with it, I am hampered up in it. It is my curse of curses, the curse of Eve. The curse of Eve is upon me, my eyes are like hooks, my knowledge is like a fish-hook through my gills, pulling me in spasmodic desire. Oh, who will free me from the grappling of my eyes, from the impurity of sharp sight! Daughter of Eve, of greedy vision, why don't these men save me from the sharpness of my own eyes—!" (*PS*, 184)

This is Lawrence at his least attractive—but none of this is in *Quetzalcoatl*.

In *The Plumed Serpent*, Ramón, as the mythic representative of Quetzalcoatl, seems to have power even over the elements of earth and sky, for the rituals, the drumming, the songs, and the long sermon of Ramón that follows in chapter 13

("The First Rain") seem to evoke the thunder, lightning, and tropical downpour that end this long central sequence of three chapters.

> Even as he spoke the wind rose, in sudden gusts, and a door could be heard slamming in the house, with a shivering of glass, and the trees gave off a tearing sound.
>   "Come then, Bird of all the great sky!" Ramón called wildly. "Come! Oh Bird, settle a moment on my wrist, over my head, and give me power of the sky, and wisdom." (*PS*, 198)

Soon, after more of Ramón's sermon, the rain comes.

All this symbolizes the change that is coming over the land through the religious power of Ramón, "Lord of the Two Ways," downward and upward, uniting earth and sky and men and women in one irresistible unity, where the women are always subordinate to the rediscovered manhood of the followers of Quetzalcoatl, with their ominous celebration of the Leader.

> In low, deep, inward voices, the guard of Quetzalcoatl began to speak, in heavy unison:
>   *"Oye! Oye! Oye! Oye!"*
>   The small, inset door within the heavy doors of the church opened and Don Ramón stepped through. In his white clothes, wearing the Quetzalcoatl sarape, he stood at the head of his two rows of guards, until there was a silence. Then he raised his naked right arm.
>   "What is God, we shall never know!" he said, in a strong voice, to all the people.
>   The guard of Quetzalcoatl turned to the people, thrusting up their right arm.
>   "What is God, we shall never know!" they repeated.
>   Then again, in the crowd, the words were re-echoed by the guard of Huitzilopochtli.
>   After which there fell a dead silence, in which Kate was aware of a forest of black eyes glistening with white fire.

"With his words," Lawrence adds, "Ramón was able to put the power of his heavy, strong will over the people. The crowd began to fuse under his influence" (*PS*, 336–37).[16]

No one who has heard the roar of Nazi rallies or has seen the staged rituals of Hitlerism can avoid wincing here. But we know, as I have said, that Lawrence hated fascism: Cipriano himself scorns it in *Quetzalcoatl* (chapter 15), calling

---

16. The corresponding scene in *Q* is quite different. The opening words are spoken by a priest, not by Ramón, who then sings a song about Quetzalcoatl, "not in chant, and in the queer, naive, blind way of the people" (*Q*, 230–31). The hypnotic effect of Ramón in *PS* is therefore absent.

fascism a "great bully movement" (*Q*, 248). *The Plumed Serpent* attempts to suggest that such mass movements may be controlled and justified by religious belief. But in the early version of the novel, the questioning presence of Kate suggests that the European consciousness ultimately cannot accept such primitive mass movements, although near the close, in the climactic chapter 18, she comes very close to accepting a role in the movement, as Ramón, in the strange initiation ritual, puts upon her all the immense pressure of his mysterious rhetoric. His long symbolic sermon here may well strike us as an abrupt and alien intrusion upon the scene, for its terms are derived from the sort of occult theosophy that Lawrence had become familiar with in England. And indeed the appearance of this episode may be due to the accidental impact of an outside force: the arrival of the manuscript of Frederick Carter's theosophical and astrological treatise, *The Dragon of the Apocalypse,* on June 15, 1923, just as Lawrence was nearing the conclusion of his "rough draft." Lawrence at once read the treatise; his long letter to Carter on June 18 and the introduction that he later wrote for a version of the treatise show how deeply he was impressed by it. The ending of Lawrence's letter indeed contains the essence of Ramón's sermon: "I should like to see the end of this Return. The end of the Little Creation of the Logos. A fresh start, in the first great direction, with the polarity downwards, as it was in the great pre-Greek Aeons, all Egypt and Chaldea."[17]

Nevertheless, the episode has its important function: it reveals the religious depths of Ramón's mission and represents the ultimate appeal of primitive symbols to Kate's sophisticated European consciousness. She very reluctantly and with intense fear drinks from the cup of wine that is pressed upon her, but she at once shudders away into the solitude of her room and renounces the implied pledge. " 'I can't!' said Kate, standing rigid before the window, 'I can't! I can't! I can't!' " (*Q*, 310). And she does not: she refuses to marry Cipriano and carries out her resolve to return to England. She does not promise to return to Mexico, although that possibility is left open.

Thus the entire development of the early version remains true to the principle of open-ended weaving that Cipriano explains (in chapter 10) to Kate in their first serious discussion of her remaining in Mexico. He explains what he has found wrong in England: that it was "all made and finished." Then he presents his central metaphor, drawn from Indian life in the north; but here the image is a blanket, not a drum:

> "You know the Navajo women, the Indian women, when they weave blankets, weave their souls into them. So at the end they leave a place, some threads coming down to the edge, some loose threads where their souls can come out. And it seems to me your country has woven its soul into its fabrics

17. *Letters*, 4:461. For Lawrence's introduction to Carter's *Dragon of the Apocalypse,* see Lawrence, *Apocalypse and the Writings on Revelation,* ed. Mara Kalnins, 45–46.

and its goods and its books, and never left a place for the soul to come out. So all the soul is in the goods, in the books, and in the roads and ways of life, and the people are finished like finished sarapes, that have no faults and nothing beyond. Your women have no threads into the beyond. Their pattern is finished and they are complete."

Kate objects that she is Irish, not English, and Cipriano concedes that she may be different.

> "I did not say that every English woman, or Irish woman, was finished and finished off. But they wish to be. They do not like their threads into the beyond. They quickly tie the threads and close the pattern. In your women the pattern is usually complete and closed, at twenty years."
> "And in Mexico there is no pattern—it is all a tangle," said Kate.
> "The pattern is very beautiful, while there are threads into the unknown, and the pattern is never finished. The Indian patterns are never quite complete. There is always a flaw at the end, where they break into the beyond— nothing is more beautiful to me than a pattern which is lovely and perfect, when it breaks at the end imperfectly on to the unknown—" (*Q*, 162–63)

Kate says, "rather venomously," "Well, it may be I am old, and my pattern is finished." And he replies, "You are not old . . . and your pattern is not finished. Your true pattern has yet to be woven." The early version of this novel is the story of the weaving of Kate's pattern. In *The Plumed Serpent* this conversation about the blanket is reduced to one-fifth of its original length, and it is applied to the weaving of Mexico's soul, not Kate's (*PS*, 234).

Such an open design is quite in accord with the view that Lawrence described in an angry letter to Carlo Linati in January 1925, just as he had nearly finished *The Plumed Serpent*. "Well well, in a world so anxious for outside tidiness, the critics will tidy me up, so I needn't bother. Myself, I don't care a button for neat works of art":

> But really, Signor Linati, do you think that books should be sort of toys, nicely built up of observations and sensations, all finished and complete?— I don't. To me, even Synge, whom I admire very much indeed, is a bit too rounded off and, as it were, put on the shelf to be looked at. I can't bear art that you can walk round and admire. . . . You need not complain that I don't subject the intensity of my vision—or whatever it is—to some vast and imposing rhythm—by which you mean, isolate it on to a stage so that you can look down on it like a god who has got a ticket to the show. . . . But whoever reads me will be in the thick of the scrimmage, and if he doesn't like it—if he wants a safe seat in the audience—let him read somebody else.[18]

18. *Letters*, 5:200–201.

The early version of his novel fits this description better than does *The Plumed Serpent,* with Kate's reluctant acceptance of the religion of Quetzalcoatl. In the early version Kate is at first a spectator, but she plunges into the midst of the scrimmage and carries us with her throughout, until at the close she emerges with her fate not decided but open. On the last page of the early version we find her surrounded by the chattering Felipa and her children, yet "Under these trying circumstances Kate tried to get on with her packing." It is a typical Lawrentian open end. The religion of Quetzalcoatl, in this version of the novel, is a myth of the future that the world needs to create, as the soul escapes from the loose threads in the weaving.

The final chapter of the early version sums up the effect of this weaving within Kate, in a springtime scene with all the landscape coming to life after the rains, which have here come on their own, without any association with Ramón. Kate has just returned from a visit with Ramón and the new "dark" Mexican wife, Teresa, whom Ramón has so surprisingly taken. The tender relationship between the two has made Kate a bit jealous: the marriage has the effect of bringing Ramón down to earth. At the same time this episode with Teresa, coming in the next-to-last chapter, has the effect of liberating Kate from Ramón's spell: for in the concluding chapter Ramón is nowhere present. Kate stands alone looking at the springtime scene; she feels refreshed, she feels renewed strength and vision:

> The lake had come alive with the rains, the air had come to life, the sky was silver and white and grey, with distant blue. There was something soothing and, curiously enough, paradisal about it, even the pale, dove-brown water. She could not remember any longer the dry rigid pallor of the heat, like memory gone dry and sterile, hellish. A boat was coming over with its sail hollowing out like a shell, pearly white, and its sharp black canoe-beak slipping past the water. It looked like the boat of Dionysos crossing the seas and bringing the sprouting of the vine. (*Q,* 321)

The mythical touch prepares the way for the brilliantly presented scene that follows as the peons urge a cow and "a huge black-and-white bull" into the interior of the boat. The bull is magnificent in his "unutterable calm and weighty poise," as the men urge him toward the boat in ritual, balletlike movements: "with the loose pauses and the casual, soft-balanced rearrangements at every pause."

> There he stood, huge, silvery and dappled like the sky, with snake-dapples down his haunches, looming massive way above the red hatches of the roof of the canoe. How would such a great beast pass that low red roof and drop into that hole? It seemed impossible.

And then in the end he leaps down to join the cow, and the boat moves off "softly on the water, with her white sail in a whorl like the boat of Dionysos, going across the lake. There seemed a certain mystery in it. When she thought of the great dappled bull upon the waters, it seemed mystical to her" (*Q,* 322–23).

The symbolism is clear: the men have captured, with ritual reverence, the very principle of potency. The wretched bullfight, with its "stupid" bulls, that formed the novel's opening chapter has been redeemed by recognition of a divinity that looms within this noble creature once worshiped by the ancients. The incident is retained in the middle of the last chapter of *The Plumed Serpent,* along with details of the earlier springtime scene, but it is placed in November and surrounded by the presence of Ramón. Thus the mythological power of the symbolic bull is associated with Ramón, along with the other activities of nature.

In the springtime scene of *Quetzalcoatl,* Kate sees everywhere the signs of creative life: "A roan horse, speckled with white, was racing prancing along the shore, and neighing frantically." "A mother-ass" has just given birth to a foal, and Kate watches the foal rise on its "four loose legs."

> Then it hobbled a few steps forward, to smell at some growing green maize. It smelled and smelled and smelled, as if all the aeons of green juice of memory were striving to awake. Then it turned round, looked straight towards Kate with its bushy-velvet face, and put out a pink tongue at her. She broke into a laugh. It stood wondering, lost in wonder. Then it put out its tongue at her again. And she laughed again, delighted. It gave an awkward little new skip, and was so surprised and rickety, having done so. It ventured forward a few steps, and unexpectedly exploded into another little skip, itself most surprised of all by the event. (*Q,* 324–25)

It seems almost the perfect image of Kate's own rebirth. She is leaving Mexico, but the "green juice" of the memory of what she has witnessed will stay with her. Her whole Mexican experience now seems like a myth of Dionysus, the fiction of a possibility. It is almost as though she had dreamed the whole experience, in answer to her need. That is why the memories of her life in England have, in the preceding chapter, come back so strongly to her. England, however "finished," is her reality, just as the enduring memory of her beloved husband remains with her until the end, helping to draw her home.

One of the most significant differences between the two versions lies in Lawrence's treatment of Kate's married life. In *Quetzalcoatl* she has one husband (the father of her two children), bearing the simple Scotch-Irish name Desmond Burns. In the final version she has two husbands, the first of whom she remembers with respect but not with love, and by this divorced husband she has had her two children. Then she marries an Irish patriot bearing the name James Joachim Leslie, a symbolic name that suggests James the apostle, as well as Joachim the father of Mary and the medieval mystic and prophet Joachim of Flora, in whom Lawrence was deeply interested. So the second husband bears the aura of an evangelist and a prophet, whereas Desmond Burns is a beloved man—but no more than a man.

One of the most moving scenes in *Quetzalcoatl* occurs in the third chapter when Kate, in the midst of a dinner party, breaks down weeping before all the company at the memory of her dead husband. She never loses that link with her past: again, in the middle of chapter 12, she weeps bitterly at the memory of her husband's failure and death. The earlier incident of her weeping is retained in *The Plumed Serpent,* but here it occurs only in the presence of Cipriano and thus serves to indicate the possibility of a closer relation between the two.[19]

To prepare for Kate's acceptance of Cipriano, Lawrence has made a drastic change in his treatment of the general. In the third chapter of *Quetzalcoatl* we hear the story of how, when he was a small boy, he saved the life of the mistress of his hacienda by sucking out the poison of a snake that had bitten her, with the result that she sent him to England to be educated. "Oh, by the way," says Owen in reporting the story, "beware he doesn't bite you, because the natives have a superstition that his bite is poisonous" (*Q,* 33). This image of the snake reaches its climax in the latter part of chapter 18. In the initiation ritual, as Kate is about to drink the wine, she feels Cipriano's "black, bright, strange eyes on her face, in a strange smile that seemed to hypnotise her, like a serpent gradually insinuating its folds round her" (*Q,* 310).

And soon her memories of England stress the unlikelihood of her staying in Mexico and marrying the general. Near the close of this chapter, she refuses Cipriano's urgent pressure for her to stay, although she tells him that once she gets to England she may be able to choose. He offers her an old ring, possibly Aztec, with "a flat serpent with scales faintly outlined in black, and a flat green stone in its head" (*Q,* 316). But Kate accepts it only with the understanding that it does not constitute a commitment.

As he rides away she sees him as "The rider on the red horse"—an ominous allusion to the sixth chapter of the Book of Revelation, where "there went out another horse that was red: and power was given to him that sat thereon to take peace from the earth, and that they should kill one another: and there was given unto him a great sword."[20] This is quite in accord with Kate's frequently expressed fear of Cipriano, and in accord also with the long passage that ends the chapter, where Kate watches a snake withdraw into a hole in the wall:

> The hole could not have been very large, because when it had all gone in,
> Kate could see the last fold still, and the flat little head resting on this fold,
> like the devil with his chin on his arms looking out of a loop-hole in hell.
> There was the little head looking out at her from that hole in the wall, with
> the wicked spark of an eye. Making itself invisible. Watching out of its own

---

19. See *Q,* 38, 199–200; *PS,* 71.
20. *Q,* 319; the phrase is emphasized by being given a separate paragraph.

invisibility. Coiled wickedly on its own disappointment. It was disappointed
at its failure to rise higher in creation, and its disappointment was poisonous.
Kate went away, unable to forget it. (*Q*, 319–20)

The disappointment belongs to Cipriano, with Kate's rejection of his proposal:
"his bite is poisonous." After this, it seems, there can be no real possibility that
Kate will ever accept his offer.

A version of this passage is retained in *The Plumed Serpent* at the close of
chapter 26, "Kate Is a Wife." The effect is utterly different, partly because the
phrase "The rider on the red horse" does not appear, but mainly because the
early and persistent association of the general with the poisonous serpent has
been removed. In *The Plumed Serpent* the story of how Cipriano sucked out the
poison from the hacienda's mistress is gone, replaced by the story of Cipriano's
becoming the favorite of an English bishop in Mexico, who sent him to England
for his education, in the hope that he might become a priest. "So you see,"
Cipriano explains to Kate, "I have always been half a priest and half a soldier" (*PS*,
69–70). With his venom thus removed, the way is clear for Kate to marry him.

So here at the close of chapter 26 the serpent image takes a different turn:

> So she wondered over it, as it lay in its hidden places. At all the unseen
> things in the hidden places of the earth. And she wondered if it was disap-
> pointed at not being able to rise higher in creation: to be able to run on four
> feet, and not keep its belly on the ground.
>
> Perhaps not! Perhaps it had its own peace. She felt a certain reconciliation
> between herself and it. (*PS*, 425)

She has already married Cipriano, twice, in the ceremony performed by Ramón
and in a legal ceremony. The reconciliation has been difficult but it is happening,
as we are told at the outset of this very chapter: "She felt a great change was
being worked in her, and if it worked too violently, she would die. It was the end
of something, and the beginning of something, far, far inside her: in her soul
and womb. The men, Ramón and Cipriano, caused the change, and Mexico"
(*PS*, 414).

By this marriage, and by her agreement to join the new movement as the
representative of the goddess Malintzi, Kate denies the essence of the individual
character that she maintains throughout *Quetzalcoatl*, and throughout the earlier
portion of *The Plumed Serpent*. Kate thus controls the action and the meaning
of *Quetzalcoatl*, whereas in *The Plumed Serpent* Ramón and Cipriano have their
way. True, she keeps a strong measure of inner resistance up to the very end of
the final version, but at the close it is clear that she has decided to stay. "She had
come to make a sort of submission: to say she didn't want to go away." " 'You
don't want me to go, do you?' she pleaded" with Cipriano. Then in the final
version's closing line she continues her pleading in words that variously imply

that she will and wants to stay: " 'You won't let me go!' she said to him." That is to say: "Your strength is overpowering me: I can't get free." Or, "You won't let me go; this reassures me that I will stay." Or, "You won't ever let me go, will you?"

In all these ways, while making his final expansion, Lawrence transformed *Quetzalcoatl* from a psychologically plausible narrative, focused on and through Kate, into a work that places much greater stress upon the transcendent element, in accord with the rumination in the middle of the crucial chapter 6 of *The Plumed Serpent,* where Kate is overwhelmed by "the great seething light of the lake":

> So in her soul she cried aloud to the greater mystery, the higher power that hovered in the interstices of the hot air, rich and potent. It was as if she could lift her hands and clutch the silent, stormless potency that roved everywhere, waiting. "Come then!" she said, drawing a long slow breath, and addressing the silent life-breath which hung unrevealed in the atmosphere, waiting. (*PS,* 106)

And she says to herself, "There is something rich and alive in these people. They want to be able to breathe the Great Breath"—a term suggestive of current theosophical thought. Lawrence knows exactly what he is doing here; he stresses the shift in her tone:

> She was surprised at herself, suddenly using this language. But her weariness and her sense of devastation had been so complete, that the Other Breath in the air, and the bluish dark power in the earth had become almost suddenly, more real to her than so-called reality. Concrete, jarring, exasperating reality had melted away, and a soft world of potency stood in its place, the velvety dark flux from the earth, the delicate yet supreme life-breath in the inner air. Behind the fierce sun the dark eyes of a deeper sun were watching, and between the bluish ribs of the mountains a powerful heart was secretly beating, the heart of the earth. (*PS,* 108–9)

So Chapala becomes Sayula, and most of the other actual names of places around the lake (which are retained in *Quetzalcoatl*) are likewise changed to fictitious names, where the myth of the gods' return can move beyond "concrete, jarring, exasperating reality" into the "velvety dark flux" of the earth and the "supreme life-breath of the inner air."

While the amount of material dealing with landscape and local life remains substantially the same in both versions, because of the much greater size of *The Plumed Serpent,* the native matter has proportionately less impact. In *Quetzalcoatl* the local and the mythological are closely wrought together, evenly balanced in emphasis. But in *The Plumed Serpent* the additional mythic and transcendent elements—sermons, ruminations, expanded hymns, expanded ritual—tend to dominate the landscape and local detail preserved from the early version;

in the new context these exist as a thin, transient layer of temporal life, lying between two greater modes of being. *The Plumed Serpent,* as in the passage just quoted, frequently creates abrupt shifts from the local to the transcendental: a strategy appropriate to the prophetic novel designed to shock the reader into an awareness of the need for a religious awakening and renewal. But *Quetzalcoatl* works in another way, with more stress on the concrete details indicative of "spirit of place"—a way illustrated by the scene in chapter 10 in which Cipriano escorts Kate to her home. They come to a corner where there are "several reed huts of the natives":

> Kate was quite used to seeing the donkeys looking over the low dry-stone wall, the black sheep with the curved horns tied to a pole, the boy naked save for his shirt, darting to the corner of the wall that served as a W.C. That was the worst of these little clusters of huts, they always made a smell of human excrement. (*Q,* 159)

But there is something beyond all this: "Kate was used, too, to hearing the music of guitars and fiddles from the corner not far from her house. When she asked Felipa what the music meant, Felipa said it was a dance." Now once again music is emerging from the huts, and "by the light of the moon many figures could be seen, the white clothes of the men."

> "Look!" said Kate. "They are having a baile—a dance!"
> And she stood to watch. But nobody was dancing. Someone was singing— two men. Kate recognized the hymns.
> "They are singing the hymns to Quetzalcoatl," she said to Viedma.
> "What are those?" he replied laconically.
> "The boys sing them to me at the house."
> He did not answer.

Like Felipa, the general is reluctant to speak of the hymns.

> The song ceased, and he would have moved on. But she stood persistently. Then the song started again. And this time it was different. There was a sort of refrain sung by all the men in unison, a deep, brief response of male voices, the response of the audience to the chant. It seemed very wild, very barbaric in its solemnity, and so deeply, resonantly musical that Kate felt wild tears in her heart. The strange sound of men in unanimous deep, wild resolution. As if the hot-blooded soul were speaking from many men at once.
> "That is beautiful," she said, turning to him.

And he proceeds to mythologize the song: " 'It is the song of the moon,' he answered. 'The response of the men to the words of the woman with white breasts, who is the moon-mother' " (*Q,* 159–60).

In this way, throughout *Quetzalcoatl*, the mythological element is closely related to the native scene, with all its local detail. In *The Plumed Serpent* the musical portion of the above scene is omitted: the final version jumps from "a smell of human excrement" to "Kate and Cipriano sat on the verandah of the House of the Cuentas" (*PS*, 233). Then follows a conversation in which Cipriano attempts to persuade Kate to accept the role of "a goddess in the Mexican pantheon." For such a role the preservation of human individuality ceases to matter; what is important is to be swept away into the realms of transcendent being.

One can understand, then, why Katherine Anne Porter in her early review said that *The Plumed Serpent* "seems only incidentally a novel."[21] While this judgment is extreme, it points the way toward a valid distinction between the two versions, or rather, the two novels. If *The Plumed Serpent* is not a traditional novel, what is it? In its combination of prose and poetry, its mingling of narrative and description with songs and hymns, lyrical sermons and eloquent authorial ruminations, in all this *The Plumed Serpent* comes to resemble the mingling of such elements in the prophetic books of the Bible. Indeed *The Plumed Serpent* strives to be such a prophetic book, denouncing the evils of the day and exhorting the people to return to true belief in transcendent powers. From the standpoint of a reader who expects a traditional novel, *The Plumed Serpent* may seem to have grave flaws: we may wish that Ramón's sermons were shorter, Lawrence's own ruminations more restrained, the insistence on Kate's submission moderated, and the cult of the Leader subject to deeper questioning. But all these aspects of the book are part of its prophetic message. Read as a novel of prophecy, with all the abrupt shifts of tone and technique that prophecy manifests, *The Plumed Serpent* may be judged a success, within its own mode of existence.[22]

But *Quetzalcoatl* works in another mode, based upon Lawrence's conception of "the spirit of place," as set forth in the first version of his essay by that title in 1918. During his stay at Chapala, Lawrence was correcting the proofs for this essay as it appeared, greatly revised, in the American edition of his *Studies in Classic American Literature* (1923). This conception of "place" was therefore very close to the center of his mind as he was composing *Quetzalcoatl*. This early version breathes the very spirit of place: the people and the landscape express the emergence of the new consciousness that Lawrence longed to feel arising in the New World. "For every great locality has its own pure daimon," says Lawrence in this essay, "and is conveyed at last into perfected life."

> Every great locality expresses itself perfectly, in its own flowers, its own birds and beasts, lastly its own men, with their perfected works. Mountains

21. "Quetzalcoatl," *New York Herald Tribune Books*, March 7, 1926: sect. 6, pp. 1–2.
22. See John Worthen, *D. H. Lawrence and the Idea of the Novel*, chap. 9, for an account of *The Plumed Serpent* as a work of "prophetic art."

convey themselves in unutterable expressed perfection in the blue gentian flower and in the edelweiss flower, so soft, yet shaped like snow-crystals. The very strata of the earth come to a point of perfect, unutterable concentration in the inherent sapphires and emeralds. It is so with all worlds and all places of the world. We may take it as a law.

"So now," he concludes, "we wait for the fulfillment of the law in the west, the inception of a new era of living. . . . We wait for the miracle, for the new soft wind . . . we can expect our iron ships to put forth vine and tendril and bunches of grapes, like the ship of Dionysos in full sail upon the ocean."[23]

This is the ship that Kate sees in the final chapter of *Quetzalcoatl*, "like the boat of Dionysos crossing the seas and bringing the sprouting of the vine."

---

23. *The Symbolic Meaning: The Uncollected Versions of Studies in Classic American Literature,* ed. Armin Arnold, 30.

14.

D. H. Lawrence

The Second Lady Chatterley

I

*I*T IS A PITY that one of Lawrence's best novels should
have appeared under the inappropriate title *John Thomas
and Lady Jane*. Of course we are told that this is the title
that Lawrence preferred; and it is true that in his letters of 1928 he was doggedly
insisting upon this title, instead of *Lady Chatterley's Lover*.[1] But the change of title
does not refer to the second version, finished in 1927; it refers to the drastically
different third version, for which the title *John Thomas and Lady Jane* might
in some ways seem appropriate, since it is only in the third version that these
names are used. The change in title represented an act of defiance, motivated,
as Lawrence tells us, by Juliette Huxley's dislike of the final manuscript. She
"read the MS. and was very cross, morally so," Lawrence reports, and then she

---

1. *The Letters of D. H. Lawrence,* vol. 6, ed. James T. Boulton and Margaret H. Boulton
with Gerald M. Lacy (Cambridge: Cambridge University Press, 1991), 308, 314–16, 321.
Part I of this essay is reprinted exactly as it appeared in *The Spirit of D. H. Lawrence: Centenary
Studies,* ed. Gāmini Sālgado and G. K. Das, 106–24, except for minor changes in styling and
references to Lawrence's letters, which are now made to the new Cambridge edition. The
essay was composed and accepted for publication in 1982, but publication was delayed until
1988 by the illness and death of Gāmini Sālgado. A note (appended to the proofs) briefly
acknowledged the appearance of the important study by Michael Squires, but revising the
essay was at that time impossible. I have taken account of recent scholarship on the subject,
and have developed in greater detail some of the views broached in the first essay, by adding
here an entirely new part II.

"suggested rather savagely I should call it: John Thomas and Lady Jane." "Many a true word spoken in spite," he adds, "so I promptly called it that. Remains to be seen if Secker and Knopf will stand it."[2] But later he decided, or was persuaded, to use the names only as a subtitle; and finally he agreed to expunge even the subtitle from the proofs of the first, Florentine edition.[3]

The point to remember is that Lawrence never contemplated any title other than *Lady Chatterley's Lover* for his second version, a title that he thought "nice and old-fashioned sounding," and hence apparently, in his view, highly appropriate to this novel, for which Lawrence in his letters shows a remarkably old-fashioned and protective affection: "To me it is beautiful and tender and frail as the naked self is—and I shrink very much even from having it typed."[4] The phrase "old-fashioned sounding" is perhaps a valid clue to the peculiar composition of this version, and a key to its essential difference from the novel that Lawrence ultimately printed. In the second version Lawrence returned to the tradition of George Eliot and Thomas Hardy, both of whom, in their own ways, had written novels of sexual conflict involved with problems of class. *Adam Bede* and *Tess* are the immediate precursors of what is best called (as in the Italian translation) *The Second Lady Chatterley*.[5] It is as though Lawrence had asked himself: how would a novel in this English tradition have developed if George Eliot and Thomas Hardy had been able to present the explicit details of sexual experience and all the language that the common characters really would have used? Such an approach would explain why Lawrence could compose his "English novel" so "patiently,"[6] sitting amid the trees and flowers of the Tuscan countryside, and remembering the country of his youth, which, as he tells Earl Brewster, he had revisited in 1926 with affection and a strange feeling of hope:

> Curiously, I like England again, now I am up in my own regions. It braces me up: and there seems a queer, odd sort of potentiality in the people, especially the common people. One feels in them some odd, unaccustomed sort of plasm twinkling and nascent. They are not finished. And they have a funny sort of purity and gentleness, and at the same time, unbreakableness, that attracts one.[7]

Thus, after experimenting with the draft of the short novel that we know as *The First Lady Chatterley*, Lawrence proceeded to flesh out a full novel of character in the nineteenth-century tradition, with Constance, Clifford, and Parkin developed into fully motivated, fully realized characters who stir a sympathetic

2. *Letters*, 6:315.
3. Ibid., 6:321, 352–53.
4. Ibid., 5:638, 6:29.
5. *Le Tre "Lady Chatterley,"* trans. Carlo Izzo and Giulio Monteleone.
6. Frieda Lawrence, *Not I, but the Wind* (New York: Viking, 1934), 220; *Letters*, 5:601.
7. *Letters*, 5:519–20.

response and draw the reader gradually into a story that deals with the basic problems of English and Western society in the "tragic age"[8] following upon World War I. In the third version, however, which was written after months of miserable illness, the novel becomes a bitter polemic against a dead society, interspersed with glimpses of the fugitive happiness available to two alienated figures who find their lonely consolation in sexual love.

The difference is clear in Connie's motor trip through the Midland landscape, a long passage occupying some ten pages near the middle of the last two versions, a position that allows the passage to act as a revelation of each novel's basic themes and attitudes. In both the scene is dismal, dreary, blackened, oppressive; but in *The Second Lady Chatterley* the scene has still some life, as in Lawrence's letter to Brewster:

> Yet, gradually, it came to have a certain hold over her. It was sad country, with a grey, almost gruesome sadness. Yet it was not dead. It was alive, labouring under a queer, savage weight of dismalness and acquiescence. It was not cowed nor broken, either. No, the very ugliness seemed to have preserved a manly relentlessness in the men, a sort of slow, smouldering courage of death and desperation. But no hope. No immediate hope.[9]

Is there then some hope in the future? Connie, looking at the colliers "going home from the pit, in their underworld grey clothes, with underworld grey faces," is overcome with "fear and dread":

> The future! The far future! Out of the orgy of ugliness and of dismalness and of dreariness, would there, could there ever unfold a flower, a life with beauty in it? . . . After all this that existed at present was gone, smashed and abandoned, repudiated for ever—could the children of miners make a new world, with mystery and sumptuousness in it? Her own children's children, if she had a child to Parkin? She shuddered a little, at the awful necessity for transition. (*2LC*, 156–57)

The word *transition* marks the basic difference between the last two versions, for in Connie's relation to Parkin lies the basis of the transition, the possibility of a sympathy, even a love, between individuals of the now severed classes. That is why Parkin, however rebellious, must still be one of the people, must be seen living with his mother and the Tewsons, must speak their dialect consistently. Connie herself makes the point neatly in *The First Lady Chatterley*, when she says that she "must not try to make" of Parkin, "even in the mildest form, a gentleman. It would only start a confusion. No! She must not even try to make him develop along those lines, the lines of educated consciousness. She must

8. The phrase occurs in the opening sentence of all three versions.
9. *John Thomas and Lady Jane* (London: Heinemann, 1972), 150; hereafter cited as *2LC*.

leave him to his own way. His instinct was against education. His instinct made him refuse to speak King's English, even to her."[10] And again, a few pages later in this version, as she thinks of the impossibility of her becoming a "working man's wife": "He would probably begin speaking King's English—and that would be the first step to his undoing. No no! He must never be uplifted. He must never be brought one stride nearer to Clifford" (*1LC,* 62). And yet in the third version, Lawrence proceeds with every step in Parkin's undoing.

In the second version, which clings to this initial principle of Parkin's creation, Connie thinks of Parkin with a mingling of compassion and desire as she drives through the region, while her feelings flow out to embrace the whole "disfigured countryside, and the disfigured, strange, almost wraithlike populace. . . . Ugliness incarnate, they seemed. And yet alive!" (*2LC,* 157). And as her feelings embrace the scene, she is able to express her struggling hope in the words of one of Lawrence's most moving and beautiful visions of prophecy:

> She shuddered again at the thought of them: and even her Parkin was one of them. Creatures of another element, they did not really live, they only subserved the coal, as the steel-workers subserved the steel, the workers in the potteries, the clay. Men not men, but merely the animae of coal and steel, iron and clay. Strange fauna of the mineral elements, of carbon and iron and silicon!
>
> If ever they did emerge, it would be with weird luxuriance, something in heavy contrast to what they were now. From ugliness incarnate, they would bring forth, perhaps, a luxuriant, uncanny beauty, some of the beauty that must have been in the great ferns and giant mosses of which the coal was made: some of the beauty of the weight and the resistance of iron, and the blueness of steel, and the iridescence of glass. When at last they had risen from subservience to the mineral elements, and were really animate, when they really *used* the iron, for the flowering of their own bodies and anima, instead of, as now, being used by it. Now the iron and the coal used them, not they the iron and the coal. (*2LC,* 158)

In the third version of the novel, however, all this atmosphere of sympathy and tenderness and half-hope is extinguished: the last paragraph above is removed, while some of its details are absorbed into an expansion of the earlier paragraph that sees the men as "fauna of the mineral elements." Now Lawrence concludes: "They had perhaps some of the weird, inhuman beauty of minerals, the lustre of coal, the weight and blueness and resistance of iron, the transparency of glass. Elemental creatures, weird and distorted, of the mineral world! They belonged to the coal, the iron, the clay, as fish belong to the sea and worms to dead wood. The anima of mineral disintegration!"[11]

10. *The First Lady Chatterley* (London: Heinemann, 1972), 53; hereafter cited as *1LC.*
11. *Lady Chatterley's Lover* (London: Heinemann, 1960), 146–47; hereafter cited as *3LC.* I have left the citations to this edition as they originally appeared, but I have compared the

In the third version, Connie's love for a man of the people is unable to spread out over the landscape and the populace, for Parkin has been transformed into Mellors, a grammar-school boy, a lieutenant (almost a captain) in the army, a man who can, and frequently does, speak "King's English," a man who has lived in India and Egypt—"quite the gentleman, really quite the gentleman!" as Ivy Bolton says (*3LC*, 133)—and thus a man deracinated from the region, the people, and the landscape of his birth. Lawrence stresses the significance of the change:

> She felt again in a wave of terror the grey, gritty hopelessness of it all. With such creatures for the industrial masses, and the upper classes as she knew them, there was no hope, no hope any more. . . .
> Yet Mellors had come out of all this!—Yes, but he was as apart from it all as she was. Even in him there was no fellowship left. It was dead. The fellowship was dead. There was only apartness and hopelessness, as far as all this was concerned. (*3LC*, 140–41)

Thus the love affair loses the basic function in the novel which Lawrence seems to have discovered near the very close of his first, experimental version, as he tries to sum up the direction in which his thoughts are moving. Connie, he writes, "wanted to pity Parkin and be maternally kind to him, keeping her deeper self shut off and the mysterious stream that can flow all the time between man and woman walled back." This is the "stream of desire," which, he adds, "is the stream of life itself." "It is that which unites us. It is that, even, which makes a nation a nation: the soft, invisible desire of people making a great swarm like a hive of bees. The clue is some unconscious, living idea which draws multitudes of men in a stream of desire" (*1LC*, 198). Therefore, in *The Second Lady Chatterley*, the love affair must constantly be related, not only to birds, beasts, and flowers, but also to the novel's prophetic hope for a new civilization, replacing the one that the war has left in ruins. For the war is only the precipitating, immediate cause of the disaster: the true cause lies deeper, in the barriers of class and industry that sever the flow of life.

In all three versions, Clifford is treated not simply as a wounded victim of the war, but also as a man wounded in his psyche by his upper-class breeding and position. As Lawrence explains rather awkwardly in the first draft, through the thoughts of Constance:

> She thought she had loved Clifford. And she had loved him. But, she knew it now, not with her heart. Her heart had never wakened to him, and left to him, never would have wakened. No, not if he had never been to the war at all.—His terrible accident, his paralysis or whatever it was, was really

---

quoted passages with the new Cambridge edition; there are numerous variations in punctuation and phrasing, but none that affect the argument.

> symbolical in him. He was always paralysed, in some part of him. That part
> in a man which can wake a woman's heart once and for all was always dead
> in him. As it is dead in thousands of men like him. All the women who have
> men like him live with unawakened hearts. (*1LC,* 69)

Although this idea underlies all three versions, the treatment of Clifford in the
second version is remarkably different from that in the other two, where Clifford's "symbolical" function is stressed throughout, and stressed with particular
bitterness in the final version. But in *The Second Lady Chatterley,* in accord with its
mode as a novel of character in the English tradition, the symbolical function of
Clifford emerges only tacitly and gradually, while for most of the novel Lawrence
makes a great effort to hold the reader's sympathy with Clifford, as the victim
of a disaster that has wounded a whole society. The presence of the war, as a
constant memory, is kept before us persistently, by dozens of large and small
reminders, in a way that is not characteristic of the other two versions. The war
thus runs through the second version like a disease in the stream of life. This is
part of the naturalistic action and motivation of this version: the suffering has a
realistic cause.

In keeping with this naturalistic mode, the breaking of Connie's relationship
with Clifford is gradual, as, more and more, the frustration of her natural instincts
drains her vitality, and the constant tending of Clifford becomes an unbearable
burden. And when at last a nurse is hired, we are told that Clifford "resented"
the change "deeply." "It made a cleavage through his feeling for her, that she
had relinquished his wrecked body into the hands of a stranger. He never any
more felt the close oneness between himself and his wife."

> Constance knew, but did not really mind. It was a relief to her. That other
> oneness had almost destroyed her. Sometimes, upstairs, she would sing to
> herself the song: 'Touch not the nettle!' It has a refrain: 'for the bonds of
> love are ill to loose.' She had never quite understood that, till lately, when
> she was trying to extricate herself from the intense personal love that was
> between her and Clifford. (*2LC,* 79)

Lawrence is distinguishing an "intense personal love" from a sexual love—but
in the third version even this kind of intense love is gone. Indeed, the handling
of the revised passage here is indicative of the ways in which, throughout the
final version, Lawrence goes about removing all sympathy from Clifford and
trivializing the "love" that once existed between the pair. Now, we hear, Clifford,
"never quite forgave Connie for giving up her personal care of him to a strange
hired woman." It is one thing to "resent"; something else never to forgive. It
is one thing to remember Clifford's "wrecked body"; quite something else to
speak of "personal care," as in a nursing home. And finally, it is one thing to
resist turning one's body over to a stranger; but there is an added element of
class antagonism in resisting the attention of a "hired woman." "It killed, he

said to himself, the real flower of the intimacy between him and her. But Connie didn't mind that. The fine flower of their intimacy was to her rather like an orchid, a bulb stuck parasitic on her tree of life, and producing, to her eyes, a rather shabby flower" (*3LC*, 76). After this, the bonds of love may still be "ill to loose," but they come apart much more easily.

In the second version the loosing of these bonds is shown to be disastrous for Clifford: "It was Connie's gradual abandonment of all her intimate duties towards him, that had finally hardened Clifford's heart, and cut him off from her, emotionally" (*2LC*, 134–35). The relation with Parkin has now begun, and Clifford feels the change, though not knowing the cause. But he notices when, for the first time, she forgets to kiss him goodnight:

> He gazed angrily at the door-panels, too angry to ring as yet for Mrs Bolton. Ah well! Let the last vestiges of the old love disappear! He could not make love to her! and therefore she was withdrawing every tiny show of love. She forgot, no doubt. But the forgetfulness was part of her whole intention.
>
> Ah well! He was a man, and asked charity from nobody, not even his wife! He was a net-work of nerves, it is true, and suffered terrible nervous torments of fear and gloom, dread of death, dread of the future. (*2LC*, 135)

Throughout the middle of the second version, Clifford's suffering and torment are borne in upon us, especially in the episode where Connie returns from a visit with Parkin, and Clifford meets her in his wheelchair at the top of the drive, amid "the wild, uncanny disturbance of an English spring." "Suddenly she struck him as lovely": she has now all the freshness and vitality of the season itself. She tells him she "went fast asleep," "in the keeper's hut, sitting in the sunshine." Of course, it was not the hut where the pheasants are tended: it was the keeper's own cottage, where, in a tranquil, nonerotic scene, she has played the role of wife, as the destruction of the picture of Parkin and Bertha has suggested.

> 'And was the keeper there?' asked Clifford.
> 'Not at the hut,' she said. 'Why didn't you come and meet me? I kept expecting to hear the chair.'
> 'I didn't know where you'd gone,' he said. 'And on a day like this— especially an evening like this—' he looked up into the sky—'I was by no means sure you would want me and my chair.'
> 'Why not?' she said quickly. 'I was thinking of you, as I came home, and wondering if you were out of doors, as you ought to be.'

But the only possible thought of Clifford has been contained in Parkin's warning: "I won't come to th' gate with you, for fear there's somebody in th' park."

> 'If there were any point in my being out of doors!' [Clifford] said, with a touch of bitterness. 'You look so lovely this evening, Connie! You want something different from me to come and meet you.'

> She stopped, and looked at him.
> 'Why, Clifford?' she said.
> 'Why!' he answered ironically. 'A bath-chair, in the month of May! There goes the cuckoo, he's at it all day! I can't bear May.'

And again, as she tries to restrain his bitterness: "The cuckoo only jeers at me, even the rooks. . . . Why doesn't somebody shoot me!" Though Clifford has earlier suggested that she ought to take a lover, if she must, the cry of the cuckoo can only intensify his "nervous anger and misery" as he says, "I ought to be shot, as a horse with broken legs is shot" (*2LC*, 186–88).

This whole episode is removed in the third version, with the result that the subsequent episode where Clifford loses his temper with the balky motorized chair stands out starkly as an example of utterly outrageous behavior. Lawrence has also taken steps to make Clifford even more unpleasant, for in the final version he has accentuated the anger by repeating the word "snapped" and adding phrases like "savage impatience" and "rigid with anger" (*3LC*, 172–74). Most important, however, is the removal of one significant aspect of the second version that adds a touch of humanity to the scene—and at the same time reminds us of the war. Connie has been sitting on a bank and watching the men work with the chair:

> But she was amused once more by the busy, interested freemasonry of men, as soon as it was a question of machinery. Then indeed class differences broke down a little. Parkin was no longer a gamekeeper: he was much freer and more active, perhaps as when he was in the war, and drove a lorry. And Clifford was the officer, a little impatient with the Tommy, a bit out of temper, but not at all the employer. (*2LC*, 209)

This takes a great deal of the sting out of the anger, and it follows naturally to hear that Clifford "commanded" Parkin to let go of the machine, that "the keeper dropped a pace into the rear," and that "Parkin stepped smartly aside, like a soldier" (*2LC*, 210–11). But in version three, "commanded" is replaced by "snarled," and the "soldierly" phrases are gone (*3LC*, 174–75). Finally, Clifford's effort at an apology comes through rather well in version two, with a little help from Connie:

> 'I'm afraid I rather lost my temper with the infernal thing!' said Clifford at last.
> 'It is annoying!' said Constance.
> 'Do you mind pushing me home, Parkin?' said Clifford. 'And excuse anything I said,' he added rather offhand.
> 'It's nothing to me, Sir Clifford!' (*2LC*, 211)

But in version three, everything becomes stiff and haughty, on both sides:

'I expect she'll have to be pushed,' said Clifford at last, with an affectation of *sang froid*.

No answer. Mellors' abstracted face looked as if he had heard nothing. Connie glanced anxiously at him. Clifford too glanced round.

'Do you mind pushing her home, Mellors!' he said in a cold, superior tone. 'I hope I have said nothing to offend you,' he added, in a tone of dislike.

'Nothing at all, Sir Clifford! Do you want me to push that chair?'

'If you please.' (*3LC*, 174–75)

Thus Mellors has his revenge by forcing Clifford to ask him, in effect, three times, if he will push the chair. But then, we remember, Mellors was himself an officer in the army. This is almost a contest of equals; in the end, neither Clifford nor Mellors can win our sympathy here, whereas the power of the earlier version of this incident lies in the way in which Parkin and Clifford, as well as Connie, display subtle and complex human responses in their difficult relationship.

Even at the close of version two Lawrence manages to maintain something of the earlier view of Clifford as victim. When Connie returns to Wragby after her journey to the continent, as she has promised (and it is significant that in this version she has enough vestigial feeling for Clifford to keep this promise), Clifford goes into a total collapse after his effort to meet her at the station and demonstrate his new accomplishment at walking with crutches. Mrs. Bolton explains his collapse in terms that link Clifford with his whole wounded generation of men:

'Was it too much for him?' asked Connie, fear-struck.

'Oh, I don't think so! But he suffers from these lapses of energy. You remember he always did. It seems as if men do suffer that way since the war, even men who were never touched, or never even in the war at all. But their energy collapses, without anything being wrong with them.' . . .

Connie was frightened. . . . Clifford seemed as if his very soul were paralysed; and he knew it, his eyes were haunted with fear and irritable horror. He hated Connie to see him like that. She had to leave him. (*2LC*, 313)

The episode thus hovers ambiguously between the feelings of Connie and Clifford, as though some threads were still remaining of those old bonds. The whole scene forms the strongest possible contrast with the long scene of "male hysteria" that we are forced to watch in version three, after Clifford receives the letter telling him that she will not return to Wragby because she is in love with another man (*3LC*, 266–69).

Forced to watch: this phrase has perhaps unconsciously given my own impression of how one is likely to read the third version, after a careful reading of version two. The changes made in the third version may well come to seem almost acts of vandalism—the deliberate destruction of the bonds of sympathy that gradually weave version two into an impressive unity, in tune with the forces of nature. *The Second Lady Chatterley* develops a natural rhythm of growth and change, as the forces of nature work gradually to slough off, however painfully, the dying and useless remnants of the old consciousness. But in version three the old consciousness does not thus die away: it is violently rejected, by the authorial voice, as well as by the voices of Connie and Mellors.

The result is a pervasive withdrawal of sympathy, even in minor scenes, such as the visit that Connie pays to Mrs. Flint at Marehay Farm. In version two this is a happy visit. Connie likes Mrs. Flint, plays with the baby, finds "the quiet female atmosphere . . . infinitely soothing." "And the two women enjoyed themselves, talking about the baby, and everything that came up" (*2LC*, 125). But in version three we learn that Connie at the outset "suspected" Mrs. Flint "of being rather a false little thing," and the baby becomes "a perky little thing" with "cheeky pale-blue eyes," and the child is "surrounded with rag dolls and other toys in modern excess" (*3LC*, 118–19). Mrs. Flint, described as a former schoolteacher in both versions, is at the close of version three made to put on schoolteacherly airs, with regard to her farmer-husband. In version two, as Connie is leaving, she sees the auriculas blooming in the front garden and exclaims simply, "Oh, how pretty!" "The recklesses?" Mrs. Flint replies. "Yes, aren't they a show!" But in version three Connie sees the flowers and remarks, "Lovely auriculas." " 'Recklesses, as Luke calls them,' laughed Mrs. Flint." In version two the local word passes unremarked in an atmosphere of sympathy and intimacy. The episode thus prepares the way for the domestic scene where Connie sleeps in Parkin's lap: she has in fact much in common with the farmer's wife.

More serious in its impact upon the novel is the hardening of attitude that occurs when Parkin is transformed into Mellors, with the difference that comes out near the close, when the gamekeeper, Connie, and her sister Hilda meet in the keeper's cottage. In version two the conversation is tense, embarrassed, uncomfortable; everyone is making a great effort to keep the situation under control. Flashes of anger or resentment or worry leap out, but at the end:

> Suddenly Hilda leaned over the side of the car, holding out her hand.
> 'Good-night, Mr Parkin!' she said. He strode up, and took her hand.
> 'Good-night!' he said.
> 'If you feel you're right—' she said, 'I suppose nobody has any business to interfere.' (*2LC*, 269)

In version three Mellors and Hilda quarrel violently, with Mellors lashing out at Hilda in a furious tirade that covers half a page (*3LC*, 226). After this, there can be no handshake at the end.

Such examples are symptoms of a hardening of attitude that is making its way through the entire body of version three. We sense the difference in the opening chapter of the final version, where the two-and-a-half-page prelude to life at Wragby has been expanded to eight pages, in which Connie and Hilda are introduced to sexual life in prewar Germany, while most of the chapter is given over to a satirical account of how "ridiculous" everything seemed in the prewar years and even during the early years of the war itself—"ridiculous" because of the superficiality and triviality of all emotions and relationships:

> And the authorities felt ridiculous, and behaved in a rather ridiculous fashion, and it was all a mad hatter's tea-party for a while. Till things developed over there, and Lloyd George came to save the situation over here. And this surpassed even ridicule, the flippant young laughed no more.
>
> In 1916 Herbert Chatterley [the elder brother] was killed, so Clifford became heir. He was terrified even of this. (*3LC*, 11)

Lawrence saves his final touch of ridicule for the contemptuous final sentence of the chapter: "But early in 1918 Clifford was shipped home smashed, and there was no child. And Sir Geoffrey [the father] died of chagrin."

This acrid sense of the "ridiculous" plays no part in the opening chapter of *The Second Lady Chatterley*. After two and a half pages of prelude, Lawrence takes the couple at once to Wragby, with these ominous words: "But by the time the *Untergang des Abendlands* appeared, Clifford was a smashed man, and by the time Constance became mistress of Wragby, cold ash had begun to blanket the glow of the war fervour. It was the day after, the grey morrow for which no thought had been taken" (*2LC*, 3). The allusion to Spengler sets the theme: the war has set in motion, or rather, has accelerated, the decline of the West, and what lies before us is the story of human beings caught in that decline. Connie's deep unhappiness is gradually revealed by her decline in vitality, worrisome to her father, her sister, and her aunt, and ultimately to Clifford, after her father has spoken to him about Connie's health.

The long opening movement of version two is brought to a climax in the powerful chapter 5, which begins with Connie's feeling of "indefinable dread" at the approach of Christmas. "But perhaps that was because Clifford had been wounded on Christmas day" (*2LC*, 52). It is a brief touch, but enough. Clifford is a victim, like his whole generation of men—as the conversations in this chapter will reveal, especially in the prophetic words of Tommy Dukes, the sensitive brigadier general, who is "fond of Clifford," has a sort of "tenderness" for Lady Eva, and understands at once Connie's desire to be "where a bit of life flowed."

> 'You're quite right, Connie!' said Dukes, looking at her with his shrewd eyes. 'A flow of life, and contact! We've never had proper human contact— we've never been civilised enough. We're not civilised enough even now, to be able to touch one another. We start away, like suspicious hairy animals. The next civilisation will be based on the inspiration of touch: believe me—But we shall never live to see it, so why talk about it?'

But when Connie reminds him that he never seems to want "to touch anybody," Dukes looks at her in such a way that she is emotionally touched: "He looked at her oddly, and her heart gave a queer lurch. This man might have been in love with her—if he'd had enough hope, if the weight of disillusion hadn't been too heavy." Like the miners, Dukes has still some spark of life inside the covering ashes; and so he is given a speech that expresses the heart of Lawrence's evangelistic mission:

> there *will* be a new civilisation, the very antithesis of tabloids and aeroplanes: believe me! There will be a civilisation based on the mystery of touch, and all that that means; a field of consciousness which hasn't yet opened into existence. *We're* too much afraid of it—oh, stiff as wood, with fear! . . . Oh, there'll be a democracy—the democracy of touch. For the few who survive the fear of it. (*2LC,* 57–58)

Then, as the conversation turns upon one of Lawrence's favorite biblical texts, the *noli me tangere,* Connie says to Dukes, "You mean you're not touchable, either," thus setting in flow a current of thought that lies at the heart of this version: "I suppose that's what I do mean," Dukes answers. "Don't touch me! for I am not yet ascended unto the Father! Perhaps that's about where we stand."

> The dance came to an end, and he left her. But vaguely in her conscious-ness the words of Jesus were moving: '*Noli me tangere!* Touch me not! for I am not yet ascended unto the Father!' What did they mean?
> It meant they had died, these men. In the war, finally, they had died. And though they were still walking about in the flesh, and were still struggling for the life that should be theirs, after the resurrection, they had not yet got the body of the new life. . . .
> How terrible the story of Jesus! It was the epitome of the story of all men. They had all been crucified, these men: all except Jack, who had balked it. But Clifford and Tommy Dukes and even Winterslow, they had all been killed, in some subtle way. And it was the strange, dim, grey era of the resurrection, with them, before the ascension into new life.
> And perhaps they would never ascend really into life. They would remain the shadowy, almost incorporeal beings of the era between the rolling open of the tomb, and the ascending into the firmament of a new body. They lived and walked and spoke, but theirs was still the old, tortured body that could not be touched. (*2LC,* 61–62)

In version three all this apocalyptic talk is removed—and is replaced by empty conversation satirizing the utter desiccation of the upper classes and the intellectuals, a fierce attack brought to a climax by the introduction of the playwright Michaelis and the nasty episode of Connie's "affair" with him. A reading of chapter 5 in version two along with chapters 4 and 5 in version three is in itself enough to show the immense difference between the two novels—yes, different novels, not truly versions, for they do not connect at heart. It is clear from the above passage that *The Second Lady Chatterley* is working from the heart of Lawrence's deepest hopes and beliefs: it leads inevitably into *The Man Who Died* and *Apocalypse*. *The Third Lady Chatterley* is, by comparison, a series of symbolic events, with commentary.

We have, then, essentially, two different novels, two different kinds of novel. Each defines its own nature in ways that indicate how clearly Lawrence knows his craft. The clue in *The Second Lady Chatterley* is given in the conversation, two-thirds of the way through the book, where Connie and Clifford discuss his liking for "the ultra-modern, so-called futuristic writers, who grouped round Joyce or Proust," and Connie declares that *Ulysses* "is a perverse activity of the will." "My dear Connie," Clifford replies, "I know your nature is evangelical." The point is so important that Clifford repeats it three times here, saying that she speaks "like an angel and an evangel," calling her "my evangelical little wife" and "an evangelist by profession" (*2LC*, 217–18). It seems right, then, to see *The Second Lady Chatterley* as an "evangelical" novel, a work that enters deeply into the woes of the human race, feels the inevitable forces of change at work, knows the agony of change, and yet foresees the possibility of a new, brighter, happier age ahead—however far in the future. Although this mode of writing will allow some measure of denunciation and bitterness (as in the gospels), the central tendency will be much gentler, in accord with the warning that Lawrence issues about a third of the way through: "Whoever wants life must go softly towards life, softly as one would go towards a deer and a fawn that was nestling under a tree. One gesture of violence, one violent assertion of self-will, and life is gone" (*2LC*, 107).

In *The Third Lady Chatterley*, Lawrence has chosen to compose a polemical, frequently satirical novel, in which all figures, except Connie and to some extent Mellors, operate as types or symbols, with all the life concentrated in the now considerably extended sexual episodes. Again, Lawrence makes his method clear, in a little essay on the novel that comes about one-third of the way along, as Lawrence declares that "even satire is a form of sympathy."

> It is the way our sympathy flows and recoils that really determines our lives. And here lies the vast importance of the novel, properly handled. It can inform and lead into new places the flow of our sympathetic consciousness, and it can lead our sympathy away in recoil from things gone dead. Therefore, the novel, properly handled, can reveal the most secret places of life: for it is in the passional secret places of life, above all, that the tide of sensitive awareness needs to ebb and flow, cleansing and freshening. (*3LC*, 92)

This novel, then, is being constructed in episodes of flow and recoil, in an effort to move all sympathy toward Connie's torment and her rediscovery of life in the sexual episodes.

This procedure is revealed quite early in *The Third Lady Chatterley,* where Connie, though afflicted by a "sense of deep physical injustice," goes on with her intimate tending of her husband's needs. But, we hear, "The physical sense of injustice is a dangerous feeling, once it is awakened. It must have outlet, or it eats away the one in whom it is aroused. Poor Clifford, he was not to blame. His was the greater misfortune. It was all part of the general catastrophe" (*3LC,* 65). So far, this echoes the sympathetic approach of *The Second Lady Chatterley.* But now Lawrence deliberately turns the reader in another direction: "And yet was he not in a way to blame? This lack of warmth, this lack of the simple, warm, physical contact, was he not to blame for that? He was never really warm, nor even kind, only thoughtful, considerate, in a well-bred, cold sort of way!" And then, as Connie's "sense of rebellion" smolders, the recoil moves into bitter denunciation and ridicule, her voice blending with the authorial voice:

> Even Clifford's cool and contactless assurance that he belonged to the ruling class didn't prevent his tongue lolling out of his mouth, as he panted after the bitch-goddess [success]. After all, Michaelis was really more dignified in the matter, and far, far more successful. Really, if you looked closely at Clifford, he was a buffoon, and a buffoon is more humiliating than a bounder.
>
> As between the two men, Michaelis really had far more use for her than Clifford had. He had even more need of her. Any good nurse can attend to crippled legs! And as for the heroic effort, Michaelis was a heroic rat, and Clifford was very much of a poodle showing off. (*3LC,* 66)

It is important to note how all these changes, and especially the introduction of Michaelis, alter the "evangelical" conception of Connie's character that runs throughout *The Second Lady Chatterley:* her basic innocence, her sensitive response to nature, her instinctive sympathy with other human beings, including Clifford, her longing for "a God" to whom she could open her heart, and the epiphany of this possibility as she glimpses Parkin washing his body behind the cottage: "And she felt again there was God on earth; or gods." "The sudden sense of pure beauty, beauty that was active and alive, had put worship in her heart again" (*2LC,* 34, 44). It is her evangelical nature that makes it right for Lawrence to retain, as part of his conclusion, the visit of Connie to Parkin at the Tewsons' home in Sheffield, for the episode is essential in showing the effort to create a sympathy between the classes—and at the same time the impossibility of breaking through the barriers, right now. Finally, the pathetic meeting of the lovers at Hucknall is imbued with Connie's evangelical sadness ("Jesus wept"): "They went into the dark church together. It was empty. And she looked at the little slab behind which rests the pinch of dust which was Byron's heart: in that thrice-dismal Hucknall Torkard. The sense of the greatness of human mistakes made her want to cry" (*2LC,* 367–68). The image of Byron's withered heart sets the necessary somber undertone. Despite their efforts to achieve a union, the time has not yet come, as Dukes has said.

In contrast with the nuances of this finale, we have the long, explicit closing letter from Mellors to Connie, with its contempt for "the mass of people" and its view of love as a refuge from a doomed society:

> There's a bad time coming. There's a bad time coming, boys, there's a bad time coming! If things go on as they are, there's nothing lies in the future but death and destruction, for these industrial masses. I feel my inside turn to water sometimes, and there you are, going to have a child by me. But never mind. All the bad times that ever have been, haven't been able to blow the crocus out: not even the love of women. So they won't be able to blow out my wanting you, nor the little glow there is between you and me. We'll be together next year. (*3LC*, 328)

Probably so: after all, Mellors can pass for a gentleman.

II

The preceding essay was written in 1982, before the appearance of the detailed study of all three versions of the novel by Michael Squires (1983), a work preceded by his separate essay on the final version as a pastoral novel (1974); these were followed by his edition of the third version in the Cambridge series (1993) and by his Penguin edition of this same version (1994).[12] These are all excellent works, performed with fine scholarly and critical intelligence, and giving, on the whole, a balanced comparison of the last two versions. Squires sees many of the virtues of the second version, particularly the complex and appealing characterization of Parkin, and he notes that one may often wish "that Lawrence had preserved the fluency and inspiration of version two, where his methods best discover Connie's rich responses." At the same time he recognizes many flaws in the final version: the flattening and hardening of Clifford's character, and the presence of a narrative voice that is frequently strident, cynical, and dogmatic, along with the use of Mellors as a similar voice of denunciation. He suggests that Lawrence might have written a better novel if he had chosen

---

12. Michael Squires, *The Creation of Lady Chatterley's Lover* and *The Pastoral Novel: Studies in George Eliot, Thomas Hardy, and D. H. Lawrence;* D. H. Lawrence, *Lady Chatterley's Lover: A Propos of "Lady Chatterley's Lover,"* ed. Michael Squires; references are to the Penguin edition, hereafter cited by the number 3 before page numbers.

Other comparisons of the three versions have been given by Philip M. Weinstein, "Choosing between the Quick and the Dead: Three Versions of *Lady Chatterley's Lover*"; by Kingsley Widmer, "The Pertinence of Modern Pastoral: The Three Versions of *Lady Chatterley's Lover*"; by Peter Scheckner, *Class, Politics, and the Individual: A Study of the Major Works of D. H. Lawrence,* chap. 4; and by Worthen, *D. H. Lawrence and the Idea of the Novel,* chap. 10, where Worthen stresses the "polemic," "crusading" qualities of version three. An effective appraisal of the weaknesses in the final version has been given by Ian Gregor, "The Novel as Prophecy: *Lady Chatterley's Lover* (1928)."

simply to revise version two, instead of rewriting the novel from a different perspective.[13]

Nevertheless, Squires comes out strongly in praise of the "fine symmetry of the novel's design" in the final version: "Lawrence unifies the novel by blending the voices and thoughts of the characters with the narrator's darker tones," with the result that "the ending of version three, though imperfect, is strongest, sounding again the novel's central concerns" in the long closing letter by Mellors.[14] This favorable judgment, surprising after Squires's shrewd account of the novel's flaws, may be valid, but only when we consider that Lawrence, in creating version three, had decided to produce a polemical novel, replacing the pastoral and evangelical novel that constitutes version two. Pastoral and evangelical: we should examine first the pastoral aspect that Squires has well explored in relation to the traditional pattern of withdrawal from a corrupt society into a healing and renewing center of natural vitality, with return to a better life.[15] What we have in version three is only the remnant of the full pastoral action set forth in version two, which remedies the serious lack that Squires at one point discerns in version three. Lawrence, he says,

> wanted to demonstrate the relation between a phallic marriage and the larger cosmos, to show that sexuality must acknowledge its roots in the daily and seasonal rhythms of the cosmos. *Lady Chatterley*'s concern with tenderness and touch ought to express this "cosmic" dimension of sexuality; it ought to make fully persuasive the connection between opening leaves and opening desire, between daily rhythms and the progression of desire, between religious ritual and sexual rite.

"In this crucial way," he concludes, "the novel fails."[16]

But version two does not thus fail: it fulfills the need that Lawrence describes in a passage from *A Propos of "Lady Chatterley's Lover"*:

> Augustine said that God created the universe new every day: to the living, emotional soul, this is true. Every dawn dawns upon an entirely new universe, every Easter lights up an entirely new glory of a new world opening in utterly new flower. . . . The long neuter spell of Lent, when the blood is low, and the delight of the Easter kiss, the sexual revel of spring, the passion of midsummer, the slow recoil, revolt, and grief of autumn, greyness again, then the sharp stimulus of winter, of the long nights. Sex goes through the rhythm of the year, in man and woman, ceaselessly changing: the rhythm of the sun in his relation to the earth.[17]

13. Squires, *Creation*, 141, 104.
14. Ibid., 15, 52.
15. Squires, *Pastoral Novel*, chap. 9.
16. Squires, *Creation*, 177.
17. Quoted from the Penguin edition, 323.

This is the pastoral action that runs throughout version two, following explicitly the movement of the seasons and the planets. The movement begins in chapter 3, when, in "the late autumn . . . came a few very beautiful sunny days," and Lawrence creates the pastoral vision of a harmony that once prevailed:

> The soft, warm wooliness of the uncanny November day seemed utterly unreal to her, in its thick, soft-gold sunlight and thick gossamer atmosphere. The park, with its oak-trees and sere grass, sheep feeding in silence on the slope, and the near distance bluey, an opalescent haze showing through it the last yellow and brown of oak-leaves, seemed unreal, a vision from the past. It was a ghost-day returned from the late eighteenth century, a day such as lingers in the old English aquatints. The English landscape had revealed itself then, in its real soft beauty. And sometimes the revelation stealthily disclosed itself again, like a ghost, a *revenant*.[18]

"To the left," Lawrence continues, "the wood was thick with hazels and trees." But "to the right, up to the knoll, it was bare save for a few stalky, ricketty-looking oak saplings. All the timber had been cut up by Sir Geoffrey, for the war. Naked and forlorn the big hill looked" (2:26). The scene becomes a symbol of the war's destructive effects upon nature and human life, and particularly upon Clifford—opening a theme that runs relentlessly throughout this version.

Into this damaged pastoral scene strides a new force, "the gamekeeper, dressed in greenish velveteen corduroy" (2:34), who then pushes the chair, helping it up the incline. A glance reveals to Parkin the "unconscious spark of appeal" (2:35) in the eyes of Connie, who admires the antique garb of Parkin and his strength: "Constance liked the colour of his greenish velveteen corduroys, with the fawn cloth leggings. It was the old colour for gamekeepers, but one rarely saw it nowadays. What a strong back the man had!" (2:36).

Version three delays the couple's viewing of this landscape until chapter 5 (3:41), where it occurs "on a frosty morning with a little February sun," in a scene that has lost its "unreal" vision. When Mellors appears the stress falls, not upon his "dark green velveteen," but upon his dignified appearance, "like a gentleman." "He might almost be a gentleman." "He looked like a free soldier rather than a servant" (3:46–47). Thus Lawrence begins to close the gap between the gamekeeper's class and Connie's, begins the process of changing Parkin into an educated army officer with worldwide experience, a figure who can dominate his setting and his lover, and who can utter fierce denunciations of society.

In version two the calendar now moves in chapter 4 from the "last days of autumn . . . into the gloom of winter" (2:40), as Connie's desperate inner rage is revealed, her "evil days." This mood is continued when Connie intervenes in the quarrel between the keeper and his daughter over the shooting of a cat—a scene

---

18. *John Thomas and Lady Jane: The Second Version of Lady Chatterley's Lover* (London and New York: Penguin Books, 1973), 25; hereafter cited by the number 2 before page numbers.

that reinforces her "dislike of the common people" (2:49). But soon, when she goes on her errand to the keeper's cottage, she has her vision of Parkin washing himself, "stripped to the waist," revealing "the white arch of life" described in phallic terms. It is a pagan vision of "the world of gods, cleaving through the gloom like a revelation" (2:50–51). The depth of Connie's despair has produced an extravagant rebound into an atmosphere of "worship."

All this in version two prepares the way for the powerful chapter 5, firmly set in the Christmas season by the whole opening paragraph, which concludes thus: "The approach of Christmas always inspired her with indefinable dread, as if something bad were going to happen. But perhaps that was because Clifford had been wounded on Christmas day. Anyhow, she had to prepare for mild festivities" (2:58). Then she remembers: "In the wood she had seen a holly tree with many red berries. It was very bright, and very gay, with the jolliness of the pre-christian Christmas, the heathen mid-winter excitement." The keeper appears, bearing the holly, confirming his association with nature and ancient ritual: "The gamekeeper, in his dark velveteens and red face, seemed part of the wild outdoors, as he stood and watched" (2:59). "Since the war, Christmas nauseated her" (2:59), but Connie gradually comes to realize, through the prophetic utterances of Tommy Dukes, that the season holds more than the memory of death, more than the thought of Jesus and these men as victims. Dukes, as we have seen in the first part of this essay, brings a message of hope, belief that somehow, sometime, a "new civilization" with a "democracy of touch" will come to be (2:65). Connie broods over the prophecy of "touch," remembering the *noli me tangere,* the words spoken by the risen Christ to Mary Magdalene. "What did they mean?"

> It meant they had died, these men. In the war, finally, they had died. And though they were still walking about in the flesh, and were still struggling for the life that should be theirs after the resurrection, they had not yet got the body of the new life. . . .
> And perhaps they would never ascend really into life. They would remain the shadowy, almost incorporeal beings of the era between the rolling open of the tomb, and the ascending into the firmament of a new body. (2:68–69)

But Dukes now asserts his belief "in the resurrection of Man, and the Son of Man," though what he has in mind is not the traditional view; what he is preaching is the Lawrentian view of the renewal of the body in this life. Dukes does not exactly deny the traditional view of the survival of the spirit, but this is not for him "a poignant truth." The "poignant truth, for me is the resurrection of the body. . . . ultimately, to me there is one body: the body of men and the animals and the earth! And if this body is capable of newness, then that is my resurrection" (2:70–71). Nearly all of this redemptive conversation is removed from version three, except for four lines in chapter 7 (3:75), where Dukes is allowed to assert his belief in the coming "democracy of touch," with a two-line echo in Connie's consciousness.

Instead of the prophetic chapter 5 Lawrence has inserted a new chapter 4 at this early point in version three, giving a different conversation, with empty thoughts about sex and bolshevism, set in no particular time (though the season is presumably winter); this conversation represents, as Lawrence says, the sort of talk that Connie has heard for "many evenings," presumably over many months. From this we move in version three to the "frosty morning with a little February sun" where Lawrence presents his revision of the opening landscape scene and the introduction of Mellors. Christmas has been ignored; the movement of the seasons has been obscured. But now in version two the seasons and the months come alive, each with its specific identification in the natural process. First, in chapter 6 comes the early spring of the daffodils, as Connie makes her first two visits to the hut, "a sacred place, silent and healing" (2:101). Then, in chapter 7 of version two "Spring was here. In the green light of an April evening, blackbirds were whistling with the old triumph of life" (2:114). And a vivid description of flourishing life in nature follows. After Connie talks with Parkin as he builds a house for the pheasants, "as she went home she saw a new moon bright as a splinter of crystal in the sky" (2:117). As Lawrence says in *A Propos* (3:322–23), human life, the seasons, and the planets must all work in harmony.

The sequence of the months is marked by Connie's witty but silent answer to Clifford's query about a possible child. She had said "it might be." " 'When might changes to may,' he said, 'then I'll tell you how I feel.' " "But inside herself, she was thinking, 'You perhaps need only wait till April changes to May' " (2:154). It is in "May, but cold and wet again" (2:154), that she makes her drive through the mining countryside, with her feeling that, despite its ugliness, "it was not dead" (2:156). Above all, this is the time when Parkin, "walking in the wood when the night deepened to a magnificent night of May, felt a peculiar surging joy" (2:176), and when Connie, amid all the flowery "abundance of May" (2:180), finds a rich fulfillment, first at the hut, then at the cottage, where she falls asleep in Parkin's arms, with Connie and the sun at one: "And the sun moved slowly, slowly across the room, shortening, lingering, gathering itself to depart" (2:186).

It is after this episode that we come to the scene, canceled in version three, where Connie meets Clifford in his chair, and he breaks out in bitter agony: "A bath-chair, in the month of May! There goes the cuckoo, he's at it all day! I can't bear May, I wish it was always winter, and dark and rainy" (2:192). The canceled episode here has two functions: to stress the vitality of Maytime life in nature and the lovers, and the deep misery of Clifford, drawing the reader's sympathy.

Now, in version two, when "a half-moon was shining" (2:224), Connie makes her first nighttime visit to the cottage and has her rhapsody over the "phallus"— with the words *phallus* and *phallic* repeated no less than thirty times in the space of five pages (2:236–41). This is surely excessive, even grotesque. But we can see what Lawrence was trying to do here: create a sense of pagan religion, the old sexual world of the Dionysiac festivals, as the climax of all this Maytime life, before Connie's departure with Hilda, planned for "7th June" (2:245). Before she leaves Connie makes another visit to the hut, in a flowery setting under the "quick pattering of June rain" (2:256). This is the famous scene of running naked and making love in the downpour, followed by the scene of decorating their bodies with flowers gathered from the landscape. Here the latter scene is brief and done discreetly, in a pastoral mode, without any of the "taboo words" that mark this scene in version three; in version two the scene serves well to celebrate the union of humankind with nature, and it leads to talk of marriage and life together on a farm.

As Connie and Hilda drive through France, returning from their trip abroad, the calendar is again clearly marked: "It was full summer, end of hay-harvest, almost time to cut the corn, but the grapes were not yet dark under the leaves. But in some places, apricots and peaches were ripe and warm from the sun" (2:309). As she approaches Wragby, the "car was running on through the well-known landscape, in the grey, cool evening of July" (2:316). The next day Connie pays her visit to Parkin at his mother's home, and a week or so later she visits Parkin at the Tewsons' home, set in "the grey August dismalness of the town" (2:348). Then the very last scene, in Lawrence's own loved countryside, is set in "a grey but warm August day" (2:370). Connie will go to her sister "in September" (2:370), but what will the harvest be?

In version three a truncated movement of the seasons is maintained by the descriptions of the landscape, but the months are mentioned sporadically and, with one exception, without relation to the landscape. March is mentioned as the time of Hilda's visit (3:76); May is stressed only in relation to Connie's ride through the dismal countryside (3:151–52); June is mentioned as the time for Connie's departure abroad (3:151, 214), and as her answer to Clifford's query about her pregnancy—she has known "since June" (3:296); July is mentioned as the time of her promised return, by "the twentieth of July" (3:215); and September is mentioned in the heading of Mellors's final letter (3:298). In version two the consistent naming and describing of the months acts as a frame for the descriptions of the landscape and the actions of the lovers: moving from autumn to autumn, this version enacts the full cycle of the year. Version three, by opening in February, fragments the cycle, just as the weakened naming of the months weakens the seasonal movement that remains. In version three Lawrence's attention has drifted away from the pastoral design and has turned toward the creation of a different kind of novel, filled with satire and invective against a corrupt society and its ruling class.

From the outset of version three Lawrence has made his different mode clear, by revising and expanding what Squires calls the "negation" of the opening movement.[19] Lawrence altered the first chapter by describing Connie's sexual

---

19. Squires discerns three major sections or movements in the novel: "toward negation, toward regeneration, and toward resolution and escape." See his Cambridge edition, xxv, and *Creation*, 29; for his analysis of the movement toward negation, see *Creation*, 30–36.

experience in Germany and by bringing in the rasping authorial voice that
finds everything in England "ridiculous" until "Lloyd George came to save the
situation over here" (3:11). Chapter 2 is then devoted to the "hopeless ugliness"
of the village, to the "gulf impassable" between the upper and the lower classes, to
Clifford's "success" as a writer of superficial stories, and to the decline in Connie's
vitality. Chapter 3 creates the new and rather despicable character of Michaelis—a
part of Lawrence's satire against the triviality of the intellectual scene in London,
with everyone pursuing the "bitch-goddess," success. Despite the unpleasant
account of Michaelis—"this Dublin mongrel!"—there was, Lawrence insists,
"something about him Connie liked" (3:22). So she engages in her sexual affair
with him, showing herself to be the sort of woman that Lawrence dislikes: "She
still wanted the physical, sexual thrill she could get with him, by her own activity,
his little orgasm being over" (3:29).

This is not at all the Connie of the second version, who basically acts in accord
with the pastoral description of her appearance that is found in both versions:
"a ruddy, country-looking girl, with soft brown hair and sturdy body and slow
movements full of unused energy. She had big, wondering blue eyes and a slow,
soft voice, and seemed just to have come from her native village" (2:10). But,
Lawrence adds, "It was not so at all." She has had "a cultured-unconventional
upbringing" with visits to the Continent. Lawrence does not, however, mention
any sexual experience here, though in a later chapter he notes parenthetically,
and once only, that "she has had brief experience of other men" (2:54). This
parenthesis barely registers because of the emphasis that Lawrence places upon
her existence as "a married nun, become virgin again by disuse" (2:18). Although
hidden depths lie beneath her "modest-maiden, ruddy appearance" (2:11), the
stress on her modesty and innocence is borne out by her reluctance to follow
the advice of those who urge her to take a lover. Essentially, in version two,
she has the basic qualities of a pastoral heroine waiting for her awakening by a
woodland lover.

Chapter 4 of version three, as we have seen, carries on the satire of intellectual
life, while Lawrence here introduces, so early in the novel,[20] some of his "taboo
words," which have the effect of coarsening the character of Tommy Dukes, who
has in version two been presented as a sensitive and visionary character. Here he
speaks quite differently:

'Love's another of those half-witted performances today. Fellows with sway-
ing waists fucking little jazz girls with small boy buttocks like two collar-studs?
Do you mean that sort of love? Or the joint-property, make-a-success-of-it,

20. It is noteworthy that Lawrence in the second version delays his first use of the "taboo
words" until much later, in chapter 10, where two uses of the word *cunt* are explained as
Parkin's use "of one of the indefinable words of the dialect" (2:175). The difficulty, of course,
is that these words are not limited to the local dialect, but are in general use as derogatory
epithets or meaningless expletives.

my-husband, my-wife sort of love? No my fine fellow, I don't believe in it at all!'

'But you do believe in something.'

'Me! Oh, intellectually, I believe in having a good heart, a chirpy penis, a lively intelligence, and the courage to say shit! in front of a lady.'

'Well, you've got them all,' said Berry.

'You angel boy! If only I had! If only I had! No, my heart's as numb as a potato, my penis droops and never lifts his head up, I dare rather cut him clean off than say shit! in front of my mother or my aunt . . .' (3:39)

Lawrence's "negative" design has led him to coarsen the atmosphere, as he has done with the introduction of Michaelis.

Chapter 5 of version three, after the first appearance of Mellors, presents a powerful passage about "the bruise of the war, that had been in abeyance, slowly rising to the surface and creating the great ache of unrest, the stupor of discontent."

> The bruise was deep, deep, deep—the bruise of the false and inhuman war. It would take many years for the living blood of the generations to dissolve the vast black clot of bruised blood, deep inside their souls and bodies. And it would need a new hope. (3:50)

But version three does not offer this hope: it is not the function of a polemical novel to provide hope, but to satirize and denounce evil, in the belief that the clearing away of corruption may open the way for new forces of life. Lawrence does not continue with this vision of the war as the cause of distress in society and its individuals; as the first part of this essay has pointed out, Lawrence deliberately discards this theory and shifts the blame to the character of Clifford and his class. In preparation for this change of view, the end of chapter 5 brings us back to Michaelis, returning to Wragby "in summer" (3:51)—a further breaking of the seasonal movement. He is writing a play with "Clifford as a central figure" (3:50), both men now in full pursuit of the "bitch-goddess." The chapter appropriately ends with an "unexpected piece of brutality," Michaelis's ugly, stunning attack on Connie's sexual selfishness (3:54). This attack is vicious in its crudity, but it is not without some justification. For Lawrence has just been describing "the wild tumult and heaving of her loins" (3:53). Connie's character has been coarsened by this contact; she can no longer play the role of modest heroine in a pastoral romance.

But what of the second term that I have used to describe the peculiar quality of *The Second Lady Chatterley*—evangelical? The term is taken from Clifford's fourfold use of the words *evangelical, evangel,* and *evangelist* to describe his wife, in a conversation where she expresses her dislike of the novels of Joyce and Proust (2:222–23). In this context, the word *evangelical* suggests Lawrence's full awareness that he is writing a kind of novel that might be called "evangelical"

—a novel with a message, bearing some gospel.[21] As applied to Connie—"your nature is evangelical"—the word may serve accurately to describe her role and bearing throughout version two: she carries a message of compassion and love— for Parkin, for the whole generation of miners, for Clifford, as long as she can stand the deprivation of physical passion. Her sympathy extends even to Bertha Coutts, whom she attempts to defend in her letter to Parkin: "You mustn't altogether blame Bertha Coutts, perhaps in her way she loved you more than you loved her, and so she despised herself for being the one who had to love more than she was loved, and she went wrong, trying to get even" (2:301).

Nothing in the novel displays her evangelical nature better than the scene in chapter 14 where Connie has her last meeting with Parkin in the wood, where "Everything was green, green, with aching, over-riding vegetation of branched fern, and the smell of fern-seed" (2:329). In this potentially redemptive setting Connie now consoles and encourages the beaten Parkin in his mood of "acute depression," "infinite sadness," and "intense bitterness" (2:329, 332). His despair comes in part from his feeling that his mother was right in saying "as I was on'y ha'ef a man." "If I've got too much of a woman in me, I have, an' I'd better abide by it. And if I can't fend for myself, I'll come to you—." "The idea that he was too womanly was terribly humiliating to him," Lawrence adds. Now Connie brings forth the full measure of her evangelical wisdom and understanding:

> 'Why do you mind?' she said, tears coming to her eyes. 'It's foolish! You say you have too much of a woman in you, you only mean you are more sensitive than stupid people like Dan Coutts. You ought to be proud that you are sensitive, and have that much of a woman's good qualities. It's very good for a man to have a touch of woman's sensitiveness. I hate your stupid hard-headed clowns who think they are so very manly—' (2:333)

The whole scene (2:329–38) shows Parkin's complete dependence on Connie's strength of love and her belief in his essential goodness. "You have got a gift," she says, "a gift of life."

> 'Don't spoil it. And don't take it away from me. You've got to help me to live, too. Don't have silly ideas about being manly. You've got a gift of life, which so few men have. . . . Promise me not to spoil the life in you. Promise me you'll trust me. Promise me faithfully you'll come to me, before you let yourself be really damaged.' (2:333)

The gift of life is what every true evangelist promises.

---

21. In version three Lawrence applies these words three times to Connie in a different conversation (3:193–94). But this aspect of her character does not develop because of the change of Parkin to Mellors, a strong, independent, and dominant figure.

Then, in chapter 15 of *The Second Lady Chatterley,* comes the climactic scene where Connie pays her visit to the damaged Parkin at the home of the Tewsons—a scene that draws together three major themes that have run throughout the book: the impact of the war, the gap between the classes, and the evangelical nature of Connie, here displayed in what might well be called a missionary visit. Parkin and Tewson are especially close because of the war: "a pal's a pal—especially one as was in France with yer—" (2:356). Ethics in the factory has changed: now the supervisors might well accept a bribe: "afore t'war, you'd ha' got sack for tryin' it on. But you never know nowadays. Things is so different—" (2:355). And just because there was a bit of fellowship between officers and men "in the war," things seem to be worse now:

> 'Some of the officers was very friendly like, sort of a bit pally. But you knew it wasn't going to last. You knew they were goin' back to their own lives, an' we were goin' back to work, an' it'd be same as before. Worse! I allers knowed they laughed at us, for the way we talked.' (2:360)

This is part of the long conversation on the problem of the chasm between the classes, launched by Tewson's blunt question: "Do you think it is possible for people in a very different walk of life to be friends—really friends?" (2:358). Connie at once illustrates the difficulty by referring to "Parkin," a usage bitingly corrected by Mrs. Tewson: "You aren't friends with Mr. Seivers—Parkin, as you say!—like we are, as one of us-selves." "Connie looked at her, rather puzzled. She didn't realize that to Mrs. Tewson, for a woman to call a man merely 'Parkin' was as good as an insult" (2:359). This is as big a blunder as her coming to the front door instead of the back, and then knocking down the hat in the hallway. These are small things, but indicative of the truth of what Tewson says—the classes do not know each other; they have no contact. So how can the breach ever be mended, for all the goodwill of people such as Connie? This whole scene, subtle and revealing, is one of the finest that Lawrence ever wrote—but it could play no part in the final version, since it bears no relation to the newly conceived character of Mellors.

One should compare the relationship between Parkin and Connie in these closing scenes with the relationship between Mellors and Connie in chapters 12 and 15 of the final version, where Mellors is dominant in every way. In chapter 12 she at first shows considerable resistance to "the peculiar haste of his possession"—"Cold and derisive her queer female mind stood apart" (3:171–72). But before long she awakens to "the strange potency of manhood upon her," and she "clung to him with a hiss of wonder that was also awe, terror" (3:174–75). Then the chapter ends with Mellors reverting to dialect and bringing in a cluster of the "taboo words" (3:177–78). In chapter 15 Mellors shows his intellectual power and his social views in four pages of a bitter tirade upon the evils of society—speeches to which Connie is "hardly listening," for she is uncovering "his belly" and toying with his private parts (3:217–20). Her sudden naked lunge into the rain seems like an impetuous effort to escape from his speeches. The scene of the twining of the flowers in their hair then follows, extended to twice the original length and accompanied by Mellors's reversion to dialect and the use of clusters of "taboo words," including of course John Thomas and Lady Jane, who do not make their appearance in version two.

What is the effect of all this enormous increase in the use of the taboo words? It seems to be a part of Lawrence's technique of polemic—to throw these words in the teeth of the public, to shock, to unsettle, though in *A Propos* (3:334) Lawrence denies that this is his aim. Conceding that the published version is "obviously a book written in defiance of convention," Lawrence says "the silly desire to *épater le bourgeois,* to bewilder the commonplace person, is not worth entertaining. If I use the taboo words, there is a reason. We shall never free the phallic reality from the 'uplift' taint till we give it its own phallic language, and use the obscene words." With the words moderately used, as in version two,[22] this argument will hold, but the concentrated use of the words in chapters 12 and 15 of the final version creates an effect of aggression, especially when coupled with Mellors's reversion to dialect. Lawrence was perhaps attempting to create an effect of intimacy, but the result is quite different, both for the reader and for Connie, who goes home with a feeling of humiliation: "She never knew how to answer him when he was in this condition of the vernacular. So she dressed herself and prepared to go a little ignominiously home to Wragby. Or so she felt it: a little ignominiously home" (3:229). Parkin's consistent use of the vernacular, with very few exceptions, makes it his natural language, whereas when Mellors shifts from "King's English" to dialect, the language seems like a deliberate effort to overwhelm Connie with an awareness of their different backgrounds.

The dominance of Mellors is then maintained in the final scene at the cottage, where Mellors launches his violent verbal attack on Connie's sister, while Connie listens without attempting to intervene (3:244–45). And finally, by closing the novel with the long letter by Mellors, with its political denunciation and its cluster of taboo words, Lawrence makes it plain that Mellors has come to play the dominant role. The contrast here is somewhat similar to the difference we have noted between the early and the final versions of *The Plumed Serpent.* In the early version the heroine is able to fend off the demands of Don Ramón and Cipriano and emerges at the close with her individuality intact. But in the final version, however reluctantly, she does submit to the pressures of the two men. These differences are characteristic of the ambiguity in Lawrence's attitude toward women that runs throughout his career. He admired women immensely for their creative vitality; yet he at the same time resented this power and attempted to assert the domination of "manhood."

22. The word *phallus,* used so immoderately by Lawrence, does not count as one of the "taboo words": it is carefully defined in standard dictionaries of the time.

But no such domination is asserted in the ending of *The Second Lady Chatterley*, where Connie's evangelical nature extends her pity to all humanity: "And she looked at the little slab behind which rests the pinch of dust which was Byron's heart: in that thrice dismal Hucknall Torkard. The sense of the greatness of human mistakes made her want to cry" (2:372).[23] These are the mistakes that blend to create the novel's themes and strength: the terrible mistake of the war, the mistake of allowing the classes to develop a destructive antagonism, the mistake of industrial development that has brutalized the common people and brought them to the verge of violence. From this setting of mistakes the lovers attempt to seize one final moment of peace and union in a pastoral setting: the Annesley wood that Lawrence knew so well. But it cannot be done: the keeper comes to disturb their furtive idyll, and the scene shifts to "The dead countryside! and the grisly live spots, the mining settlements!" Nothing, it seems, can be done at present to heal these wounds, but at least one man may be saved:

> 'If I really want you to do anything, will you do it?' Connie asked him. 'You mustn't think you can just leave me. Will you come to me if I need you, even if you never get your divorce? If I can't bear it, will you come and live with me—even next month? We can go to Italy if you like.'
> 'If you feel it's the best, I will. I'll do anything you like, for the best. I don't reckon it's any good layin' the law down, not for myself or anybody—But I can go on lookin' for some farmin' work, like, an' then—'
> 'You'll come to me if I can't bear it?'
> 'Yes,' he said.

With these final words in *The Second Lady Chatterley,* Lawrence achieved one of his finest open endings and accomplished what he accused others of refusing to do, in the first sentence of his novel: "Ours is essentially a tragic age, so we refuse to take it tragically." This version of the novel sets forth the tragedy of human mistakes.

---

23. Weinstein has given an appreciative account of the ending of version two: "The ending is lyrical and almost hopeless; Byron's heart haunts these pages with its implication of passion gone to waste." He sees the Parkin of version two as "a tragic gamekeeper: a man inextricably enmeshed in class, and yet superior to class, isolated within its confines" ("Choosing," 277–78).

Appendix

Pound, Blake, and Dante

*T*HE SIMILARITY IS striking between the running figure of Blake in Canto 16 and the running figure of Dante in the first of Blake's drawings for the *Divine Comedy* (see Fig. 3). But the question remains: could Pound have seen these drawings? They remained in the possession of the Linnell family until they were sold at auction in 1918 to a consortium of five institutions. Fortunately, before the series was dispersed, the consortium arranged to have the whole series reproduced in a monochrome portfolio "Printed Privately for The National Art-Collection Fund and Issued to the Subscribers only" (London: Hertford House, 1922)—a handsome edition of 250 copies. Pound was living in Paris in 1922, but, with his deep interest in Dante, he may have made a special effort to gain access to the portfolio (though I can find no evidence in his letters that he did so). In any case, the figure of Dante in the first drawing of the series ("Dante Running from the Three Beasts") bears a close resemblance to Pound's running figure, for the arms might be seen as "whirling" and the head is certainly "held backward to gaze on the evil / As he ran from it." Plate 2 in the series then shows "Dante and Virgil Penetrating the Forest"; but in plate 3 ("The Mission of Virgil") the figure of Dante appears again, still running, as in Pound's canto, with a facial expression of revulsion and hands flattened outward at his sides to indicate a vehement horror of the beasts. In both drawings the figure is not "naked" but clothed in the transparent garment characteristic of Blake.

Wendy Stallard Flory has argued for an analogy with the figure of Charon in plate 6 of the series (see her *Ezra Pound and the Cantos*, 90–92). Certainly the eyes of Charon here fully accord with Pound's description of Blake's "eyes rolling / Whirling like flaming cart-wheels," for in Blake's drawing Charon's eyes are prominently drawn in wheeling circles, in accord with Dante's description of Charon's eyes as surrounded by "di fiamme rote" ("wheels of flame") in *Inferno* 3.99. But the figure of Charon is not running; he is standing on the gunwhale of his boat, arms stretched upward as he shouts the "cruel words" to the condemned host, "beating with his oar whoever lingers" (*Inf.* 3.82–111, trans. Singleton). Instead of an oar Blake shows Charon grasping a trident in his left hand.

George Kearns (*Guide to Ezra Pound's Selected Cantos*, 71) has pointed out a possible analogy with the naked, agonized figure of Cain as he attempts to flee from Abel's grave in Blake's "The Body of Abel Found by Adam and Eve" at the Tate; see Martin Butlin, *William Blake* (Tate Gallery Collections, vol. 5, 1990, p. 169). But the arms are not whirling and the face is presented directly to the viewer. Naked running figures are frequent in Blake's drawings for the *Inferno:* see plates 25, 26, 29, 32, 33. The whole series, along with the seven engravings that Blake made, is now easily available in two publications: Albert S. Roe, *Blake's Illustrations to the Divine Comedy* (Princeton: Princeton University Press, 1953), which reproduces the designs from the limited edition of 1922; and Milton Klonsky, *Blake's Dante: The Complete Illustrations to the Divine Comedy* (New York: Harmony Books, 1980), which reproduces forty-six of the drawings in color.

Still another possible analogy might be noted: plate 4 in Blake's *Illustrations of the Book of Job,* with its anguished running messenger; another messenger appears on the curving road far below, as in Pound. See David Bindman, *The Complete Graphic Works of William Blake* (London: Thames and Hudson, 1978), 629.

It seems possible that some of the mountainous backgrounds in Blake's drawings for the *Inferno* may have suggested to Pound the unusual conception of *two* purgatorial mountains. See especially plate 11 ("The Circle of the Gluttons with Cerberus"), where two mountain ridges appear, with a valley in between. Similarly, in plate 58 ("The Circle of the Falsifiers") two images appear that look like mountains, though they are really rock-bridges. The resemblance to two mountains here is more pronounced in Blake's engraving for this scene (see Bindman, *Graphic Works,* plate 652). And finally, to complete this series of conjectures, one should note the curving ascent that matches Pound's description ("The angle almost imperceptible / so that the circuit seemed hardly to rise") in plate 42 ("The Circle of the Corrupt Officials"), where, above the fighting devils, Dante and Vergil may be seen walking along a very gradual ascent; this effect is also more pronounced in the engraving (see Bindman, plate 649). For a complete catalog of the drawings for the *Divine Comedy* see Martin Butlin, *The Paintings and Drawings of William Blake,* 2 vols. (New Haven and London: Yale University Press, 1981), Text, 554–94.

Bibliography

Manuscript Sources

H.D. Archive, Beinecke Rare Book and Manuscript Library, Yale University.
Bryher Papers, Beinecke Library. Yale University.
Ezra Pound Archive, Beinecke Library, Yale University.
D. H. Lawrence Collection, Harry Ransom Humanities Research Center, University of Texas at Austin. (*Quetzalcoatl* mss.)
Houghton Library, Harvard University. (*Quetzalcoatl* ts.)

Primary Texts

Dante Alighieri. *The Divine Comedy*. Trans., with commentary, by Charles S. Singleton. 6 vols. Princeton: Princeton University Press. *Inferno,* 1970; *Purgatorio,* 1973; *Paradiso,* 1975.

———. *The Divine Comedy*. Temple Classics. *Inferno,* trans. John Carlyle; rev. H. Oelsner. London: Dent, 1900. *Purgatorio,* trans. Thomas Okey. London: Dent, 1901. *Paradiso,* trans. Philip Wicksteed. London: Dent, 1899.

———. *Vita Nuova*. Trans. Mark Musa. Bloomington: Indiana University Press, 1973.

Eliot, T. S. *Collected Poems, 1909–1935*. New York: Harcourt, 1936.

———. *Collected Poems, 1909–1962*. New York: Harcourt, 1963.

———. *Inventions of the March Hare: Poems, 1909–1917*. Ed. Christopher Ricks. London: Faber, 1996.

⸺. *The Letters of T. S. Eliot.* Vol. 1. Ed. Valerie Eliot. New York: Harcourt, 1988.

⸺. *On Poetry and Poets.* London: Faber, 1957.

⸺. *The Waste Land: A Facsimile and Transcript of the Original Drafts, Including the Annotations of Ezra Pound.* Ed. Valerie Eliot. New York: Harcourt, 1971.

H.D. *Bid Me to Live: A Madrigal.* With a memoir, "A Profound Animal," by Perdita Schaffner, an afterword by John Walsh, and excerpts from H.D.'s "Notes on Recent Writing." Redding Ridge, Conn.: Black Swan Books, 1983.

⸺. *Collected Poems, 1912–1944.* Ed. Louis L. Martz. New York: New Directions, 1983.

⸺. *Helen in Egypt.* New York: New Directions, 1974.

⸺. *Ion: A Play after Euripides.* Rev. with an afterword by John Walsh and excerpts from H.D.'s notes on Euripides. Redding Ridge, Conn.: Black Swan Books, 1986.

⸺. *Selected Poems.* Ed. Louis L. Martz. New York: New Directions, 1988.

⸺. *Tribute to Freud: Writing on the Wall, Advent.* With a foreword by Norman Holmes Pearson. New York: New Directions, 1984. The first complete edition was published by David R. Godine, Boston, 1974, with an introduction by Kenneth Fields.

Joyce, James. *Ulysses.* New York: Random House, 1934.

Lawrence, D. H. *Apocalypse and the Writings on Revelation.* ed. Mara Kalnins. Cambridge: Cambridge University Press, 1980.

⸺. *The Complete Poems of D. H. Lawrence.* Ed. Vivian de Sola Pinto and Warren Roberts. Harmondsworth and New York: Penguin Books, 1977.

⸺. *The Escaped Cock.* Ed. Gerald M. Lacy. Los Angeles: Black Sparrow Press, 1973.

⸺. *The First Lady Chatterley.* London: Heinemann, 1972.

⸺. *John Thomas and Lady Jane: The Second Version of Lady Chatterley's Lover.* London: Heinemann, 1972; New York and London: Penguin Books, 1977.

⸺. *Lady Chatterley's Lover.* London: Heinemann, 1960.

⸺. *Lady Chatterley's Lover: A Propos of "Lady Chatterley's Lover."* Ed. Michael Squires. Cambridge: Cambridge University Press, 1993; London and New York: Penguin Books, 1994.

⸺. *The Letters of D. H. Lawrence.* Ed. Aldous Huxley. London: Heinemann, 1932.

⸺. *The Letters of D. H. Lawrence.* Ed. James T. Boulton et al. 7 vols. Cambridge: Cambridge University Press, 1979–1993.

⸺. *The Man Who Died.* New York: Knopf, 1931.

⸺. *Phoenix.* Ed. Edward D. McDonald. London: Heinemann, 1936.

⸺. *The Plumed Serpent.* Ed. L. D. Clark. Cambridge: Cambridge University Press, 1987.

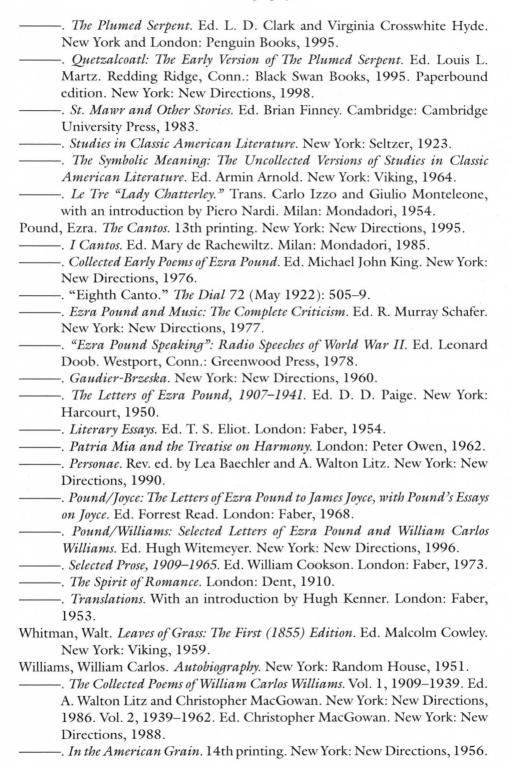

———. *The Plumed Serpent*. Ed. L. D. Clark and Virginia Crosswhite Hyde. New York and London: Penguin Books, 1995.

———. *Quetzalcoatl: The Early Version of The Plumed Serpent*. Ed. Louis L. Martz. Redding Ridge, Conn.: Black Swan Books, 1995. Paperbound edition. New York: New Directions, 1998.

———. *St. Mawr and Other Stories*. Ed. Brian Finney. Cambridge: Cambridge University Press, 1983.

———. *Studies in Classic American Literature*. New York: Seltzer, 1923.

———. *The Symbolic Meaning: The Uncollected Versions of Studies in Classic American Literature*. Ed. Armin Arnold. New York: Viking, 1964.

———. *Le Tre "Lady Chatterley."* Trans. Carlo Izzo and Giulio Monteleone, with an introduction by Piero Nardi. Milan: Mondadori, 1954.

Pound, Ezra. *The Cantos*. 13th printing. New York: New Directions, 1995.

———. *I Cantos*. Ed. Mary de Rachewiltz. Milan: Mondadori, 1985.

———. *Collected Early Poems of Ezra Pound*. Ed. Michael John King. New York: New Directions, 1976.

———. "Eighth Canto." *The Dial* 72 (May 1922): 505–9.

———. *Ezra Pound and Music: The Complete Criticism*. Ed. R. Murray Schafer. New York: New Directions, 1977.

———. *"Ezra Pound Speaking": Radio Speeches of World War II*. Ed. Leonard Doob. Westport, Conn.: Greenwood Press, 1978.

———. *Gaudier-Brzeska*. New York: New Directions, 1960.

———. *The Letters of Ezra Pound, 1907–1941*. Ed. D. D. Paige. New York: Harcourt, 1950.

———. *Literary Essays*. Ed. T. S. Eliot. London: Faber, 1954.

———. *Patria Mia and the Treatise on Harmony*. London: Peter Owen, 1962.

———. *Personae*. Rev. ed. by Lea Baechler and A. Walton Litz. New York: New Directions, 1990.

———. *Pound/Joyce: The Letters of Ezra Pound to James Joyce, with Pound's Essays on Joyce*. Ed. Forrest Read. London: Faber, 1968.

———. *Pound/Williams: Selected Letters of Ezra Pound and William Carlos Williams*. Ed. Hugh Witemeyer. New York: New Directions, 1996.

———. *Selected Prose, 1909–1965*. Ed. William Cookson. London: Faber, 1973.

———. *The Spirit of Romance*. London: Dent, 1910.

———. *Translations*. With an introduction by Hugh Kenner. London: Faber, 1953.

Whitman, Walt. *Leaves of Grass: The First (1855) Edition*. Ed. Malcolm Cowley. New York: Viking, 1959.

Williams, William Carlos. *Autobiography*. New York: Random House, 1951.

———. *The Collected Poems of William Carlos Williams*. Vol. 1, 1909–1939. Ed. A. Walton Litz and Christopher MacGowan. New York: New Directions, 1986. Vol. 2, 1939–1962. Ed. Christopher MacGowan. New York: New Directions, 1988.

———. *In the American Grain*. 14th printing. New York: New Directions, 1956.

————. *The Last Word: Letters between Marcia Nardi and William Carlos Williams*. Ed. Elizabeth Murrie O'Neil. Iowa City: University of Iowa Press, 1994.

————. *Paterson*. Rev. ed. by Christopher MacGowan. New York: New Directions, 1992; New Directions Paperbook, 1995, with same pagination and a few corrections.

————. *Selected Letters of William Carlos Williams*. Ed. John C. Thirlwall. New York: McDowell, Obolensky, 1957.

Secondary Studies

In view of the large amount of commentary available for all the authors here concerned, the following list is, of necessity, highly selective. Except for a few standard books, the list is limited to studies that have seemed most germane to the issues considered in the present book.

Adams, Stephen J. "Are the *Cantos* a Fugue?" *University of Toronto Quarterly* 45 (1975): 67–74.

Alexander, Michael. *The Poetic Achievement of Ezra Pound*. Berkeley: University of California Press, 1979.

Altieri, Charles. *Painterly Abstraction in Modernist American Poetry: The Contemporaneity of Modernism*. Cambridge: Cambridge University Press, 1989.

Bacigalupo, Massimo. "Ezra Pound's Cantos 72 and 73: An Annotated Translation." *Paideuma* 20 (1991): 9–41.

————. *The Forméd Trace: The Later Poetry of Ezra Pound*. New York: Columbia University Press, 1980.

Balbert, Peter, and Phillip L. Marcus, eds. *D. H. Lawrence: A Centenary Consideration*. Ithaca and London: Cornell University Press, 1985.

Ballerini, Luigi. "Exile From and To, and Williams' Sense of Belonging." In *The Rhetoric of Love in the Collected Poems of William Carlos Williams*, ed. Cristina Giorcelli and Maria Anita Stefanelli, 71–98. Rome: Edizioni Associate, 1993.

Baumann, Walter. *The Rose in the Steel Dust: An Examination of the Cantos of Ezra Pound*. Coral Gables: University of Miami Press, 1970.

Bedient, Calvin. *He Do the Police in Different Voices: The Waste Land and Its Protagonist*. Chicago and London: University of Chicago Press, 1986.

Bernstein, Michael André. *The Tale of the Tribe: Ezra Pound and the Modern Verse Epic*. Princeton: Princeton University Press, 1980.

Blasing, Mutlu Konuk. *American Poetry; The Rhetoric of Its Forms*. New Haven and London: Yale University Press, 1987. See chaps. 7 and 8, on Whitman and Pound.

Bornstein, George, ed. *Ezra Pound among the Poets.* Chicago and London: University of Chicago Press, 1985.

Breslin, James E. *William Carlos Williams: An American Artist.* New York: Oxford University Press, 1970.

Brooke-Rose, Christine. *A ZBC of Ezra Pound.* London: Faber, 1971.

Buck, Claire, *H.D. and Freud: Bisexuality and a Feminine Discourse.* New York and London: Harvester Wheatsheaf, 1991.

Burnett, Gary, *H.D. between Image and Epic: The Mysteries of Her Poetics.* Ann Arbor: UMI Research Press, 1990.

Bush, Ronald. *The Genesis of Ezra Pound's Cantos.* Princeton: Princeton University Press, 1976.

———. "Modernism, Fascism, and the Composition of Ezra Pound's *Pisan Cantos.*" *Modernism/Modernity* 2 (1995): 69–87.

———. *T. S. Eliot: A Study in Character and Style.* New York and Oxford: Oxford University Press, 1983.

Carswell, Catherine, *The Savage Pilgrimage: A Narrative of D. H. Lawrence.* London: Chatto, 1932.

Cavitch, David. *D. H. Lawrence and the New World.* New York: Oxford University Press, 1969.

Chisholm, Dianne. *H.D.'s Freudian Poetics: Psychoanalysis in Translation.* Ithaca and London: Cornell University Press, 1992.

Clark, L. D. *Dark Night of the Body.* Austin: University of Texas Press, 1964.

———. *The Minoan Distance.* Tucson: University of Arizona Press, 1980.

Comens, Bruce, *Apocalypse and After: Modern Strategy and Postmodern Tactics in Pound, Williams, and Zukofsky.* Tuscaloosa and London: University of Alabama Press, 1995.

Conarroe, Joel. *William Carlos Williams' Paterson: Language and Landscape.* Philadelphia: University of Pennsylvania Press, 1970.

Conrad, Bryce. *Refiguring America: A Study of William Carlos Williams' In the American Grain.* Urbana and Chicago: University of Illinois Press, 1990.

Cooper, John Xiros. "Music as Symbol and Structure in Pound's *Pisan Cantos* and Eliot's *Four Quartets.*" In *Ezra Pound and Europe,* ed. Richard Taylor and Claus Melchior, 177–89. Amsterdam: Rodopi, 1993.

———. *T. S. Eliot and the Ideology of Four Quartets.* Cambridge: Cambridge University Press, 1995.

Cowan, James C. *D. H. Lawrence's American Journey: A Study in Literature and Myth.* Cleveland and London: Press of Case Western Reserve University, 1970.

Cowan, Laura, ed. *T. S. Eliot: Man and Poet.* Vol. 1. Orono: National Poetry Foundation, University of Maine, 1990. Vol. 2. *An Annotated Bibliography of a Decade of T. S. Eliot Criticism: 1977–1986.* Compiled and annotated by Sebastian D. G. Knowles and Scott A. Leonard, 1992.

Cushman, Stephen. *Fictions of Form in American Poetry*. Princeton: Princeton University Press, 1993. See chaps. 2 and 4, on Whitman and Pound.

Daleski, H. M. *The Forked Flame: A Study of D. H. Lawrence*. Evanston: Northwestern University Press, 1965.

Dasenbrock, Reed Way. *The Literary Vorticism of Ezra Pound and Wyndham Lewis*. Baltimore: Johns Hopkins University Press, 1985.

Davenport, Guy. *Cities on Hills: A Study of I–XXX of Ezra Pound's Cantos*. Ann Arbor: UMI Research Press, 1983.

Davie, Donald. *Ezra Pound: Poet as Sculptor*. New York: Oxford University Press, 1964.

———. *Studies in Ezra Pound*. Manchester: Carcanet, 1991.

Davis, Kay. *Fugue and Fresco: Structures in Pound's Cantos*. Orono: National Poetry Foundation, University of Maine, 1984.

Delaney, Paul. *D. H. Lawrence's Nightmare: The Writer and His Circle in the Years of the Great War*. New York: Basic Books, 1978.

D'Epiro, Peter. "Whose Vanity Must Be Pulled Down?" *Paideuma* 13 (1984): 247–52.

de Rachewiltz, Mary. *Discretions*. Boston: Little, Brown, 1971.

Dijkstra, Bram. *Hieroglyphics of a New Speech*. Princeton: Princeton University Press, 1969.

———. Introduction to *A Recognizable Image: William Carlos Williams on Art and Artists*. New York: New Directions, 1978.

Dodd, Elizabeth. *The Veiled Mirror and the Woman Poet: H.D., Louise Bogan, Elizabeth Bishop, and Louise Glück*. Columbia: University of Missouri Press, 1992.

Doyle, Charles. *William Carlos Williams: The Critical Heritage*. London: Routledge, 1980.

———. *William Carlos Williams and the American Poem*. New York: St. Martin's Press, 1982.

Duffey, Bernard. *A Poetry of Presence: The Writing of William Carlos Williams*. Madison: University of Wisconsin Press, 1986.

Duncan, Robert. "The H.D. Book." For a list of installments see *H.D.: Woman and Poet*, ed. Michael King, bibliography, items 9–10, 12–13, 15–18, 21–24. Orono: National Poetry Foundation, University of Maine, 1986. Also *Southern Review* 21 (1985): 26–48.

DuPlessis, Rachel Blau. *H.D.: The Career of That Struggle*. Bloomington: Indiana University Press, 1986.

———. "Romantic Thralldom in H.D." *Contemporary Literature* 20 (1979): 178–203. Included in *Signets: Reading H.D.*, ed. Susan Stanford Friedman and Rachel Blau DuPlessis, 406–29. Madison: University of Wisconsin Press, 1990.

DuPlessis, Rachel Blau, and Susan Stanford Friedman. " 'Woman Is Perfect': H.D.'s Debate with Freud." *Feminist Studies* 7 (1981): 417–30.

Edmunds, Susan. *Out of Line: History, Psychoanalysis, and Montage in H.D.'s Long Poems*. Stanford: Stanford University Press, 1994.

Edwards, John Hamilton, and William W. Vasse. *Annotated Index to the Cantos of Ezra Pound: Cantos I–LXXXIV*. Berkeley: University of California Press, 1957.

Ellis, Steve. *The English Eliot: Design, Language, and Landscape in Four Quartets*. London and New York: Routledge, 1991.

Ellmann, Richard. *James Joyce*. Rev. ed. New York: Oxford University Press, 1982.

Emery, Clark. *Ideas into Action: A Study of Pound's Cantos*. Coral Gables: University of Miami Press, 1958.

Firchow, Peter. "Rico and Julia: The Hilda Doolittle–D. H. Lawrence Affair Reconsidered." *Journal of Modern Literature* 8 (1980): 51–76.

Flory, Wendy Stallard. *The American Ezra Pound*. New Haven and London: Yale University Press, 1989.

———. *Ezra Pound and the Cantos: A Record of Struggle*. New Haven and London: Yale University Press, 1980.

French, William. " 'Saint Hilda,' Mr. Pound, and Rilke's Parisian Panther at Pisa." *Paideuma* 11 (1982): 79–87.

Friedman, Susan Stanford. "Creating a Women's Mythology: H.D.'s *Helen in Egypt*." *Women's Studies* 5 (1977): 163–97. Included in *Signets: Reading H.D.*, ed. Susan Stanford Friedman and Rachel Blau DuPlessis, 373–405. Madison: University of Wisconsin Press, 1990.

———. "Exile in the American Grain: H.D.'s Diaspora." *Agenda* 25 (1987–1988): 27–50. Included in *Women's Writing in Exile*, ed. Mary Lynn Broe and Angela Ingram, 87–112. Chapel Hill: University of North Carolina Press, 1989.

———. *Penelope's Web: Gender, Modernity, H.D.'s Fiction*. Cambridge: Cambridge University Press, 1990.

———. *Psyche Reborn: The Emergence of H.D.* Bloomington: Indiana University Press, 1981.

Friedman, Susan Stanford, and Rachel Blau DuPlessis, eds. *Signets: Reading H.D.* Madison: University of Wisconsin Press, 1990.

Fritz, Angela DiPace. *Thought and Vision: A Critical Reading of H.D.'s Poetry*. Washington, D.C.: Catholic University Press, 1988.

Froula, Christine. *To Write Paradise: Style and Error in Pound's Cantos*. New Haven and London: Yale University Press, 1984.

Fulker, Teresa. "Not-War and the Inspiration of the *Gloire* in H.D.'s *Bid Me to Live*." *Sagetrieb* 12 (1993): 51–82.

Gallup, Donald. *Ezra Pound: A Bibliography*. Charlottesville: University Press of Virginia, 1983.

———. "The William Carlos Williams Collection at Yale." *Yale University Library Gazette* 56 (1981): 50–59.

Gardner, Helen. *The Art of T. S. Eliot.* New York: Dutton, 1950.

————. *The Composition of Four Quartets.* New York: Oxford University Press, 1978.

Gelpi, Albert. *A Coherent Splendor: The American Poetic Renaissance, 1910–1950.* Cambridge: Cambridge University Press, 1987. See chapters on Eliot, Pound, H.D., and Williams.

————. "Hilda in Egypt." *Southern Review* 18 (1982): 233–50.

————. "Re-membering the Mother: A Reading of H.D.'s *Trilogy.*" In *H.D.: Woman and Poet,* ed. Michael King, 173–90. Orono: National Poetry Foundation, University of Maine, 1986. Included in *Signets: Reading H.D.,* ed. Susan Stanford Friedman and Rachel Blau DuPlessis, 318–35. Madison: University of Wisconsin Press, 1990.

Gilbert, Sandra M., and Susan Gubar. *No Man's Land: The Place of the Woman Writer in the Twentieth Century.* Vol. 3. New Haven and London: Yale University Press, 1994.

Glendening, John. "Ezra Pound and Ezra Pound's Blake: Method in Madness, Madness in Method." *Paideuma* 20 (1991): 95–106.

Gordon, Lyndall. *Eliot's New Life.* New York: Farrar, Straus, Giroux, 1988.

Graham, Theodora R. " 'Her Heigh Compleynte': The Cress Letters of William Carlos Williams' *Paterson.*" In *Ezra Pound and William Carlos Williams: The University of Pennsylvania Conference Papers,* ed. Daniel Hoffman, 164–93. Philadelphia: University of Pennsylvania Press, 1983.

Gregor, Ian. "The Novel as Prophecy: *Lady Chatterley's Lover* (1928)." In Ian Gregor and Brian Nicholas, *The Moral and the Story,* 217–48. London: Faber, 1962.

Gubar, Susan. "The Echoing Spell of H.D.'s *Trilogy.*" *Contemporary Literature* 19 (1978): 196–218. Included in *Signets: Reading H.D.,* ed. Susan Stanford Friedman and Rachel Blau DuPlessis, 297–317. Madison: University of Wisconsin Press, 1990. Also in *Shakespeare's Sisters,* ed. Sandra M. Gilbert and Susan Gubar, 153–64. Bloomington: Indiana University Press, 1979.

Guest, Barbara. *Herself Defined: The Poet H.D. and Her World.* Garden City, N.Y.: Doubleday, 1984.

Halter, Peter. *The Revolution in the Visual Arts and the Poetry of William Carlos Williams.* Cambridge: Cambridge University Press, 1994.

Hesse, Eva, ed. *New Approaches to Ezra Pound: A Co-ordinated Investigation of Pound's Poetry and Ideas.* London: Faber, 1969.

Holland, Norman N. "H.D. and the 'Blameless Physician.' " *Contemporary Literature* 10 (1969): 474–506.

Hollenberg, Donna Krolik. *H.D.: The Poetics of Childbirth and Creativity.* Boston: Northeastern University Press, 1991.

Hyde, Virginia. *The Risen Adam: D. H. Lawrence's Revisionist Typology.* University Park, Pa.: Pennsylvania State University Press, 1992.

Kearns, George. *Guide to Ezra Pound's Selected Cantos.* New Brunswick, N.J.: Rutgers University Press, 1980.

Kenner, Hugh. "*Drafts and Fragments* and the Structure of the *Cantos.*" *Agenda* 8 (1970): 7–18.

———. *The Invisible Poet: T. S. Eliot.* New York: Citadel Press, 1959.

———. *The Poetry of Ezra Pound.* Norfolk, Conn.: New Directions, 1951.

———. *The Pound Era.* New York: New Directions, 1971.

———. "The Rose in the Steel Dust." *Hudson Review* 3 (1950): 66–123.

King, Michael, ed. *H.D.: Woman and Poet.* Orono: National Poetry Foundation, University of Maine, 1986. See "Annotated Bibliography of Works about H.D.: 1969–1985" by Mary S. Mathis and Michael King, 393–511.

Kinkead-Weekes, Mark. *D. H. Lawrence: Triumph to Exile, 1912–1922.* Cambridge: Cambridge University Press, 1996.

Kloepfer, Deborah Kelly. "Mother as Muse and Desire: The Sexual Poetics of H.D.'s *Trilogy.*" In *H.D.: Woman and Poet,* ed. Michael King, 191–206. Orono: National Poetry Foundation, University of Maine, 1986.

———. *The Unspeakable Mother: Forbidden Discourse in Jean Rhys and H.D.* Ithaca and London: Cornell University Press, 1989.

Laity, Cassandra. *H.D. and the Victorian Fin de Siècle.* Cambridge: Cambridge University Press, 1996.

Leary, Lewis, ed. *Motive and Method in the Cantos of Ezra Pound.* New York: Columbia University Press, 1954.

Litz, A. Walton. *The Art of James Joyce.* London: Oxford University Press, 1961.

———. "Lawrence, Pound, and Early Modernism." In *D. H. Lawrence: A Centenary Consideration,* ed. Peter Balbert and Phillip L. Marcus, 15–28. Ithaca and London: Cornell University Press, 1985.

Litz, A. Walton, ed. *Eliot in His Time: Essays on the Occasion of the Fiftieth Anniversary of "The Waste Land."* Princeton: Princeton University Press, 1973.

Lloyd, Margaret Glynne. *William Carlos Williams' Paterson: A Critical Reappraisal.* Rutherford, N.J.: Fairleigh Dickinson University Press, 1980.

Longenbach, James. *Modernist Poetics of History: Pound, Eliot, and the Sense of the Past.* Princeton: Princeton University Press, 1987.

———. *Stone Cottage: Pound, Yeats, and Modernism.* New York: Oxford University Press, 1988.

Luhan, Mabel Dodge. *Lorenzo in Taos.* New York: Knopf, 1932.

Makin, Peter. *Pound's Cantos.* London: Allen and Unwin, 1985; Baltimore and London: Johns Hopkins University Press, 1992.

Mariani, Paul. *William Carlos Williams: A New World Naked.* New York: McGraw-Hill, 1981.

Marling, William. *William Carlos Williams and the Painters, 1909–1923.* Athens: Ohio University Press, 1982.

Martz, Louis L. "*Quetzalcoatl:* The Early Version of *The Plumed Serpent.*" *D. H. Lawrence Review* 22 (1990): 286–98.

Materer, Timothy. *Vortex: Pound, Eliot, and Lewis.* Ithaca and London: Cornell University Press, 1979.

McGann, Jerome. "The *Cantos* of Ezra Pound." *Critical Inquiry* 15 (1988): 1–25.

Milicia, Joseph. "*Bid Me to Live:* Within the Storm." In *H.D.: Woman and Poet,* ed. Michael King, 279–98. Orono: National Poetry Foundation, University of Maine, 1986.

Miller, James E., Jr. *The American Quest for a Supreme Fiction: Whitman's Legacy in the Personal Epic.* Chicago and London: University of Chicago Press, 1979. Chapters on Whitman, Pound, Eliot, and Williams.

Moody, A. David. *Thomas Stearns Eliot, Poet.* 2d ed. Cambridge: Cambridge University Press, 1994.

Moody, A. David, ed. *The Waste Land in Different Voices.* London: Arnold, 1974.

Moore, Harry T. *The Priest of Love: A Life of D. H. Lawrence.* Rev. ed. Harmondsworth and New York: Penguin Books, 1981.

Morris, Adalaide. "The Concept of Projection: H.D.'s Visionary Powers." *Contemporary Literature* 25 (1984): 411–36. Included in *Signets: Reading H.D.,* ed. Susan Stanford Friedman and Rachel Blau DuPlessis, 273–96. Madison: University of Wisconsin Press, 1990.

―――. "Signaling: Feminism, Politics, and Mysticism in H.D.'s War Trilogy." *Sagetrieb* 9 (1990): 121–33.

Nassar, Eugene Paul. *The Cantos of Ezra Pound: The Lyric Mode.* Baltimore and London: Johns Hopkins University Press, 1975.

Ostriker, Alicia. "No Rule of Procedure: The Open Poetics of H.D." *Agenda* 25 (1987–1988): 145–54. Included in *Signets: Reading H.D.,* ed. Susan Stanford Friedman and Rachel Blau DuPlessis, 336–51. Madison: University of Wisconsin Press, 1990.

―――. "The Poet as Heroine: Learning to Read H.D." In *Writing Like a Woman,* 7–41. Ann Arbor: University of Michigan Press, 1983.

Ostrom, Alan. *The Poetic World of William Carlos Williams.* Carbondale: Southern Illinois University Press, 1966.

Parini, Jay, and Brett C. Millier. *The Columbia History of American Poetry.* New York: Columbia University Press, 1993. See esp. the essays by William Pritchard on Eliot, by Christopher MacGowan on Williams, and by Lynn Keller on "The Twentieth-Century Long Poem."

Parmenter, Ross. *Lawrence in Oaxaca: A Quest for the Novelist in Mexico.* Salt Lake City: Peregrine Smith Books, 1984.

Pearce, Roy Harvey. *The Continuity of American Poetry.* Princeton: Princeton University Press, 1961.

Pearlman, Daniel D. *The Barb of Time: On the Unity of Ezra Pound's Cantos.* New York: Oxford University Press, 1969.

Perloff, Marjorie. *The Dance of the Intellect: Studies in the Poetry of the Pound Tradition.* Cambridge: Cambridge University Press, 1985.

Peterson, Walter Scott. *An Approach to Paterson.* New Haven and London: Yale University Press, 1967.

Pichardie, Jean-Paul. *D. H. Lawrence: La Tentation Utopique de Rananim au Serpent à Plumes.* Rouen: Publications de l'Université de Rouen, 1988.

Pondrom, Cyrena N. "H.D. and the Origins of Imagism." *Sagetrieb* 4 (1985): 73–97. Included in *Signets: Reading H.D.,* ed. Susan Stanford Friedman and Rachel Blau DuPlessis, 85–109. Madison: University of Wisconsin Press, 1990.

———. "*Trilogy* and *Four Quartets:* Contrapuntal Visions of Spiritual Quest." *Agenda* 25 (1987–1988)): 155–65.

Quinn, Sister Bernetta. *Ezra Pound: An Introduction to the Poetry.* New York: Columbia University Press, 1972.

Quinn, Vincent. *Hilda Doolittle (H.D.).* New York: Twayne, 1967.

Rainey, Lawrence S. *Ezra Pound and the Monument of Culture: Text, History and the Malatesta Cantos.* Chicago and London: University of Chicago Press, 1991.

Riddel, Joseph N. *The Inverted Bell: Modernism and the Counterpoetics of William Carlos Williams.* Baton Rouge: Louisiana State University Press, 1974.

Robinson, Janice. *H.D.: The Life and Work of an American Poet.* Boston: Houghton Mifflin, 1982.

Rosenthal, M. L., and Sally M. Gall. *The Modern Poetic Sequence.* New York: Oxford University Press, 1983. Chapters on Whitman, Eliot, Pound, and Williams.

Rossman, Charles. "D. H. Lawrence and Mexico." In *D. H. Lawrence: A Centenary Consideration,* ed. Peter Balbert and Phillip L. Marcus, 180–209. Ithaca and London: Cornell University Press, 1985.

Russell, Peter, ed. *An Examination of Ezra Pound.* New York: New Directions, 1950.

Sagar, Keith. *The Art of D. H. Lawrence.* Cambridge: Cambridge University Press, 1966.

———. *D. H. Lawrence: A Calendar of His Works.* Manchester: Manchester University Press, 1979. Includes "Checklist of the manuscripts of D. H. Lawrence," by Lindeth Vasey.

———. *D. H. Lawrence: Life into Art.* Athens: University of Georgia Press, 1985.

———. *The Life of D. H. Lawrence.* New York: Pantheon, 1980.

Salgādo, Gāmini, and G. K. Das, eds. *The Spirit of D. H. Lawrence: Centenary Studies.* With a foreword by Raymond Williams. London: Macmillan, 1988.

Sankey, Benjamin. *A Companion to William Carlos Williams' Paterson.* Berkeley: University of California Press, 1971.

Sayre, Henry M. *The Visual Text of William Carlos Williams*. Urbana and Chicago: University of Illinois Press, 1983.

Scheckner, Peter. *Class, Politics, and the Individual: A Study of the Major Works of D. H. Lawrence*. Rutherford, N.J.: Fairleigh Dickinson University Press, 1985.

Schmidt, Peter. *William Carlos Williams, the Arts, and Literary Tradition*. Baton Rouge: Louisiana State University Press, 1988.

Schweik, Susan. *A Gulf So Deeply Cut: American Women Poets and the Second World War*. Madison: University of Wisconsin Press, 1991.

Sicari, Stephen. *Pound's Epic Ambition: Dante and the Modern World*. Albany: State University of New York Press, 1991.

Slatin, Myles. "A History of Pound's Cantos I–XVI, 1915–1925." *American Literature* 35 (1963): 183–95.

Smith, Grover. *T. S. Eliot's Poetry and Plays*. 2d ed. Chicago and London: University of Chicago Press, 1974.

Squires, Michael. *The Creation of Lady Chatterley's Lover*. Baltimore and London: Johns Hopkins University Press, 1983.

———. *The Pastoral Novel: Studies in George Eliot, Thomas Hardy, and D. H. Lawrence*. Charlottesville: University Press of Virginia, 1974.

Squires, Michael, and Dennis Jackson, eds. *D. H. Lawrence's "Lady": A New Look at Lady Chatterley's Lover*. Athens: University of Georgia Press, 1985.

Stock, Noel. *The Life of Ezra Pound*. London: Routledge, 1970.

———. *Poet in Exile: Ezra Pound*. Manchester: Manchester University Press, 1964.

———. *Reading the Cantos: A Study of Meaning in Ezra Pound*. London: Routledge, 1967.

Surette, Leon. *A Light from Eleusis: A Study of Ezra Pound's Cantos*. Oxford: Clarendon Press, 1979.

Sword, Helen. "Orpheus and Eurydice in the Twentieth Century: Lawrence, H.D., and the Poetics of the Turn." *Twentieth Century Literature* 35 (1989): 407–28.

Tapscott, Stephen. *American Beauty: William Carlos Williams and the Modernist Whitman*. New York: Columbia University Press, 1984.

Tashjian, Dickran. *William Carlos Williams and the American Scene, 1920–1940*. New York: Whitney Museum and Berkeley: University of California Press, 1978.

Taylor, Richard, and Claus Melchior, eds. *Ezra Pound and Europe*. Amsterdam: Rodopi, 1993.

Terrell, Carroll F. *A Companion to the Cantos of Ezra Pound*. 2 vols. Berkeley: University of California Press, 1980, 1984.

Terrell, Carroll F., ed. *William Carlos Williams: Man and Poet*. Orono: National Poetry Foundation, University of Maine, 1983. Includes "An Annotated

Bibliography of Works about William Carlos Williams, 1974–1982," by Joseph Brogunier, 453–585.

Traversi, Derek. *T. S. Eliot: The Longer Poems*. New York and London: Harcourt, 1976.

Tryphonopoulos, Demetres P. *The Celestial Tradition: A Study of Ezra Pound's The Cantos*. Waterloo, Ontario: Wilfrid Laurier University Press, 1992.

Unger, Leonard. *T. S. Eliot: Moments and Patterns*. Minneapolis: University of Minnesota Press, 1966.

Waggoner, Hyatt H. *American Visionary Poetry*. Baton Rouge: Louisiana State University Press, 1982.

Wagner, Linda Welshimer. *The Poems of William Carlos Williams: A Critical Study*. Middletown, Conn.: Wesleyan University Press, 1964.

Walker, Jeffrey. *Bardic Ethos and the American Epic Poem: Whitman, Pound, Crane, Williams, Olson*. Baton Rouge: Louisiana State University Press, 1989.

Weaver, Mike. *William Carlos Williams: The American Background*. Cambridge: Cambridge University Press, 1971.

Weinstein, Philip. "Choosing between the Quick and the Dead: Three Versions of *Lady Chatterley's Lover*." *Modern Language Review* 43 (1982): 267–90.

Whitaker, Thomas R. *William Carlos Williams*. 2d ed. Boston: Twayne, 1989.

Widmer, Kingsley. "The Pertinence of Modern Pastoral: The Three Versions of *Lady Chatterley's Lover*." *Studies in the Novel* 5 (1973): 298–313.

Wilhelm, James J. *The American Roots of Ezra Pound*. New York: Garland, 1985.

———. *Dante and Pound: The Epic of Judgement*. Orono: University of Maine Press, 1974.

———. *Ezra Pound: The Tragic Years, 1925–1972*. University Park: Pennsylvania State University Press, 1994.

———. *Ezra Pound in London and Paris, 1908–1925*. University Park: Pennsylvania State University Press, 1990.

———. *The Later Cantos of Ezra Pound*. New York: Walker, 1977.

Witemeyer, Hugh, "Clothing the American Adam: Pound's Tailoring of Walt Whitman." In *Ezra Pound among the Poets*, ed. George Bornstein, 81–105. Chicago and London: University of Chicago Press, 1985.

Wojcik, Jan, and Raymond-Jean Frontain, eds. *Poetic Prophecy in Western Literature*. Rutherford, N.J.: Fairleigh Dickinson University Press, 1984.

Woodward, Anthony. *Ezra Pound and The Pisan Cantos*. London: Routledge, 1980.

Worthen, John. *D. H. Lawrence and the Idea of the Novel*. London: Macmillan, 1979.

Acknowledgments

GRATEFUL ACKNOWLEDGMENT is given to New Directions Publishing Corporation and Faber and Faber Ltd. for permission to quote from the following copyrighted works of Ezra Pound: *The Cantos* (copyright © 1934, 1937, 1940, 1948, 1956, 1959, 1962, 1963, 1966, and 1968 by Ezra Pound); *Collected Early Poems* (copyright © 1976 by the Trustees of the Ezra Pound Literary Property Trust); *Gaudier-Brzeska* (copyright © 1970 by Ezra Pound); *Literary Essays* (copyright © 1918, 1920, 1935 by Ezra Pound); *Personae* (copyright © 1926 by Ezra Pound); *Pound/Joyce* (copyright © 1967 by Ezra Pound); *Selected Letters, 1907–1941* (copyright © 1950 by Ezra Pound); *Selected Prose, 1909–1965* (copyright © 1960, 1962 by Ezra Pound, copyright © 1973 by the Estate of Ezra Pound); *The Spirit of Romance* (copyright © 1968 by Ezra Pound); *Translations* (copyright © 1954–1963 by Ezra Pound).

Previously unpublished material by Ezra Pound: copyright © 1998 by Mary de Rachewiltz and Omar Pound.

Grateful acknowledgment is given to New Directions Publishing Corporation for permission to quote from the following copyrighted works of H.D.: *Bid Me to Live* (copyright © 1960 by Norman Holmes Pearson); *Collected Poems, 1912–1944* (copyright © 1925 by H.D., copyright © 1957, 1969 by Norman Holmes Pearson, copyright © by the Estate of H.D., copyright © 1983 by Perdita Schaffner); *Helen in Egypt* (copyright © 1961 by Norman Holmes Pearson); *Ion* (copyright © 1937 by Hilda Aldington, copyright © 1986 by Perdita Schaffner); *Tribute to Freud* (copyright © 1956, 1974 by Norman Holmes Pearson); *Trilogy* (copyright © 1956, 1974 by Norman Holmes Pearson).

The Flowering of the Rod, copyright 1946 by Oxford University Press; *Tribute to the Angels,* copyright 1945 by Oxford University Press, copyright renewed 1973 by Norman Holmes Pearson; *The Walls Do Not Fall,* copyright 1944 by Oxford

University Press, copyright renewed 1972 by Norman Holmes Pearson.

Previously unpublished material by H.D. (Hilda Doolittle) copyright © 1998 by Perdita Schaffner; used by permission of New Directions Publishing Corporation, agents.

Grateful acknowledgment is given to New Directions Publishing Corporation and Carcanet Press Ltd. for permission to quote from the following copyrighted works of William Carlos Williams: *The Autobiography of William Carlos Williams* (copyright © 1948, 1951 by William Carlos Williams); *Collected Poems: Volume I, 1909–1939* (copyright © 1938 by New Directions Publishing Corporation, copyright © 1982, 1986 by William Eric Williams and Paul H. Williams); *In the American Grain* (copyright © 1925 by James Laughlin, copyright © 1933 by William Carlos Williams); *Paterson* (copyright © 1946, 1948, 1949, 1958 by William Carlos Williams); *Selected Letters of William Carlos Williams* copyright © 1957 by William Carlos Williams).

Grateful acknowledgment is given to Harcourt Brace and Company and to Faber and Faber Ltd. for permission to reproduce material by T. S. Eliot as follows: Excerpts from *Four Quartets,* copyright 1943 by T. S. Eliot and renewed 1971 by Esme Valerie Eliot; excerpts from *Collected Poems, 1909–1962,* copyright © 1963, 1964, by T. S. Eliot.

Grateful acknowledgment is also extended to the following for permission to reproduce works of art and photographs: Yale University Art Gallery; Freud Museum; the Harry Ransom Humanities Research Center of the University of Texas at Austin; the Department of Special Collections, University Research Library, UCLA; the National Gallery of Victoria, Melbourne, Australia; and the Yale Collection of American Literature, Beinecke Rare Book and Manuscript Library, Yale University.

Grateful acknowledgment is also extended to the following for permission to reprint materials that have appeared in the following journals and collections: *Yale Review, Journal of Modern Literature, Thought* (Fordham University Press), *William Carlos Williams Review, D. H. Lawrence Review, T. S. Eliot: Man and Poet* (National Poetry Foundation, University of Maine), *The Spirit of D. H. Lawrence* (Macmillan, London), and *Words in Time* (Athlone Press).

The photograph of Isadora Duncan is reproduced from *Isadora Duncan: Twenty-four Studies by Arnold Genthe* (New York and London: Mitchell Kennerley, 1929).

I wish to thank Patricia Willis, Curator of the Yale Collection of American Literature, for her generous assistance in gaining access to manuscript materials and for providing photographs of materials in this collection.

I wish also to thank Donald Gallup, distinguished collector and former Curator of the above Yale Collection, for a lifetime of friendship that has included many illuminating conversations about Eliot, Pound, Williams, and H.D.; to him I owe, for example, the latest information about recent translations of *The Waste Land* and the dating of one of Pound's letters according to the *Little Review* calendar.

Finally, I wish to express my appreciation to Jane Lago, Managing Editor of the University of Missouri Press, for her patience with my many revisions, along with her skill in guiding the manuscript through the press, and to Beverly Jarrett, Director of the press, who has encouraged the completion of this book over the period of some three years.

Index